Sell More Books!

Book Marketing and Publishing for Low Profile and Debut Authors

Rethinking Book Publicity after the Digital Revolutions

J. Steve Miller and Cherie K. Miller

With Blythe Daniel, Brian Jud, John Kremer, and Stephanie Richards

Wisdom Creek Press, LLC

What People Are Saying About Sell More Books!

"Whether you're traditionally published or self-published, the author must do the promotion. This book provides solid guidance and is full of valuable tips."

- Dan Poynter, best-selling author of over 125 books and revisions, recognized authority on book marketing, promoting and distributing, author of *The Self-Publishing Manual*

"...a comprehensive guide to marketing a book...[a] well-written, engaging resource that's loaded with specific tips.... Brimming with creative ideas, *Sell More Books!* should prove to be a low profile author's best friend."

- ForeWord Reviews

"While there are many books out there that will give you the old clichés about how to market your book, none of them has the up-to-date expertise of Steve and Cherie Miller's *Sell More Books*! They not only know how to sell books in these times, but give easy explanations to both novice and long-time professional alike. If you buy one book to improve and update your book marketing skills, buy this one."

- A. Louise Staman, Editor of Tiger Iron Press, winner of ten national literary awards

"This book will be my desk reference for helping my book marketing clients sell more of their books. I will use it as a textbook to help student writing interns working with the *Georgia Writers Association* and will recommend it to our members. It is a valuable tool for authors in this digital environment, whether they are traditionally or self-published."

- Lisa M. Russell – freelance book marketer, online content writer and curricula writer – serves as administrator for the *Georgia Writers Association*, working in English Education at Kennesaw State University

"This book is chock full of helpful information, delightfully communicated. It's very user-friendly, no matter what stage of the writing/publishing/marketing process the author is in. I've read quite a few books on marketing your books and this one is by far the best. I can't wait to pass it on to my author friends!"

- Catherine McCall, blogger for *Psychology Today,* marriage and family therapist, author of *When the Piano Stops*

"Highly recommended! The Millers took a wealth of experience, knowledge, and research and packed them into one place. *Sell More Books!* takes the mystery out of marketing, and provides resources that would normally have taken weeks or months to uncover. Yet, for a typically 'boring but necessary' topic, they held my interest until the end. The face of publishing has changed, and whether you are an independent author or traditionally published, marketing is now the responsibility of the author. Every writer should own a copy."

- Eddie Snipes, President of the Christian Authors Guild, author of *I Call Him Dancer*

"Far from a rehash of the same old stuff, *Sell More Books!* gives the up-to-date details of how authors are actually selling books in a digital age. While the extensive research and careful documentation give it authority, the easy-to-read style and refreshing candor (e.g., personal marketing initiatives that sold no books at all) made it a delight to read."

- Lorilyn Roberts, media professional, author of *Children of Dreams*

"Steve and Cherie Miller have put together a powerful and much-needed resource for the 21st century author. In this competitive, fast-changing publishing environment, you can't go wrong if you follow their practical, proven advice on getting your book out there and noticed. The Millers are the best friends and mentors that today's motivated authors could ever have."

- Peter Wallace, host of "Day1" radio program and author of eight books, including *Living Loved* and *Connected*

Sell More Books! is an honest guide for authors full of candor, useful tools, and a bit of humor. The Millers blended all of these to provide a useful and easy-to-read book that will walk you through the complex maze of publishing on your journey to realize your dreams.

- Debra J. Slover, author of the U.N.I.Q.U.E. series of leadership development books for kids and adults

"I wish I'd had this book when I started writing mine. It takes a practical and insightful look at the author's entire process – from improving your writing to getting published to marketing your book. As a low profile author, I'm intimately acquainted with the unique challenges of building a platform from scratch. Steve and Cherie understand those challenges and give clear guidance to overcoming them."

- Danny Kofke, elementary special education teacher, author of *How to Survive (and Sometimes Thrive) on a Teacher's Salary*

Dedication

To every author who ever wrote a great book that nobody ever buys,
and to those writing a book that they fear will fall stillborn from the press.

Library of Congress Cataloging-in-Publication Data

Miller, J. Steve.

Sell more books!: book marketing and publishing for low profile and debut authors: rethinking book publicity after the digital revolutions /

J. Steve Miller and Cherie K. Miller ; with Blythe Daniel ... [et al.].

p. cm.

Includes bibliographical references and index.

ISBN-13: 978-0-9818756-3-7

ISBN-10: 0-9818756-3-7

1. Books--Marketing. 2. Selling--Books.

I. Miller, Cherie K. II. Title.

Z285.6.M55 2011 002'.068'8

QBI10-600250

Library of Congress Control Number: 2011923631

WISDOM CREEK PRESS, LLC

5814 Sailboat Pointe, NW

Acworth, GA 30101

770-337-4385

www.wisdomcreekpress.com

Printed in the United States of America

First printing: May 2011

Contents

Acknowledgements

Contributors

Thanks, Cherie, for partnering with me in this venture and seeing it through to the end! Brian and John, you've mentored me from afar. Besides contributing chapters, you've given so much to authors in general and to this author in particular. Blythe (our literary agent and Colorado publicist) and Stephanie (our Georgia publicist), thanks for generously sharing your publicity expertise.

Consulting Authors, Publicists, and Publishers

Your wisdom and candor changed this book. Your vast, collective experience added new material and forced me to retract, restate, and qualify much of my advice. Experience makes such a mess out of tidy formulas.

Special thanks to those who gave input on an early draft: Ray Atkins, Stephanie Barko, Ellen Beeler, David Cady, Carole Crosby, Laura DeRiemer, Jay Earley, Tania Elfersy, Joel Friedlander, William A. Gordon, Penny Haider, Rik Isensee, Pamela Jackson, Lee Jacobus, Danny Kofke, Paul Krupin, Tim Link, Catherine McCall, Dr. Robert E. McGinnis, Marguerita McManus, Karen O'Toole, Lorilyn Roberts, Lisa Russell, Lynn Seabrook, Debra Slover, and A. Louise Staman.

The Self-Publishing Group
(http://finance.groups.yahoo.com/group/Self-Publishing)

Thanks to all the members who refined my ideas with your considerable wisdom. Your eagerness to shoot down hype saved me from a multitude of publishing sins. Thanks especially to Joel Friedlander, Kathleen Gage, Francis Grimble, Marion Gropen, Shel Horowitz, Marguerita McManus, Karen O'Toole, Claudia Pearson, Debra Slover, and Carol White.

The Book Marketing Network (http://thebookmarketingnetwork.com)

What an encouraging group! Thanks especially to Linda Weaver Clarke, Bill Frank, Penny Haider, Dr. Robert E. McGinnis, Theresa Moore, Brian Rathbone, Lorilyn Roberts, and Alberta Sequeira.

Web Gurus

Programmers Perry Brown and Terry Fritz have taught me immeasurably, as well as my Web designer, Sara Coleman. The innovators and visionaries at Gospelcom kept me abreast of Web developments through their annual conference and their listserv. Chris Ward, Kennesaw State University webmaster, also lent his valuable expertise.

Book Publicity Authors

I couldn't have viewed the landscape of book publicity without standing on the shoulders of the book marketing writers who wrote before me. I list many of these and am reviewing them at www.sellmorebooks.org.

Marketing Specialists

When I needed marketing expertise beyond book marketing, I relied on connections at the prestigious Coles College of Business at Kennesaw State University. I especially thank Lisa Bauer for making connections and supplying me with marketing texts.

Social Media Specialists

Sherry Heyl (Concept Hub) and Dr. Len Witt (The Center for Sustainable Journalism) kept me abreast of the latest social media developments through SoCon and other conferences that brought together thought leaders and allowed for debate and discussion. Noah Echols offered his keen mind to guide me through the hype and to recommend solid sources.

Editors

Many thanks to Cherie K. Miller (aka "my wife") and Ann Miller (aka "Mom") – ever and always my first line editors. And thanks to Tracy Heffner, my final editor.

Graphic Designers

Carole Mauge-Lewis, you're a creative genius and a pleasure to work with. Thanks for coming through with another extraordinary cover. Andrew Miller, thanks for your help with images and illustrations. Jessica, thanks to you and your team for a beautiful interior layout.

Mistakes

These would be mine, for which I take responsibility. As you find errors and dated information, please contact me at jstevemiller@gmail.com so that I can correct them on our site and in future editions.

Introduction

Low Profile Authors Can Win!

Today's publishing world caters to celebrities and established authors with vast followings. Query a traditional publisher and she'll want to know who you are and why readers would buy your book. As one publisher recently said, "We...are looking for authors with a 'platform' (isn't everyone?!)." How discouraging. Apparently, they're not looking for me.

This book is for the rest of us, the non-celebrities who love to write and have a passion to get our ideas out there, but are frustrated by an industry and a buying public that worships platforms.

Why Me?

My platform to write this book is that I share (or have shared) your lack of platform. As far as the world's concerned, I'm a nobody. In my early career, when I wrote my first book, I served as a youth minister – the last staff person listed on the church website below the pastor, minister of education, and minister of music. I was "Minister of Youth" at Flat Creek Baptist Church in Fayetteville, Georgia. That's worse than a platform; it's a hole in the ground.

Yet a respected, successful publisher – Tyndale House – offered me a contract to publish my book on modern music and the church, which went through several printings and was published in Dutch, German, Spanish, Romanian, and Russian. It was also used as a college textbook and sells steadily today, eighteen years after its original publication.

Yet I wasn't a musician. I didn't teach music. I had no degree in music. I was previously unpublished and had no following. How did I get a contract and why did people buy a book written by a nobody?

For the past 15 years I've been a caregiver, first to my wife who was dying of cancer, then to my four boys, then to my dad, and today to my 105-year-old grand mom and my blended family of 7 boys. Forget the nationwide book tour; I do well to venture past the mailbox. Yet, during this period I published another book, this time on personal finance. I have neither a degree in finance nor professional experience in the world of finance. My literary agent submitted it to many publishers, who rejected it due to my lack of platform. "To sell books on personal finance," they all agreed, "you need a large platform, like a national radio show."

I politely disagreed, publishing it myself. I took seriously the warnings from professional publishers, assuming that this book might be a challenge to market. So I read 25 or so books on book marketing, participated in publishing forums and listservs, and networked with fellow authors. It garnered rave reviews, won several awards, and sold as many copies on the first day of publication as the average self-published book sells in total. Two years after publication, I'm happy with its continued, growing sales.

Why This Book?

The more I studied book marketing and talked with frustrated authors, the more I sensed the need for a different kind of book – something to help authors narrow down which of the hundreds of marketing tactics might work best for their books and fit their unique personalities, talents, and interests. Most books laid out scores of ways to market books, but left me with an overwhelming feeling of "I suppose I should be doing all of this, but who has the time or money?!"

And then there's all that confusing hype. Newsletters kept promising me the "secrets" of selling tons of books – typically involving expensive seminars, building high-priced websites, and using time-consuming social media tools. "Tweet seven times a day, blog every day, post videos on Youtube, and build your following!" So if I do all that, while working a day job, raising children, and caring for Granny, when do I find time to write my next book? It sounded exhausting.

When I'd talk to people who attended these seminars, participated avidly in social media, etc., I'd ask them about concrete results in book sales. Typically, they replied vaguely, mentioning a few sales here and there. Yet, I kept crossing paths with others who were selling a lot of books using one or two simple approaches – sometimes using new technologies and sometimes not. Different approaches seemed to work for different authors and different books. It occurred to me that someone needed to help authors narrow down approaches that might work for *their* books.

Another problem I've encountered is authors assuming that in order to sell books, they must be shameless self-promoters, constantly in people's faces, with the audacity and resilience of cold-calling, cold-blooded telemarketers. Yet, especially using new media, I find those attitudes counterproductive. New technologies allow humble, caring, shy authors to get the word out about their books in unprecedented ways. This book helps authors discover and exploit those ways.

With my positive experiences in both traditional and nontraditional publishing, I have no ax to grind with either and will offer ideas that work in both arenas. And if you have yet to be published, or have another book on the horizon, you'll receive the most benefit in that you can think marketing from the very start.

Here's what I'm offering:

- **Hundreds of practical** ideas for writing, publishing, and marketing that you can implement immediately.

- **Motivational tips** that make marketing more fun. Our greatest obstacles are often our attitudes. I want authors to catch fire for marketing their books, so that they can experience the thrill of seeing their books purchased and read!

- **Outside-the-box thinking**. I question everything and offer some unique angles, often finding help outside of book marketing literature. Applying both well-established marketing principles and new insights from social media experts can save us from countless hours spent employing tactics that have little chance of selling books.

- **A "No B.S. Pledge**." Sensationalist hype dominates much of the book marketing industry. "For $350 we'll send your press release to 10,000 media giants." Cool. But will any of them actually read it? And of the past 1,000 authors who used this service, what percentage even broke even with resulting sales? I can't promise to get you on Oprah. I can't even promise that if you get on Oprah you'll sell any books (some don't). But I've kept meticulous records of my personal marketing efforts, talked to many authors about their successes and failures, and promise to tell you honestly when I put a lot of effort into something that sounded like a great idea but sold no books.

- **Help determining what marketing methods could work best for your book**, using your own unique personality, strengths, and interests. Radio isn't for everybody. Contrary to popular opinion, neither is blogging or television. Some authors detest public appearances. With thousands of ways to market books, authors desperately need principles to help them determine which methods deserve their time.

- **A bias toward cheap stuff.** I heard one author share about how she sold 20,000 copies of her book. She'd traveled to New York to do a popular TV show and done other cool promotions. Yet, at one point she mentioned as an aside, "In the end, we probably just broke even." Maybe she didn't need the money. But I'll assume you'd like to make a profit. That means controlling your publishing and promotion costs.

- **A guide to further study.** If I fail to inspire you to keep learning about selling books, I've failed. Throughout the book, I recommend other resources (books, blogs, forums, listservs, etc.) that can take you further. (Note: I'm not being paid to promote other people's resources in this book.) I plan to be a lifelong learner in this field, and hope to inspire you to keep learning as well.

I tried to make the book all the more practical by writing sections as I experienced them. Thus, when I say "As I write..." I might be speaking of a couple of years prior to writing the final manuscript. I wrote about press releases as I sent out my first press releases, about getting reviews from top blogs as I pursued them. In this way, I could more accurately report those initial frustrations and fears and delights that are often forgotten over time. As an avid spelunker, I know that caverns look very different when you look back than when you're looking forward. Since both views are valuable, I incorporate both.

Where Did I Get This Information?

Various places. Besides reading widely in book marketing, I studied general marketing and consulted with academics in the field. In specialized areas, such as social networking, I had to do specialized reading and drew from various seminars I've attended over the past four years, such as the annual SoCon social media conference, which kept me abreast of social networking from back when MySpace reigned supreme and Facebook was the new kid on the block. On Web matters, I drew upon my experiences as a webmaster – writing and selling web-based content since the late 1990s. To get the most up-to-date information, I often found myself playing the journalist by interviewing personnel at the most respected book review companies and press release companies, or calling bookstore managers to get critical information I wasn't finding elsewhere. But uppermost in my mind have been the experiences of multitudes of low-profile authors that I've gleaned from personal interviews, forums, listservs, books, articles, blogs, seminars, podcasts, webinars, etc. As authors share what's working and what's not working for them, I find that analyzing their experiences provides some of the most practical information.

Snoozer Alert!

Some authors want motivational stories to renew their zeal to write and sell books. Others need to know in sufficient detail how to mail their galleys next week. I offer something for both.

The problem with providing essential details to those who need them is that those who don't need them will be bored to tears. Tip: When you find yourself slogging through a chapter that doesn't scratch where you itch, skim the main subheadings and move on to a more relevant chapter. Otherwise, you may stop reading altogether and miss the information you desperately need today.

What's with all the Authors?

Although "I" refers to J. Steve Miller as the principal writer, my wife Cherie K. Miller is legitimately co-author in that the ideas presented here came out of a collaborative effort of researching and conversing endlessly about writing, publishing, and marketing. Brian Jud and John Kremer each contributed a chapter; but beyond that, their writings and teachings have been seminal in our thinking. Blythe Daniel has added to our understanding of the publishing industry through her strong background in traditional publishing, as well as being our literary agent and Colorado-based publicist. Stephanie Richards, our Georgia publicist, held our hands through our early publicity efforts and continues to advise us.

With this background in mind, let's plunge into the fascinating new world of book publishing and marketing!

Part I

Rethink Book Marketing in Light of the Revolutions

Chapter 1

Four Digital Revolutions that Can Make Nobodies Awesome

(Exciting Times for Writers in the New "Wild Wild West" of Publishing)

The past is a foreign country. They do things differently there.
- L.P. Hartley, from his novel, *The Go Between*

Everything you know is wrong
Black is white, up is down and short is long
And everything you thought was just so important
Doesn't matter
- "Weird Al" Yankovich

The Best of Times; the Worst of Times

On the surface, today's news points to "the worst of times" for authors.

- Many brick and mortar bookstores are failing.
- Traditional publishers are tightening their belts.
- There's more competition than ever.
- It's extremely difficult to get a contract with a traditional publisher.

But I'd argue that the revolutions that are shaking up the traditional book industry will ultimately benefit the authors and publishers who understand and harness them.

Why do I think it's the best of times for publishing?

- Traditional publishers can keep slow but steady sellers in print indefinitely through print on demand technology.
- People are still buying tons of books – $24 billion worth in 2009.[1] In 2008, 56 percent of adults in the United States bought at least one print book. That *increased* to 57 percent in 2009.[2] It's not that people aren't buying books. They simply buy less from traditional bookstores and more from alternative outlets (Wal-Mart, Kroger, Amazon, etc.).
- New technologies allow indie authors to launch out on their own and test markets themselves rather than wait for acceptance by the traditional book industry.
- Digital tools allow authors to access new media and older media that were formerly accessible only to the big players.

Times have changed, yet many well-worn pronouncements are still tossed around like dogma.

- "If you can't get distribution into bookstores, you're sunk!"
- "You've got to do a national book-signing tour!"
- "With book marketing, what really matters are the three months before publication and the three months following publication. After that, your book's no longer new."
- "You've got to be comfortable on radio and TV."
- "You must have a strong platform to get published."

Indeed, times have changed and it's time to question all dogma. It's not that these statements are without merit or that all that formerly worked is now passé. It's just that, while they have value for some authors, they certainly don't apply to all. To choose the best options to publish and market our books, we must reevaluate book marketing in the light of recent revolutions.

I know that you're here to get practical ideas for publishing and selling your books. But I urge you to bear with a quick overview of the revolutions. A couple of early readers despised this chapter, complaining that it wasn't as delightful and practical as the following chapters. Some may find it painful to rethink the old publishing paradigm. Others may find it extremely liberating. But trust me, without this background, you won't understand many of my recommendations.

Without this background, you may spend tens of thousands of dollars pursuing publishing options and marketing methods that let you down. With this background, you'll not only be able to make better decisions, but you'll be equipped to dream up better ideas for marketing your books than anything I suggest.

Behold the ever-shifting landscape of publishing and book marketing!

Four Publishing Revolutions

The Most Dramatic Advances since AD 1439 - All in the Last 15 Years

Revolution #1: Quality Print on Demand (POD) Radically Lowered Up-front Cost and Risk

In 1439 Johannes Gutenberg invented the printing press, revolutionizing the publishing world. Prior to moveable type, manuscripts had to be painstakingly copied by hand. With the printing press, thousands of copies could be made quickly, at a drastically reduced cost. Welcome to a world of affordable books, magazines, newspapers, and leaflets that reached the masses and changed the world!

Although innovators constantly improved the printing process, one limitation plagued the publishing industry for the next 550+ years – the time and cost of setting up a manuscript for print. With a traditional press, once a manuscript is set up, publishers can print 5,000 copies of a 250-page book for under $2.00 per copy, allowing them to retail it for $15.95, offer it to distributors at a 70% discount or wholesalers at a 55% discount, and still make a profit. **But this system only worked if you printed lots of copies. The fewer copies you print with a traditional press, the higher the cost of production per unit.**

Because of this limitation, publishers typically had to print a minimum of 3,000 to 5,000 copies to offer books at a competitive price and make a decent profit. But that meant that **every book they published risked large sums of money.** So a publisher does a small print run of 5,000 copies for a first-time author. Now they have $10,000 tied up in printing. But additionally they must pay for editors, designers, typesetters, storage, marketing, a slick catalogue (to promote to bookstores), and a several-thousand-dollar author advance. For the publisher to break even, your book might have to earn back $25,000 or much more.[3]

No wonder traditional publishers accept so few manuscripts from new authors! When I sent a query and a couple of example chapters to publishers back in 1991, they were accepting about one in thirty manuscripts. Today, the competition is much more fierce.[4] Today's submissions to major publishers are better conceived and better edited and include a viable marketing plan. Why the better quality? Because the large publishers accept manuscripts exclusively from literary agents, who can't make a living submitting sub-quality work. And these days, it's as difficult to get a literary agent as it is to get a publisher!

So every day, publishers reject stacks of well-written manuscripts because they can afford to take a chance on a very limited number.

Enter Print on Demand

Harry wants to write a 250-page biography of his father, assuming that only 50 or so relatives

ead it. Knowing that no traditional publisher in his right mind would consider such a book, Harry bypasses the traditional channels.

He writes it, giving each chapter to family members to check for accuracy. He lays it out in Microsoft Word, has his son design a lovely cover with PhotoShop, and asks his writers group to edit it, all free of charge. He saves it as a pdf and uploads it to CreateSpace (a print on demand subsidiary of Amazon.com), also free of charge. Within a week or so he receives a copy for review. Satisfied, he puts in an order for 10 copies at $6.50 apiece ($3.85 each with the "Pro Plan"), to send as Christmas gifts. If other relatives want to purchase additional copies from Amazon, they're available for $15.95.

Harry doesn't store the books, take orders, or ship them. Amazon orders directly from CreateSpace, ships it to buyers, and deposits a portion of each sale (royalty) into Harry's bank account each month.

POD presses churn out books as customers order them, making individual copies affordable and eliminating the cost of storage. If you were to watch the books coming out the conveyor belt, you wouldn't see 5,000 consecutive copies of the same book. Rather, a copy of one book rolls out, two copies of another, five copies of another, all printed automatically as they are ordered.

B.S. Alert! Publishing a book has never been, and will never be, as easy as this story makes it look. In real life Aunt Marie would threaten to sue Harry if he published the material on her drug habit. His brother no longer speaks to him, but won't tell Harry why. The formatting didn't work quite right in Microsoft Word and for some unexplainable reason, saving it as a pdf made all the pages too large.

CreateSpace informs you that there's not enough space on your spine, but you don't know how to correct it. You end up hiring a professional graphic artist, who's running two months behind and now won't reply to your e-mails. What should have cost nothing and taken a total of 6 months ends up taking a year and a half and costing $1000. Publishing may be revolutionized, but it's still publishing!

The implications of this new technology are astounding. Yet most of us haven't sufficiently assimilated them. Instead of a $25,000 risk, Harry risks only his time (plus his relationships with irate family members).

Does this make traditional publishing obsolete? Not at all! There are still great benefits, which we'll discuss later, for getting published through a traditional publisher. To mention a few:

- Authors get much more respect when traditionally published.
- It's much easier to get big-time reviews.
- If your dream is to sell through traditional bookstores, the big publishers have relationships and agreements with distributors, wholesalers, and bookstores that smaller presses and individuals can't leverage.

But understanding the first revolution lets us know that there are options for books that don't fit into the traditional model. This is great news for authors! The implications of print on demand are huge for both authors and publishers.

Implications of the POD Revolution

- **Risk has been significantly reduced.**
- **Major publishers will continue to use the POD model.** Lightning Source, a POD leader that works exclusively with publishers (over 9,000 of them), is used by such prestigious publishers as John Wiley & Sons, McGraw-Hill, Simon & Schuster, and Macmillan.[5]
- **If you want your book published, you can get it published.** So you've got a book burning inside of you that simply must get out. Go ahead and write it! If traditional publishers reject it, you have affordable options for printing, distribution, and marketing.
- **It's feasible for authors and publishers to print books for small niche groups and still make a profit.**
- **If you hold the rights to your out-of-print books, you can reprint them yourself and give them a new life.** I did this when my first book went out of print. BookSurge (now CreateSpace) scanned both the cover and interior (amazingly, the quality was indistinguishable from the original), and offered it on Amazon, for a total processing fee of about $350. It still meets a need and sells steadily, 18 years after its original publication.
- **Don't make decisions based upon a shallow interpretation of statistics.** Many statistics must be reinterpreted in light of the revolutions. Example: many quote statistics showing that the average POD book sells a total of 100 copies, inferring that self-published books don't sell. But many POD authors never intended to print more than 20 copies for family and

friends. And some publishers use print on demand to print niche reference books that only a limited number of specialist libraries would ever buy, charging a very high price per copy. Others are rapidly scanning and publishing thousands of out-of-print books with expired copyrights. Obviously, these books sell in low volumes and skew the statistics.

Thus, of the 764,000 titles produced in 2009 by self-publishers and micro-niche publishers, 687,000 of them were published by BiblioBazaar, Books LLC, and Kessinger Publishing LLC. These companies apparently scan and publish out-of-print books to the tune of 2,000 titles a day. By comparison, CreateSpace, targeting authors who've written new books, produced only 22,000 titles in 2009.[6]

- **Don't replicate the marketing methods for traditionally published books if you're publishing independently.** Although there's an overlap, in many respects they're vastly different. The reasons for this will become clear in later chapters.

- **The standards of success must be revised.** In a forum, an author shared how his book was selling well and another author rather arrogantly replied, "Well, if you claim your book is selling well, you must mean that it's selling at least 5,000 copies per year, as any reputable publisher would measure minimal success."[7] But even if the author is on target with his figure for the traditional model, without knowing this author's goals and through which channels he published, how can he possibly measure "minimal success?"

  A self-published author might be ecstatic about selling 500 copies of each of his 20 books per year, which, with a $5.00 profit per book, gives him $50,000 per year. Not bad. Others may publish a business book to sell at a table after speaking engagements. They're perfectly happy breaking even on the book, since they wrote it solely to give them more clout on the speaking circuit and to offer more value to their attendees.

- **Profits can be generated in different ways.** By publishing POD through either CreateSpace or Lightning Source, authors can make more money per Amazon book sale than with a traditional publisher. For example, if your book sells for $16 on Amazon and you published through Lightning Source with a 20 percent discount, you'd net $9.14 per sale, as opposed to about $1.28 per sale if you had a typical contract with a traditional publisher. (A traditional publisher might offer a new author 16 percent of their "net," which is about eight percent of the retail selling price.)

  Yet, I still occasionally submit books to traditional publishers. Why? Because if a publisher's marketing savvy, agreements with distributors, reputation, etc. would likely net me five to seven times the sales (depending on my chosen percentage discount through Lightning Source) than I'd get on my own, then why not skip the extra work involved in self-publishing?[8]

- **Self-publishers have options that free them up from mundane tasks.** Before the revolutions, if I self-published, I'd have to print thousands of copies myself, store them in my basement, take orders, wrap them, and ship them. And that's still a great model for some authors, since they're able to print copies at a reduced price per book. But if my POD publisher/printer takes care of shipping and distribution, I can concentrate on writing and publishing.

- **It's easy to spend money needlessly, since many authors don't understand the new costs of publication.** If a subsidy press says they'll publish your book for $5,000, find out specifically what you're getting for your money. Are they really providing $5,000 worth of services, or are they providing services you could better pay for yourself, or even get free of charge? If they're simply taking your manuscript (and your money) and publishing it through Lightning Source, weigh the value of skipping the middle man.

- **It's easy to get ripped off.** New "publishers" can set up shop and put up a professional-looking website on a shoestring budget. To defend yourself against the con artists, do your homework, join professional associations, and network with fellow authors and publishers. Later, I'll list some great places to network.

Revolution #2: Online sales leveled the selling field (less "pay for placement").

If a publisher had told me, back in 1993, that she could get my music book into the largest bookstore chain in the world, keep me there perpetually, and give me free tools to place my books where they would be more easily found, I'd have cackled at the whimsical joke. But substitute "Amazon.com" (launched online in 1995) for the "largest bookstore chain" and it's a reality. Book sales are quickly moving from brick and mortar stores to online stores. According to Morris Rosenthal[9], here are the figures:

Sales Growth or Loss for the Largest Booksellers

(For the two-year period: 2008-2009)

Traditional Brick and Mortar Bookstores

Borders/Waldenbooks = **down 24%**
Barnes & Noble Bookstores = **down 8%**

Online (Web-based) Sales

BN.com = **up 22%**
Amazon.com Media, North America = **up 27%**

Amazon.com is now the largest bookseller in America. Borders faces dim prospects for survival, having filed for bankruptcy protection in mid-February, 2011. If online sales continue to increase and traditional bookstore sales continue to decrease, the latter will become less and less of a concern for the average author. Before the "online sales revolution," most authors considered their success or failure to rest in the hands of brick and mortar bookstores. But even then these traditional bookstores, like the printing press, had severe limitations.

The Limitations of Traditional Bookstores

Limitation #1: Traditional bookstores can hold only so many books, and they're already filled to capacity.

The typical mall bookstore stocks 25,000 titles. The superstores (Barnes & Noble and Borders) each carry around 170,000 titles, compared to Amazon's 14 million.[10]

So not even considering the 764,000 new titles published last year by micro-niche publishers and self-publishers, **where did your local brick and mortar bookstore put the 288,000 new, traditionally published titles that were published last year?** If there's space for only 170,000 volumes, most of which stayed put, then obviously the great majority of new books couldn't be ordered.[11] Yet, when's the last time you saw a bookstore building an addition to hold more books?[12] To order more books, they must either not re-order many books that they're selling, or return non-selling books to the publishers for a refund.

This means that:

- **Many authors, even published by traditional publishers, never get into a significant number of bookstores.** A receiving manager at one of the superstores told me that she receives 40 or 50 new titles (never before ordered) per week. If she's guessing correctly with the higher number, then her store stocks 2,600 new titles every year, or **only one out of every 110 (less than one percent) of all new, traditionally published books.**[13]
- If you're fortunate enough to get your book into bookstores, you're still not home free. **If you fail to drive buyers into the bookstores with a major promotion, managers will return them unsold (typically, within four months) and won't reorder.** More than one in four books ordered by bookstores are returned.[14]
- **Even if your book is ordered and sold, it will probably not be automatically reordered unless you're a bestselling author.** I know a local, traditionally published author[15] who sells many of his novels through his local Barnes & Noble; but since he's not a bestselling author, his books aren't on automatic reorder. As a result, he has to remind the manager to reorder when they're out of stock. What then are the odds of his book

being reordered in the stores outside his geographical area, where he's not reminding them to reorder?

- This lack of space and rapid turnover results in many books going out of print after their first printing.

A Frustrating Experience

I write web-based resources for those teaching character and life skills in public schools. Some of these teachers are coaches. So when the Super Bowl contenders are decided each year, I immediately identify the highest profile players and coaches so that I can research them for character stories. What admirable traits led them to such a high level of success?

So the day after the playoffs determined that Kurt Warner would quarterback in the 2008 Super Bowl, I set out to find his autobiography. I thought, "Kurt Warner is one of the highest profile individuals of the decade – one of the top players in America's most popular sport (as far as television viewing is concerned). The Super Bowl is two weeks away – the most watched media event of the year; so surely this eight-year-old autobiography will be available in my local bookstores."

It wasn't.

I called my local *Barnes & Noble*, *Borders*, *Books-a-Million* and the local Christian bookstore. None carried it. One said he couldn't even order it. I ordered it myself from Amazon.

A Reflection

If a person with as high a profile as Kurt Warner (incredibly "high platform" with precisely the type of book which publishers are itching to publish and keep in distribution) can't keep his autobiography in the bookstores during the time of his greatest popularity (and it was truly a well-written, inspiring book), then what chance do us low-profile authors have of keeping our books in bookstores over the years? At best, especially for low-profile authors, I'd suggest that brick and mortar bookstores are typically a short-term rather than long-term strategy.

Now please don't get me wrong – I love bookstores! I love hanging out in bookstores. I love browsing in bookstores. But after a couple of experiences like that, when I needed to purchase a book, I began defaulting to Amazon. It's a time issue. A local bookstore can carry only a small percentage of the millions of books in print, even of books that are recognized classics in their fields. And after signing up for Amazon Prime, we never pay postage. Evidence suggests that many other bookstore lovers are reluctantly following suit.

Limitation #2: Small-time authors can seldom manipulate the "findability" of their books in traditional bookstores. Best-selling authors get the best placement paid for with mega bucks by their publishers. And this makes perfect sense to publishers and bookstores. After all, a high percentage of customers enter stores looking for these books, and best-selling authors are very profitable to publishers. So naturally their books should be given priority placement.

Announcement

As of today, I declare "findability" an official word and will continue to use it as such in this book. Much better than the clunky "able to be easily found." Go ahead, play it in *Scrabble*.

But that places midlist and new authors in a Catch-22 – they can't get priority placement until they're best-selling authors; but how can they become best-selling authors if people can't easily discover their books?

Because of these limitations, best selling authors and authors who can produce successful backlist books (those that sell steadily long after their original publication) would do well to continue to court traditional bookstores. But for the rest of us, they are useful outlets for people to order from, but I have no expectation that they will carry my books long-term or be a major source of sales.

Alas, this is all very depressing to all the authors who've yet to transition to the new paradigm in publishing. But here's the good news – *extremely* good news: Authors can finally break free from the severe limitations that bookstores impose. I can't overstate the importance of this revolution. Authors now have many effective ways to sell their books! A new day has arrived!

Implications of the Online Sales Revolution

- **For many publishers and authors, traditional bookstores will continue to decrease in importance to their sales, where alternative sales (of which online sales is only one part) will increase in importance.**
- **Small publishers and not-yet-famous authors have places to sell their books and compete with the large publishers and best-selling authors.**
- **Some writers won't even try to get into brick and mortar bookstores.** Although it's always advantageous to be with wholesalers so that customers can order through bookstores, if you're set up with a traditional "return policy" (without which bookstores are unlikely to carry your book), you risk losing money if a chain puts in a large order that it later returns for a refund.
- **Authors can write to niches that have large, but geographically scattered followings that wouldn't be carried by bookstores.**[16]
- **When weighing publication options, know in detail how each of these options impacts online sales.** Do you know precisely what percentage

of each online sale you will receive? Will you have any control over Amazon's retail price or discounts?

- **We should optimize our online Amazon/Barnes & Noble/etc. pages so that searchers can easily find our books.**

- **We can track sales more quickly to see which marketing efforts pay off and which don't.** The day a review comes out or an interview airs, I go immediately to Amazon to see if sales have spiked (a significant rise in rank). The next day, I check CreateSpace to check the number of direct sales from Amazon. Formerly, marketing efforts were mostly guessing games; you try multiple publicity campaigns but have to wait for six months to get sales information. In the end, you were clueless as to which efforts paid off, which produced no sales, and which you should pursue in the future.

- **We can identify key phrases that people use to search for our subject matter and consider these when choosing titles, subtitles, tags, etc.** Certain titles will sell well simply because they attract key word searches.

- **We can plan long-range marketing strategies.** In the "traditional publisher-to-bookstores" model, publishers and authors typically focus their marketing efforts on several months before publication (to get early reviews and secure bookstore orders) to a few months following publication (to drive buyers into the bookstores). After this narrow window of opportunity, the book is no longer considered new. If bookstores fail to order them initially, you may be sunk. If customers don't buy them once they're in bookstores, they'll be returned within six months for a refund and they won't re-order unless customers place a special order. Again, you're sunk. Thus when marketing to traditional bookstores, although there are exceptions, there's a narrow window of opportunity to get your book moving.

  But with online sales, I'm not competing with limited bookstore space. With the stability of knowing it's not going out of print (if a publisher drops it, I can reprint and keep selling), I can continue to build my platforms, perfect my marketing initiatives, and plan marketing strategies to span decades.

Revolution #3: Online marketing (through social networking, access to magazines and blogs, helping reporters with articles, search engine positioning, etc.) leveled the publicity field.

Interruption advertising is giving way to "I'll help you find me" positioning – a huge boon to shy authors. In the past, we relied heavily upon billboards "interrupting" our driving and advertisements "interrupting" our TV viewing. Today, those of us who loathe bugging people can concentrate on positioning our products so that people will find them when they're searching for them.

So if you've written a book on solving common cat problems, you might design a web page so that when a person types, "I'm about to murder my cat," into Google, she finds your book. The result? You not only sell a book, but have the satisfaction of knowing that you've saved a pet's life.

Social networking (through Twitter, Facebook, LinkedIn, blogs, forums, etc.) provides opportunities for authors to connect with others who are fascinated with your subject, or desperately need your information. It's much like renting a booth at a home school convention, where you display your new book, *How to Teach Your Child to Read*, and offer free advice. The attendees are already interested in your topic and are discussing it, so if you can keep from being obnoxious (no bullhorns), you're a welcome, valued expert.

The benefits of online networking over physical location networking include that people worldwide can attend at no cost, with no travel, on their own schedule, dressed in their pajamas.

Implications of the Online Marketing Revolution:

- **Authors can easily find and hang out with large groups of people who are very interested in their subject matter.**
- **Authors must understand the often-subtle "rules" of "How to Win Friends and Influence People" in a social media context.**
- **Authors need to understand the basics of search engine optimization (SEO),** in order to make it easy for people to find them on their blogs, sites, and in online stores.
- **Authors need to understand the various approaches to using social media,** so that they can better narrow down which approaches are mostly likely to work for them (with their individual interests, talents, and personalities) and their books. Example: Trying to build a following through blogging can be a time-consuming process. Is blogging worth an author's time and effort if its sole purpose is to sell more books?
- **Social networking puts word of mouth on steroids,** both allowing and encouraging people to connect and make their voices heard. Readers eagerly recommend books, write reviews, and cast votes for their favorites, helping small authors rise in visibility.

Revolution #4: Selling digital publications (e-books, white papers, members-only collections, etc.) offers more options for sales and profits.

Through November, 2010, e-book sales were up 165.6 percent for the year.[17] With new e-book readers like Amazon's *Kindle*, Barnes & Nobles' *Nook*, Sony's *Reader*, and Apple's *iPad*, many book lovers are finding that they prefer the convenience and savings of loading scores of books and newspapers onto their digital readers. And many, when searching for specific information, like

"How to Market E-Books," will pay for a downloadable document from a trusted thought leader.

This field continues to develop at lightning speed. This morning (December, 6, 2010), Google announced the opening of its Google eBookstore, offering over three million e-books.

F. Paul Wilson, author of the popular "Repairman Jack" thriller series, is taking his older, out-of-print books and publishing them as e-books. From the results so far, he estimates that he'll make $5,000 to $10,000 a month from this little maneuver.[18]

Implications of the Digital Publications Revolution

- **Authors can offer a free digital chapter to give readers a taste of the book, at no cost to the author or publisher.**

- **Authors can write and sell digital content in a way that's truly passive (without manually taking orders, shipping, or billing).** When I'm on vacation, teachers buy my web-based life skills and character curriculum online, paying with credit cards and gaining immediate access. (www.character-education.info)

- **My online presence can be as cool as the big guys.** Professional sites and blogs can be run very inexpensively.

- **The prospect of "unlimited space" offers astounding opportunities.** I remember reflecting on this with wonder during the early days of the Web, as I wrote and collected resources on a site for youth workers. I got permission to use 150 articles on youth ministry by top practitioners, offering them free of charge on my site. Those articles not only served youth workers globally, but brought people to our site. I wrote and collected 3,500 speaker illustrations and offered them through our database. I could have collected thousands of articles and millions of illustrations while using only a tiny fraction of my allotted space on the server, all for under $10 per month hosting fees.

  I still often reflect on the wonder of "unlimited space for words," and the drastic implications, which we still have difficulty grasping. The more pages you write in a traditional book, the higher the printing cost. Yet, space in a digital production is largely irrelevant to production and selling costs (beyond the writing and formatting). Digital editions of books can be offered with many advantages such as color photos, lots of white space, unlimited graphics, color interior, live links, etc., at no extra charge. I can offer thousands of pages of online character resources and offer them affordably to schools, while giving them away to disadvantaged schools and other worthy organizations at no cost to me.

- **E-books can be created quickly to address issues while the subject's hot.** Last summer, President Obama replaced General Stanley A. McChrystal, the top U.S. commander in Afghanistan, in an open-mouth-insert-foot scandal, producing a media frenzy. Two days later, Simon & Schuster published an e-book, *Truman Fires MacArthur,* to give some historical perspective.

  Two days later? Two days later?! Doesn't it take at least a year to publish a book?

  They excerpted it from David McCullough's Pulitzer Prize winning book, *Truman*. Publicity was, in all probably, cheap and easy – just throw some news releases into the media frenzy, and somebody's gonna bite. Sure enough, they got coverage from no less than the *Los Angeles Times*.[19] But what if it sells only 3,000 copies during media frenzy month and sells no more after the media moves on to the next big thing? Perhaps they take their quick profit and analyze the next media frenzy for prospects – no 5,000 copies left to dispose of, no worries about returns, minimal risk, and huge potential.[20]

Let's Rethink Book Marketing

Innovators in all industries are experimenting with these digital tools. Often, observing other industries allows us to more fully break free of the old paradigms. As web marketing guru David Meerman Scott wrote:

> "...I'm absolutely convinced that you will learn more by emulating successful ideas from outside your industry than by copying what your nearest competitor is doing."[21]

Speaking of paradigms, I think it's time to think more fully outside of the old book industry paradigm (publisher to distributors to bookstores to customers). While the old system still serves a useful function and need not be dismantled, a new paradigm would view this as only one of many ways to publish and sell books. A new paradigm would set authors free to sell their books in many exciting new ways.

It's not enough to add a couple of new features to our book marketing initiatives, like a blog campaign and an e-book version. It's time to rethink publishing and marketing from scratch in light of the revolutions. Although I don't pretend to accomplish this completely in this book, I hope to make progress in that direction.

Conclusions from the Revolutions

These are exciting times to publish and market books, filled with opportunities for both casual and professional writers. Finally, passionate writers have many wonderful options to get their works published and noticed. Those who write well and offer unique, sought-after information can attract a following. But only the well informed can take full advantage of the opportunities without getting burned in the process. Never have Al Rogers' words been more relevant:

> *"In times of profound change, the learners inherit the earth, while the learned find themselves beautifully equipped to deal with a world that no longer exists."*

So now, my fellow learners, let's get practical! In the following chapters I'll propose, step-by-step, a strategy for harnessing these revolutions to get our books into the hands of people who want and need them.

Do Something!

To put this chapter into action, I will...

1 –

2 –

3 –

Keep Learning!

Everything's changing. To keep up,

- **See my free updates** to each chapter at www.sellmorebooks.org.
- **Don't assume that the way you did it last time is the best way to do it today.** Before each step (finding a publisher, mailing review copies, sending a press release) re-study the possibilities.
- **Ask questions on forums and listserves.** I like John Kremer's *Book Marketing Forum* and the *Self Publishing Group* (a Yahoo listserv). Don't be satisfied until several sources give you the same response.
- **Publishers Weekly (http://www.publishersweekly.com) is a great site for industry news.** Subscribe to their newsletters for free delivery to your inbox.

Part Two

From Nobody to Somebody

Build Platforms with a Marketable Book and a Cool Online Presence

Chapter 2

Why Market Your Book?

Because of one basic law of book sales that most authors don't seem to understand:

People won't buy your book, unless they first know it exists.

Chapter 3

Write a Marketable Book

Don't fix the marketing first; fix your product. Once you've got a good product to talk about, the marketing's going to flow from that.

- Scott Monty, Ford Motor Company social media chief

Books don't magically fly off the press, landing in readers' laps. Somehow, people need to hear about your books. Then they'll hopefully buy them, read them, like them, and tell their friends. If we get them into enough hands, sales just might reach a tipping point where publicity takes on a life of its own as word of mouth spreads the news far and wide.

But this process assumes that, once people read your book, they'll like it enough to pass it on. Let's not assume anything. Let's begin by making sure that your book is marketable.

Marketing campaigns don't work for some books because they're simply not marketable. Sure, with slick advertising and ecstatic reviews from your mom and your best friends, you can fool a few people into buying a copy; but once general readers discover that you've misspelled five words in your first chapter, your characters aren't that likeable, your research is flawed, or you're just repeating what everybody else says about your subject, irate readers will show no mercy. They'll delightfully rip your book apart and make it their personal mission to warn other readers not to waste their time and money on a book that should have never been written. The same digital tools that so effectively spread *good* publicity are just as effective at spreading *bad* publicity. These days, any self-appointed critic can slam your book on Amazon, a popular forum, or a blog, urging potential readers to search elsewhere for a good book.

So write a great book. A great book is eminently marketable. Get out enough copies to your intended audience and some will tell their friends, others will give copies for presents, and still others will write raving reviews and blog about it, making it their mission to tell the world about this wonderful book.

So how can you ensure that your book is marketable?

1. Define Your Purpose, Audience, and Unique Selling Point

Why are you writing this book? "To have something to sell after I speak" doesn't cut it. "So that I can call myself an author" isn't good enough. Readers have plenty of books to choose from. Why should they choose yours? Millions of books are available for purchase – many more than before the revolutions. Why are you writing another one? Define that clearly and you'll not only write a better book, but you'll be more successful in pitching it to publishers and readers.

I wrote *The Contemporary Christian Music Debate* in the early 1990s because music was dividing the church and the published books on the topic didn't give enough levelheaded, well-researched direction.

- Was a rock beat physically unhealthy, as one psychiatrist claimed to have demonstrated?
- Should the church's style of music always be distinct from popular music, or is popular music simply the "musical language" that communicates most easily to the average person?
- When I work with youth, should I use the musical styles they already appreciate, or train them to appreciate traditional church styles?

In other words,

- **I recognized a need.** A controversy needed to be addressed. This gave my writing purpose.
- **I had a unique selling point.** Other books didn't adequately (objectively, with sound research) address the controversy.
- **I saw potential audiences (niches). Parents** needed wisdom to help their children make wise musical choices. **Pastors** needed to know, "Are contemporary styles harmful in themselves and to be railed against, or are they morally neutral tools that can be used for good?" **Ministers of music** needed to know whether to use old hymns and organs exclusively, or to incorporate new styles.

Thus, this book had unique qualities that made it marketable. My query letter and proposal defined the need and how I planned to meet it. My sample chapters showed that I could deliver. The result? One publisher rejected it because they didn't want to compete with another book they previously published on the topic. The acquisitions editor at another publisher loved the idea, but couldn't convince marketing that it would sell. Tyndale House, the sixth publisher I queried, loved it and published it.

Stating the need and defining an audience not only helped me get a publisher, it told me what kind of book needed to be written. To distinguish it from other books on the topic, it would require some serious research into psychology, ethnomusicology, and church history. Since I lacked authority in myself (not a recognized scholar or thought leader in the field), I needed to appeal to documented, authoritative sources. Yet, since I was writing primarily to influence church staff and parents, and only secondarily to academics, I'd write in a popular, journalistic style.

Knowing my intended audience, I could also strategize (as I wrote the book) how to market to those audiences.

So what makes *your* book different? If it's a novel, what's unique about the location, the characters, the story, or your voice? If it's nonfiction, what are you providing that's unique? If my personal finance book offered the same insights as radio sensation Dave Ramsey's books, readers would consistently choose the high profile author. The more precisely you can define your purpose, audience, and unique selling point, the more potential you have to write a great book and market it.

2. Do Your Best Writing

What Constitutes Good Writing?

Is the following sentence "good writing"? If not, how would you fix it?

> *I said "Who killed him?" and he said "I don't know who killed him but he's dead all right," and it was dark and there was water standing in the street and no lights and windows broke and boats all up in the town and trees blown down and everything all blown and I got a skiff and went out and found my boat where I had her inside of Mango Key and she was all right only she was full of water.*

I venture that most writers would deem this a sentence in trouble – obviously written by a remedial English student. Actually, I pulled it from the short story, "After the Storm," written by Ernest Hemingway, winner of a Pulitzer, and considered by many one of the greatest writers of the 1900s.

My point? Different styles work best for different purposes and different audiences. You may have to adjust your idea of "good writing" appropriately. If you're not Ernest Hemingway, and aren't writing for his audience, don't assume that you should emulate him.

- A technical journal allows (and expects) insider language, understood only by those in that discipline.

- A literary audience tends to appreciate creative description and clever sentences.
- Academics are drawn to sound deductions from solid research in their nonfiction.
- Casual readers may be less interested in clever sentences than a great story.

As simplistic as this sounds, many aspiring authors don't get it. They're still writing the generic style they learned in high school English, rather than diligently refining what their audience expects and enjoys.

James Patterson has published more New York Times Bestsellers (51 and counting) than anyone. Here's what he says about writing to his audience:

> "I have a saying. If you want to write for yourself, get a diary. If you want to write for a few friends, get a blog. But if you want to write for a lot of people, think about them a little bit. What do they like? What are their needs? A lot of people in this country go through their days numb. They need to be entertained. They need to feel something."[1]

So how does this attention to his audience impact his writing?

In Patterson's early work, he obsessed over his sentences. Now he's more interested in stories. Jonathan Mahler describes Patterson's writing as "light on atmospherics and heavy on action, conveyed by simple, colloquial sentences." Patterson says, "I don't believe in showing off. Showing off can get in the way of a good story." Thus, he writes short chapters and avoids "description, back story and scene setting whenever possible." He prefers to "hurl readers into the action and establish his characters with a minimum of telegraphic details."[2]

Am I saying that everyone should write like James Patterson? No. I'm encouraging you to find your own voice (distinct style) within the parameters of your purpose and the preferences of your intended audience. Patterson's purpose is to entertain the general public, and he's honed a writing style that succeeds in entertaining millions.

Not everyone likes Patterson's style. A *Washington Post* reviewer called one of his works "subliterate," to which Patterson responds, "Thousands of people don't like what I do. Fortunately, millions do."

So what's your purpose in writing your present book? If it's to please critics, then write for critics. But that's a rather small audience. If your ultimate purpose is to please your English professor, then publish only one copy and give it to her. If your ultimate purpose is to reach a larger audience – to inspire or to inform or to entertain – you'd do well to study writers who are popular with your intended audience and get regular input from that audience.

3. Imitate Successful Authors Who Share Your Purpose and Audience

Study great musicians and you find them starting out by imitating the techniques of their heroes. I recall an early interview with guitarist Eddie Van Halen where he challenged the interviewer, "Name me any song by *Cream* and I'll play it for you." Who was the guitarist for *Cream*? Eric Clapton. Well, Eddie certainly developed his own style, but he began by imitating his heroes. Great writers tend to follow suit.

Before I acquired a publisher for my music book, I gave the manuscript to Josh McDowell, who had written scores of successful nonfiction books. He also had a huge platform, having spoken on more university campuses than probably any living person.

Now why would he be interested in the youth minister at Flat Creek Baptist? Because he was currently on the speakers' circuit with the backing of the rock band, Petra, and was getting flack from traditional pastors. I knew he was into the subject and assumed he would be interested in my manuscript.

McDowell urged me to declare war on all academic language, editing it down for the common reader. "If you write for academics," McDowell said, "only academics will read it. If you write for a broader audience and everyone begins to read it, then the academics will have to read it to be in the know."

Wise advice.

Thus my self-editing mantra became "well-researched; simply written." Is there a place for academic writing? Certainly. But it's not the most effective style for the audiences I'm targeting and the subjects I'm tackling.

Dale Carnegie is a master of the nonfiction style I imitate. He wrote the perennial bestseller, *How to Win Friends and Influence People*. It's not "great literature" as most would define it. Rather, he wrote very plainly and simply, similar to how he speaks. I prefer that style for the non-fiction that I read, although some would snub it as dumbed down or journalese. (Books by authors who snub his style, I might add, are generally not consistently ranked in the top 125 Amazon bestsellers 70 years after publication.)

Carnegie did extensive research, but presented his findings as fascinating stories. In his book on public speaking, Carnegie notes,

> "The rules from *How to Win Friends and Influence People* can be listed on one and a half pages. The other two hundred and thirty pages of the book are filled with stories and illustrations to point up how others have used these rules with wholesome effect."[3]

It's not easy to do this style well. Breezy doesn't imply easy. Carnegie was a master organizer, master storyteller, and a master at explaining complex subjects in language everyone could understand.

Your chosen style may differ from mine. That's fine. Whatever your style, study authors who have mastered it. As Brad Thor, author of thriller novels that have reached the New York Times Bestseller List, said,

> "...it's impossible to be a great writer without being a great reader. I read everything. If someone is doing well anywhere near my genre, I want to read it, and I want to know why."

4. Get Lots of Honest Feedback

It's one thing to know the principles of great writing in your genre, quite another to be able to objectively evaluate your own writing. I want to emphasize "lots of" in this subtitle. (I could have entitled it "a plethora of," but I'm the simple writer.) Three thousand years ago, King Solomon wrote:

> "In the abundance of counselors there is safety."

The word for "abundance of" in the original Hebrew text means "lots of." Why not get input from just a few? Simply because those few may not appreciate your style or might not share your passion for the subject matter. You need a larger sampling of readers to get broad input and understand the market.

Before I decided to write the music book, I sent a thirty-page manuscript on the issue to some people I respected: a college president and a couple of successful musicians. Not "lots of." Just three. Since I never heard back, I assumed that I wasn't saying anything important and abandoned the project.

Then, a few years later, I received a letter from the college president. He wrote, "Our music department is in turmoil over the music issue and your manuscript was the best thing I've ever seen on the subject. But I've lost it. Could you send me another copy?"

Today I shudder to realize that I took the silence of three busy people as rejection. I wouldn't have written the book had this brilliant academic not lost my manuscript.

And when you get advice, don't totally rely on the opinions of a few "experts."

Catherine Lanigan grew up dreaming of becoming a writer. But in her first year of college she took a creative writing seminar, led by a traveling Harvard professor. One of the assignments was to write a short story. But the day before she was to read hers to the class, the professor called her to his office, telling her that her writing stunk. Among other things, he said,

> "You have absolutely no idea about plot structure or characterization. How you were ever recommended for this class is beyond me. You have no business being here. One thing's for sure, you'll never earn a dime as a writer."

But this pompous twit of a pseudo-professor (my characterization) encouraged her that the good news was that he'd caught her at a crossroad of life so that she wouldn't waste her time and money studying something she wasn't suited for. So he worked a bargain with her: "I will get you through my class and give you a B if you promise never to write anything ever again."

She didn't write for fourteen years.

Fortunately, after those wasted years she told her story to a journalist who replied, "Why, I'm ashamed of you. You never even tried. Here's my card. If you ever write anything, give me a call." She immediately went home, wrote her first novel, and sent it to the journalist. A month after receiving it he called her, asking if he could send a copy to his agent. The agent called her from New York, referred to her as "startlingly talented," and asked whether she thought soft cover, hard cover or trade would work best. By Christmas, she had a publisher.

Lanigan went on to write 20 novels in twenty years, including *Romancing the Stone*, *Jewel of the Nile*, and *Wings of Destiny*. But it frustrates me that she might have written 37 novels had she not trusted in the counsel of one supposed authority who just happened to be an imbecile disguised as a scholar with his professional degrees and tweed jackets.[4]

So don't base your opinion on one person's input, even a supposed expert's input, or a few people's lack of enthusiasm. The fourth person may rave over it, or have several suggestions to fix the problem that turned off the first three. Your writers group is a good place to start, but expand further.

Become Idea-Driven

Cherie and I often read stories of great businesses, searching for the characteristics that distinguish them from losers. One common characteristic we've discovered is that great businesses tend to be idea-driven, searching constantly for the best ideas for direction and improvement. Rather than listening exclusively to their formally trained MBAs, they listen to people at all levels of their organizations. They listen to their competition. They listen to their cashiers. They listen to their customers.

So we find Michael Dell (Dell Computers) listening intently to his computer customers[5], Jack Welch (General Electric) creating ways to get everyone sharing ideas openly[6], Sam Walton (Wal-Mart) waking up early on Saturday mornings to buy donuts for his truckers to get their insights on the stores they visit.[7]

This is radically different from the way most writers approach their writing. Typically, they self-edit to the best of their ability, then mail it off to a publisher "to see if it's any good," or send it to an editor to put in final form. I believe most writers could improve their manuscripts immeasurably if they'd take a hint from smart business leaders and become more idea-driven.

One reason we need input is that we aren't very objective about our own writing. One day I'm overconfident, imagining that I've discovered a brilliant angle that's never been explored in the entire history of ideas. The next day I wonder why anyone would ever buy this crappy manuscript from such a low profile amateur. This explains why Stephen King's wife found the early pages of his manuscript crumpled in the trashcan. She shook off the cigarette ashes, read them, and encouraged him to complete it and seek publication. It became his first published novel, *Carrie*, which not only sold one million copies its first year in paperback, but was adapted as a feature film and Broadway musical.[8] Apparently, even though King was teaching English at the time, he couldn't see his own manuscript objectively. We're simply too close to our writing to perceive its worth.

For *Enjoy Your Money*, after relentlessly self-editing each chapter, I passed them on to Cherie (great at "big picture" issues) and mom ("the grammar queen"). After revising accordingly, I put my manuscript into as many hands as possible – not just fellow writers, who may love cool sentences and smart analogies – but to the regular readers I'm targeting.

I gave relevant portions or entire manuscripts to about 30 people, including my children, experts in the field, and anyone who owes me one (e.g., my auto insurance agent) or might be remotely interested in the subject. I even got input on a couple of chapters from an eighth grade advanced writing class. They were honored to meet a real live author. Their input was unique, candid, and led to several important chages.

> **Tip:** If one chapter deals with a topic on which you'd like to consult a professional or scholar, consider sending that chapter alone. I sent the psychology chapter of my music book to a psychology professor I respected, resulting in a more accurate chapter. A chapter is much more doable for a busy professional than a complete manuscript.

Getting lots of input is invaluable on several levels.

- **I discover, before publication, whether or not it has a market.** Don't despair if some (even family members) quickly tire of it and never get around to finishing it. Others won't like your subject matter or style. But if some of the readers get truly excited about it, you know that they probably represent hundreds of thousands of readers. When William P. Young wrote *The Shack*, he ran off 15 copies at Kinko's for his children and a few friends. When he saw that his friends were excited enough to want to send copies to their friends, Mr. Young realized that he should consider publishing for a wider audience. Good choice. It would go on to sell millions of copies.

- **Readers give me new, interesting material to add.** One brilliant CPA sat down with me for two hours, discussing my money book and recounting stories of clients he's counseled and how he advises people.
- **I'm able to correct inaccuracies of fact, misspellings, etc.** I'm always amazed at how the 25th reader will find an "obvious" mistake that none of the first 24 noticed.
- **I discover what some people like, and others dislike, about the book.** I can't please everyone, but I prefer to know their opinions before publication than afterwards! Then I can make my final editorial decisions with full knowledge of how people might respond.
- **Besides improving my manuscript, these early readers are critical to providing me with blurbs and early reviews that will jump-start my Amazon presence and attract more readers.** More about that in later chapters.

Tip: Since it's critical to get early, positive reviews, consider these points as you recruit your critique crew:

1) Don't recruit solely high-profile, busy people, with whom you have no strong, preexisting connection. They may not have time to write a review. Many of my early readers were friends and acquaintances that were more than happy to write reviews.

2) Consider recruiting from different parts of the country. If all your reviewers are local (Amazon reviews often include where the review originated), or most share the same last name ("real names" are noted in Amazon), some savvy shoppers will suspect that your dice are loaded. (Amazon recently banned reviews by the author's family members.)

What to Do with All that Advice

Take it seriously, because each opinion likely represents a group of people. But also take it with a grain of salt. You can't please everyone. I wrote *Enjoy Your Money* in story form – more specifically, a movie script format. Some tired of the story angle and just wanted me to tell them what to do with their money. Others loved the story angle, saying it was what kept them reading. The final decisions were mine, but it was valuable to know where both sides stood.

5. Do Some Research

Before I urge you to do great research, I want to back off a bit. Don't imagine that, in order to write a great book, you must do everything I recommend. I say this to keep you from getting discouraged. Writing a book is a massive project and I don't want to weigh you down by making it even more massive.

Last summer, Cherie and I attended a panel discussion by successful mystery writers at the *Decatur Book Festival*. Phillip DePoy, author of *The King James Conspiracy*, gave a big spiel on the importance of research and how heavily he researched certain fascinating historical events. The next panelist said, in essence, "I do hardly any research at all. It's fiction. I'm a magician who makes readers believe the illusion I've created. If someone points out to me that I misnamed a New York City street, I reply, 'Hey, it's fiction; I make things up! Don't use it for a road map!'"[9]

Idea! Put Your Leftover Research to Work

Inevitably, I end up with much more fascinating, relevant research than I can squeeze into my books. In this digital age, I can blog it, turn it into white papers on specialized topics, offer it free of charge on my Website as "Additional Resources" or "Teacher Resources," use it in talks where audiences want more than a rehash of the book, etc.

As you can see in this book, I often refer readers to additional resources if they want to go deeper. This results in more people coming to my sites, more people linking to me, and more people finding my books.

Authors can be rather independent souls who make wildly different choices about the way they write. But consider the value that research can add to a book.

- **The claim of research adds interest value.** When *The DaVinci Code* first came out, I occasionally heard people quoting it as if it were nonfiction. I thought they were confusing genres, sort of like saying that Bart Simpson is a great actor. But when I read the book and saw that Dan Brown claimed it was based on researched facts, I saw why people were intrigued. While many scholars argue that his sources were questionable at best, we can't deny that his research and claim to historical accuracy added allure to his story.

- **Accurate research makes reviewers and critics happy.** People delight in pointing out errors. Make enough errors and they'll write merciless reviews. Even if I'm writing for the general public, I'd like reviews from respected experts in my field. I couldn't have gotten a review for my music book from a respected college president had it not been thoroughly researched.

- **You appeal to a wider range of people.**

- **Libraries and schools take notice.** They love documentation and indexes.

- **Fresh research adds inherent value.** People will use it for their own research and quote from it in their books and articles.

- **Research makes marketing easier.** While it's difficult for new or midlist fiction writers to get reviews from major book reviewers, they might get interviews and reviews from journalists and experts who write about their topic. Because of the research for his novel, Phillip DePoy should have many more opportunities for publicity than the writer who did no research. A California radio station interviewed me this week about my money book. Later, they asked me to return for another interview, not primarily about the book, but as an expert on a financial topic. Had my book not shown substantial research, I doubt they would have invited me back. Become known as an expert in your field and you may become the go-to person that the media seeks out for comments.

How Research Helped My Book

For my music book, I used Georgia State University's library to study decades of research on the psychological and physiological impact of music. I used Emory University's religion library to study the history of church music, discovering that many of the hymns we consider traditional were often taken from tunes already popular in the secular world.

By presenting the results of solid research, I offered something of unique value.

For the chapters of *Enjoy Your Money* on investing, I read books by the most highly regarded experts on investing, quoting them and leveraging their authority, since I had no authority on my own (no degrees in finance or economics). If you have no authority in yourself, borrow authority from someone else. Quote the recognized experts. Then, people will recognize you as a source of authoritative information and an expert in your own right.

Successful actor Johnny Depp once said that when he takes a part, he not only learns the lines and does what's expected, but he tries to add "that little something extra." Can't you see that in his films? For writers, research can add "that little something extra" to make your book stand out from others.

I believe that my objective, dogged research motivated publishers in other countries to translate my music book into their languages. It's also why magazines in both the United States and Europe published excerpts and about 30 radio stations wanted to interview me in the months following its publication. Recognized as an expert, I was invited to speak in such great locations as Holland and Moscow.

I had no platform in music or personal finance before I wrote my books. In my case, a well-researched, well-written book *became* my platform to attract radio interviews and speaking engagements.

A Great Model for Self-Help

Let's take another look at Dale Carnegie's *How to Win Friends and Influence People*. It's one of the all time international bestsellers, having been translated into most of today's written languages.

I recently attended a conference with about 250 techies. At one point, the keynote speaker asked how many of them had read Carnegie's book. From my vantage point, it looked like every hand went up. Reflect on this a bit – techies and entrepreneurs, not psychology majors and salesmen.

Doesn't that strike you as odd? Myriads of psychological and sociological studies of relationships have been done since 1937, when Carnegie originally published his book. And culture has changed significantly. Shouldn't people want to read something more current? What's the appeal?

First, it's simply a collection of well-told stories of the relational techniques of great and fascinating people. That makes it both readable and appealing. But many of today's self-help books imitate that style. A second observation is key. The author convinces me in his preface that this is no book of fluff. He did exhaustive research. Allow me to quote from Carnegie's preface, where the master influencer successfully influences me to take his book seriously:

> "In preparation for this book, I read everything that I could find on the subject – everything from newspaper columns, magazine articles, records of the family courts, the writings of the old philosophers and the new psychologists. In addition, I hired a trained researcher to spend one and a half years in various libraries reading everything I had missed, plowing through erudite tomes on psychology, poring over hundreds of magazine articles, searching through countless biographies, trying to ascertain how the great leaders of all ages had dealt with people. We read their biographies. We read the life stories of all great leaders from Julius Caesar to Thomas Edison. I recall that we read over one hundred biographies of Theodore Roosevelt alone. We were determined to spare no time, no expense, to discover every practical idea that anyone had ever used through the ages for winning friends and influencing people."[10]

But there was more to his research. He interviewed people. He prepared a short talk on people skills and encouraged the attendees to try out the principles and report back, so that his book "grew and developed out of that laboratory, out of the experiences of thousands of adults."

That kind of research sells books. One informed book buyer told me that the first place he looks in a book is the acknowledgements. There he discovers whether the author did his homework or just recorded his own ideas.

Research beyond the Library

Some authors will be inspired by that Carnegie paragraph. For others, it will have the effect of a newbie guitarist who saw a video of master shredder Yngwie Malmsteen and commented, "I never want to pick up a guitar, ever again."

But take heart, not all research has to be on such a massive, exhaustive scale.

Consider doing a survey, even if it's quite informal. So you're writing a book about pet care. Call 50 veterinarians and ask a simple question:

> "You see the heart-rending results of poor pet care every day. If you had the opportunity to address a group of pet owners and warn them about the most important aspects of pet care, which would you say are the most important?"

Also ask them how many years they've been treating animals. Let's say they average 20 years. **That means you've just collected 1,000 years of veterinary experience!** Include these results in your book and mention in your preface that your wisdom comes, not just from your personal experience and reading, but also from your collection of over 1,000 years of veterinary experience. That speaks with authority. That's new information that pet columnists and news reporters would love to interview you about.

Even if your book's already published, it's not too late to do a similar research project, send out press releases about it, and solicit interviews, with the interviewers referring to you as "the author of...."

Now, are there books that exhibit no research at all, but simply relate personal experience, that sell well? Yes. But imagine that an acquisitions editor has five proposals on her desk for books much like yours, all of which seem equally compelling and well written. But only one is documented with top authorities or includes original research. Which does she choose? It's a no brainer. So do some research to separate your book from the stack. To make your odds even better, do fabulous research.

6. Choose a Marketable Setting

When David Cady wrote his first novel, *The Handler*, about a detective attempting to rescue someone's daughter from a snake handling cult, he set it in Chattanooga, Tennessee, along the Tennessee River. That's also a popular tourist destination. Now he sells many copies in local shops that target tourists, who are interested in a book written about the region. This fall, a film crew is scheduled to begin filming the story on location.

Could a wise choice of setting make your next book more marketable?

7. Consider Involving Other Writers

Benjamin Franklin met regularly with *Junto*, a varied group of people he described as "ingenious" and "lovers of reading."[11] Members improved their writing by handing out their manuscripts for the open critique of the group. C.S Lewis and J.R.R. Tolkien met regularly with *The Inklings*, who gave input on each other's writing.[12] Sometimes writers can be private folks. But I can't urge you enough: Force yourself out of your shell and spend time with other writers.

I think screenwriters are healthy models. Study them. They're much more likely to say, "When *we* were writing this season of *Lost*..." than "When *I* wrote...."

This should be freeing to a many writers, especially those who fear that they don't have the entire package of talents. You don't have to be good at every aspect of writing. Even professional editors tend to excel in one area of writing.

In my opinion, few writers can:

- spot a grammatical error from across the room.
- discover inconsistencies.
- spell.
- "hear" the most pleasing "rhythm" of a series of sentences.
- include all the little, picky details.
- see the big picture.
- organize many details into an orderly structure that flows.
- recognize flaws in logic.
- recognize insufficient documentation.
- recognize factual errors.
- know how to develop a character that people care about.
- name characters.
- do thorough, accurate research.
- write catchy titles, including chapter titles and subtitles.

And I'm just scratching the surface.

George Lucas (*Star Wars*, etc.) can tell a great story, but sources say he's an atrocious speller.[13] Yet, who cares, as long as he keeps great spellers around? James Patterson writes out a detailed outline of the story, gives it to a co-author to flesh out, then takes the manuscript and puts it into final form.[14] If you can't or don't want to do it all, it's okay to seek help.

You may want to even consider officially co-writing, so that both names are on the book. That means two people will be eager to market the book. Jack Canfield and Mark Victor Hansen created the *Chicken Soup* series, which became a publishing phenomenon. Acquiring a publisher and doing publicity were uphill battles, but Canfield said he was aided by Hansen being more outgoing than him. Teaming up with another can add enough synergy to the writing and marketing process to make things happen.[15]

I know an author who wanted to write an illustrated children's book about a famous American. But before he started writing, he thought about marketing. He studied the various tourist centers dedicated to famous Americans to discover which ones sold books and got the most visitors. Once he decided upon one, he found out who was in charge and who were the most respected scholars concerning this great American. He got input from both the manager and a scholar, which resulted in some changes in the illustrations to reflect the period more accurately. He credited both in his book. By taking this extra step, he not only produced a better book, but he secured a source of large, ongoing sales. If you worked at this tourist center re-ordering books, wouldn't you feel obligated to keep reordering the book that had your boss' name on it? And imagine, if he didn't already have a publisher, the impact of a query saying, "I've secured a huge source of sales."

8. Learn from Great "How to Write" Books and Writing Publications

Some young writers avoid them, afraid that they'll destroy their "natural, conversational style." But remember, you don't *have* to do everything they say.

Others think they can learn all they need by imitating the great writers in their genre. Yet when I read books that I'd love to imitate (and virtually all authors agree that a steady diet of great books is essential to becoming a great writer), I find that some of their techniques are rather obvious and others aren't. I gain so much more by allowing my favorite writers to tell me about their writing process. They tell me in their "how to write" books and articles.

Although I did a lot of writing in college and graduate school, I never took a class specifically on writing. So when I began writing books, I did my own self-study. I read *The Elements of Style*--the sixty page modern classic. An acquisitions editor at InterVarsity Press suggested that anyone writing for publication should read William Zinsser's *On Writing Well* and do what he says. I read it and did what he said. I also listed some of his tips on a single page to guide me in self-editing, such as, "Am I overusing passive tense?"

Over the years, I've continued to read articles by or on great writers, read their "how I write" books, and thoroughly enjoy hearing writers talk about their craft at monthly meetings of the *Georgia Writers Association*. Cherie and I listened to the audio version of Stephen King's *On Writing* while traveling. Great tips and fun, fun, fun!

9. Take Professional Courses of Study

In her late 40s, Cherie completed an undergrad degree in Communications and a Masters in Professional Writing. I bugged her relentlessly to tell me what she was learning, so that I benefited from her experience as well. One of her texts, by Peter Rubie and Gary Provost, gave the most wonderful synopsis of a great story. They claim that it's the plot for 90 percent of the great stories in either film or ink. I pinned it up beside my desk:

> "Once upon a time, *something happened* to someone, and he decided that he would pursue a *goal*. So he devised a *plan of action*, and even though there were *forces trying to stop him*, he moved forward because there was *a lot at stake*. And just as things *seemed as bad as they could get*, he learned *an important lesson*, and when offered the prize he had sought so strenuously, he had to *decide whether or not to take it*, and in making that decision he *satisfied a need* that had been created by *something in his past*."[16]

That brilliant paragraph gave me a template for my stories. It's not that I always follow it to the letter, but typically I find that if I've missed an element, my story will improve by adding it.

This tip helped me with *Enjoy Your Money* in a way that none of my 30+ readers ever mentioned. Not enough was at stake for my characters. So these high school seniors wanted to do better than their parents with their finances. Let's all yawn. It's not exactly Luke Skywalker longing to leave the farming planet so that he could save the universe from the evil emperor with the beautiful Princess Leia.

"How can I make the stakes higher for my characters?" I wondered. So I made Akashi, my Asian character, the intellectual black sheep of her high achieving family. Her older siblings excel at Georgia Tech and MIT, while she struggles to eke out Cs. Her nonchalant, counter-cultural attitude towards school belies a relentless fear that her C average will result in a C career and a C life. She desperately needs someone to convince her that she can succeed at something.

By adding a couple of sentences here and there, I ramped up the stakes. Now readers are pulling for Akashi. Now they're emotionally invested in her future.

Learning the Craft as Platform

Earlier in my career, when I was seeking a literary agent, one snooted me soundly. She asked me what writer's conferences I had attended. I responded, "none." I think she sized me up quickly as a small time hick from Georgia who'd never make it as a writer and rudely brushed me off, moving on to talk to more important people.

Agents and publishers want to know that you're a serious writer. Prove to them that you're serious about learning your craft, and you'll be more impressive than I was.

Reading books on your craft, subscribing to writing magazines, taking classes, attending writers' conferences, and joining your local writers' association sets you apart from hordes of casual writers. Agents and publishers will take notice. They want writers who are serious about their craft and understand the industry.

Concluding Remarks

I'll let Frank Peretti, New York Times best-selling novelist with more than 12 million copies of his works in print, sum up this section:

> "Never stop learning. Learn all you can about the craft. Know what you're doing. Read books about it, take classes, read other authors, do all you can to develop your skill. Did you notice that I didn't say, 'Never give up?' Persistence comes second to learning. If you don't know what you're doing, you can persist until you're dead and never be a writer. I still consider myself a student of writing; I'm still learning."[17]

Do Something!

To make my next book more marketable, I will...

1 –

2 –

3 –

Keep Learning!

- **See my free updates** to each chapter at www.sellmorebooks.org.
- **To sharpen your nonfiction, read William K. Zinsser's classic, *On Writing Well*.** Make a checklist of ideas from his book to help your self-editing.
- **To sharpen your fiction, read Stephen King's writing memoir, *On Writing*.** Make a checklist of ideas to help your self-editing.
- **Subscribe to a writing magazine in your genre to learn from contemporary writers.**

Chapter 4

Write a Title and Subtitle that Attract Audiences

Titles: The Potential and Challenges

I wanted to title my music book *The Redemption of Rock*. It was cool, controversial, and easy to remember. Tyndale house overruled me and titled it *The Contemporary Christian Music Debate*. After the revolutions, I'm so glad they did.

I haven't publicized the book since 1995 and it's a bit dated; yet, I'm convinced that it continues to sell steadily because anyone searching for books on Google or in Amazon with the phrase "Contemporary Christian Music" will find it toward the top of their search. People searched that term 74,000 times last month in Google. Had it been called *The Redemption of Rock*, it would likely have been found on page 680 of the Google results for terms like "rock," lost in a crowd of rock music books and geological books.

Many authors of *good* books outsell authors of *great* books simply because they're more easily found. This phenomenon resulted from the seismic marketing shift from "interrupting people" to "helping searchers find you." By wisely (or fortunately) including relevant, much-searched phrases in their titles and/or subtitles, authors have done the equivalent of positioning their books open-faced by the bookstore cash register rather than hiding them away in a dark corner of aisle number twelve.

Of course there are other, often-competing priorities when considering a title. Ideally, titles should be

- memorable
- short

- clever
- enticing
- descriptive of your content.

But after the revolutions, we'd be wise to throw "findable" into this already-challenging mix, since titles can make a huge difference in helping searchers find your book. A workable compromise is to concentrate on "clever, short, enticing, and memorable" for your title, and "descriptive, including keywords" for your subtitle.

Thus, my title *Enjoy Your Money* is memorable, easy to mention on radio interviews, and unique enough to be found by a person searching specifically for that title on the web. The subtitle explains what the book is about, using words that are often searched with the term "money"; *How to Make It, Save It, Invest It and Give It*.

It appears that Amazon's search engine prioritizes helping customers find specific titles over finding the best books on a subject. In other words, imagine that you search Amazon for meteorology books on the destructive potential of wind. So you search the term "wind." If there's a novel named "Wind," you might find it, or even "Gone with the Wind" before any meteorology books that don't include "wind" in their titles.

Here's how Amazon describes its priorities for directing search traffic:

> "To ensure maximum title searchability in our store, it is important that your book listing has complete and correct title, author and subject information. When a general keyword search is performed on site, our search engine will search for those words in the title, author, and subject fields of books on our site. Then, our search engine posts the results in order based on availability, popularity, and relevance."[1]

So it's probably much more effective to include key phrases in your title/subtitle than to assume you can adequately attract relevant searches by adding key phrases in the "Tags" section of your Amazon page.

How to Find Much-Searched Phrases for Your Topic

To use popular search phrases in your title, you must first discover which phrases people most often use to find information on your topic. Say you're writing a biography of Martin Luther King, Jr. for young people. You'd like people to find your book, not only when they search "Martin Luther King, Jr.," but when they search for books on racism or prejudice or segregation. But you can't throw every related word into your title. You must narrow down which are the most important. To discover this, you need the *Google Keywords Tool*. It will tell you how many times any given word or phrase was searched in the last month. Here's how I use it for crafting my titles/subtitles.

The Boring Details

1. **Brainstorm, with family and friends, all the terms that you think people might use to search for your book's subject matter.** (This works for novels as well as nonfiction. How might people search for a book with your novel's location or dominant theme [e.g. Long Island, sharks, vampires, lawyers, espionage, etc.])

2. **Find the key words tool.** (Search "Google Key Words Tool" in Google.)

3. **Type each term into the "Word or Phrase" box and click "Search" to discover new terms and how many times they were searched last month.**

4. **Keep this information on file.** Besides helping with your title, you can use these phrases over and over as you optimize your Amazon pages, send out press releases, make your blog posts findable, etc.

Think Different

- If the most searched terms in your subject area are already overused in titles of other books by authors who are likely to outsell you (e.g., "money") **it might be more effective to target a lesser-used term/phrase** (e.g. "personal financial management"). Better to come out at the top of a search for a lesser-used term, than pages down for the most searched term.

- **Consider a long, unwieldy subtitle.** In two popular books on how to sell your books most effectively on Amazon, notice their use of titles and subtitles to capture key word searches.

  Sell Your Book on Amazon: *The Book Marketing Coach Reveals Top Secret How-To Tips Guaranteed to Increase Sales for Print on Demand and Self Publishing Writers*

  Aiming for Amazon: *The New Business of Self Publishing, or How to Publish Your Books with Print on Demand and Online Book Marketing at Amazon.com*

Let's take a closer look at these subtitles, obviously crafted to capture searches.

1) **They loaded their titles/subtitles with key words/phrases.** Here are just a few:

"How to Sell Your Book" – Searched 1,600 times last month

"Sell Your Book" – Searched 12,100 times

"Book Marketing" – 110,000 times

"Marketing Coach" – 12,100 times

"Increase Sales" – 110,000 times

"Self Publishing" – 135,000 times

The cumulative impact of these highly searched phrases indicates that several hundred thousand people could potentially find their books in any given month.

2) **A change of one letter can make a huge difference.** The plural "How to Sell Your Books" was searched 590 times, whereas the singular "How to Sell Your Book" was searched 1,600 times. How would you know this without consulting the key words tool?

3) **They provide evidence that the book selling playing field has indeed been leveled for the new authors and non-celebrities.** Neither of these books are traditionally published. Neither of the authors are household names. Yet they each have well over 100 reviews on Amazon and people are buying them (both of their Amazon rankings indicate steady sales). Why are they buying? First of all, people find these books when they search for the topic with key phrases. Second, after readers find them, the reviews assure them that the books indeed contain the information they're looking for. The reviewers typically indicate that they were pleased with their purchases.

4) **The subtitle as it reads on Amazon doesn't match the subtitle on their book covers.** Hmmm. Apparently, they didn't want to adorn their covers with such long, rambling subtitles. I didn't know you could get away with that, but if Amazon continues to allow it, authors can make use of key phrases without littering their front covers with a page of text.

Keep Thinking

Hang out with this tool for a bit. Let its awesome power sink in. We can actually know what terms people are using to search for books like ours! This is truly astounding! Rather than shamelessly hounding people who may or may not be interested in our books, we can help people who are already searching for our books to find us. Doesn't *helping* sound a lot more fun than *hounding*? But we're still learning how to fully exploit these tools. Join us in dreaming up new ways to apply them to selling our books.

Do Something!

To put this chapter into action, I will…

1 –

2 –

3 –

Chapter 5

Attract People with Your Cover

The man who said, "Don't judge a book by its cover," never sold a book in his life.

- words hanging in the office of William Shinker, publisher of Gotham Books[1]

Anybody who says, "you can't judge a book by its cover" has never met the category buyer at Barnes & Noble.

- Terri Lonier[2]

According to Dan Poynter, bookstore browsers spend four seconds looking at the front cover and fourteen seconds looking at the back cover.[3] A *Publishers Weekly* poll of 1,000 adults found two-thirds of them rating the information on the back cover and inside flaps as either "extremely important" or "very important."[4]

So imagine that someone's searching a bookstore for her next read. Something about your book's title on the spine catches her eye. She picks it up. Now you've got 18 seconds to hook her into exploring further. If you fail, she'll reshelf it and continue her search.

Make the Title Clear and Attractive on the Spine

The spine is the first part of your book that bookstore browsers typically see. Make it readable at a distance. Make it stand out! Publishing and marketing experts Arielle Eckstut & David Henry Sterry put a blurb on the spine of one of their books. That's a terrific idea, providing a high profile endorsement even before the customer pulls it off the shelf.

Don't Rest Until the Front and Back Cover are Perfect

1. Choose a designer with care. Look at her past work. Talk to some of her past clients. Does she have enough experience with book design to convince you that that she consistently puts out quality work?

2. If you're concerned with containing costs, consider a graphic arts professor. Peter Bowerman says that although many professional designers charge from $1500-2500+, "you ought to be able to get one for half that if you hunt." Cherie and I tend to pay from $200 to $250 for our cover designs and people always comment on how professional our books look. For this book and my money book, we hired a professor of graphic arts at a local university. She loves doing outside jobs. As an added incentive, professors are often urged to get out of the university and do service in the communit.

Tip for Starving Artists

If you're destitute, ask a graphic arts professor if she knows a talented student who'd love to do a low cost project, primarily to get something cool on her resume. Discuss the details over a bean burrito at Taco Bell.

3. Give general ideas to the designer up front, but give her the option of rethinking it from scratch. We like to browse stock photos for our covers on www.istockphoto.com, where we can get free digital copies (ink-marked until you pay) to play around with and to recommend to our designer before we make our final decisions and pay for the licensed copies.

4. Give your designer accurate specifications from your printer/publisher concerning dimensions, bleeds, etc.

5. Let the designer know that you want a digital copy of the cover large enough to use for a poster. That lets her know the size of the images she needs to purchase.

6. Make it look professional. People judge books by their covers. So don't make it an afterthought. And don't stop tweaking until it looks perfect.

7. I recommend using blurbs on both the front and back. Especially for low profile authors, we need others to sing our praises. Look at many covers to decide what you want and where. Typically, the back cover displays two or more of your top blurbs, a book description – with bullet points of benefits to the reader, an author photo and brief bio.

8. Get lots of input. Often, a designer will give you several options or let you look at the almost completed design for a final okay. Don't trust your own judgment. Enlist as many people as you can to look over it. We ask friends, colleagues, children, waiters, and anyone within grabbing distance to give their totally frank first impressions. Often, they disagree with one another. But I'm typically amazed at how only one out of ten may notice something significant that nobody else saw. And that person may represent one tenth of your potential audience.

Get a Professional Author Photo

In most cases, people can tell when your headshot was snapped by your middle school daughter at the kitchen table. I highly recommend a professional photographer. I really, really hate to spend money unless I have to, but in this case I'm glad I did. I use these photos not only on my books, but on displays for author appearances, in brochures, in my social media presences, and on my websites. I didn't pay big bucks for my photographer, but I looked at plenty of her photos to make sure I liked her work.

Look at author photos on their author blogs. What expressions work? What settings? What clothing? Express any ideas to the photographer and make sure she takes enough shots to give you plenty of choices. Bring informal and formal clothes. Being both color blind and fashion challenged, I get input from several people about what I should wear. And make sure the photos are large enough to be used in a poster (for author signings) and high enough dpi (dots per inch) for print, which requires a higher dpi than the web.

Tweak Your Bio to Appeal to Your Audiences

First, think about your audiences. What might they respect or find fascinating about you? If you're writing a novel for middle school boys, they may not care that you've got a PhD, but may love to know that you once played in a rock band. But the middle schoolers aren't your only audience. You're also courting distributors, bookstore managers and reviewers – many of whom respect degrees.

Second, think about your qualifications to write the book. Look over your resume. Get ideas from your friends and family. Does your education, life experience, vocation, or personal study qualify you to write on this subject? Have you taught seminars, lectured at a university, or been an active member of a related association?

Third, play around with these qualifications to see how they can put you in the best possible light with your audiences. Writing my book on music, I knew that my background was weak. Who wants to read a book on an important subject by:

> "The minister of youth at Flat Creek Baptist Church in Fayetteville, Georgia?"

So I pitched myself as:

> "Serving on the ministerial staff of a large, metro Atlanta church."

Are both accurate and truthful? Yes. In a way, my official title ("minister of youth") would mislead many, conjuring up visions of a part-time college student planning games and pizza parties for teens to keep them off the streets. Yet, most of the youth ministers I hung out with had master's degrees, with professional training in fields like psychology and education. In describing myself to the public, I felt very comfortable putting my position in terms they'd better understand and respect.

With a bit of creativity, authors can often spin liabilities into strengths. When John Gray, a former celibate monk, wrote a book about relationships, customers would obviously ask themselves, "What does a monk know about relationships with women?" He countered by turning his past into a strength, something like "I had an advantage in relationships, since I learned to be happy without someone else. This allowed me to enter relationships without expectations of others having to complete me and make me happy." His book became a New York Times Best Seller: *Men are from Mars, Women are from Venus*.

Are Academic Credentials a Must?

Although an impressive bio with academic and professional credentials can help, it's not always necessary. Alberta Sequeira lost her husband and daughter to alcoholism and wrote memoirs about dealing with the devastating effects of alcohol.

Many who live with alcoholics yearn to hear how others cope. Sure, they'll listen to the Ph.D. who specializes in addictions, but they also want to hear from the person who's been there. No wonder she finds many opportunities to speak to groups and sell her books.

If you're writing in a field where most readers expect academic credentials, but you lack them, consider not listing your schooling at all. Readers may assume that you've done your formal training. Instead, tell something interesting about yourself, your connection with the topic, or how many years you've studied the topic (if it's dramatic). Blurbs from respected academics in the field (or co-writing with one, or having one write the introduction) just might overcome your educational deficiencies.

Is there something interesting about your life that might tie into your topic? While writing my personal finance book, I was raising seven sons in a blended family while caring for elderly relatives. While that doesn't in itself qualify me to write a financial book, it lets parents who are raising a mere three or four children understand that I've probably learned a thing or two about making ends meet in difficult situations and can relate to their struggles to guide their children to independence.

Radio audiences love to hear about people's real life circumstances like how they cope with life's difficulties. So when radio hosts look for people to interview, they often look as much for what you've experienced as what you know.

If you're eminently qualified to write on your topic, either with degrees or experiences, flout them. It's no more an indication of pride than listing your degrees in a curriculum vitae. You're demonstrating your expertise and your right to teach in this field. Many readers look for these credentials.

Do Something!

To put this chapter into action, I will...

1 –

2 –

3 –

Keep Learning!

Read author bios to see the variety of ways they present themselves, jotting down elements that you think appeal to readers and might be useful in crafting your own bio.

Chapter 6

Publish through the Most Marketable Channel

Don't Let the Wrong Publisher Sabotage Your Publicity!

The fool believes everything that he hears.

- King Solomon

How many legs does a dog have if you call the tail a leg? Four. Calling a tail a leg doesn't make it a leg.

- Abraham Lincoln

I begin this chapter with fire in my eyes. This morning, a distraught author e-mailed me a heart-wrenching note, explaining how her publisher ruined her meticulously planned (months in the making) book launch by failing to have the books available at the critical location. If this were a one-time slip-up by a normally reliable publisher, it would be forgivable. But Google this publisher and you'll find report after report after report of deceptive practices, breaches of contract, and general author abuse. Because of her contract, her books will be consistently overpriced and bookstores will routinely brush her off. She chose the wrong publisher, and that one mistake will drastically impact her ability to market her book.

Her publisher's website paints a different picture – a Mother Teresa image of caring about authors, giving them the financial cut they deserve, with plenty of ecstatic testimonies to back up their claims. No wonder naïve authors flock to them by the hundreds.

Swindlers thrive in times of revolution and rapid technological advancement. With all the bewildering publishing options, many authors think, "Hey, I've completed the hard work of writing. I just need a publisher to print it and get it out there. I want to see that finished book in my hands! What difference could it make who publishes it?"

All the difference in the world.

I don't apologize for presenting this information as detailed pro and con lists. To decide which publishing options will work best for selling your books, you must understand the various options. Welcome to the business side of writing.

I'll limit my discussion of the industry to the broad strokes and big decisions that will impact your ability to sell your books.

A Brief Guide to Publishing after the Revolutions

Note: After the revolutions, we find subsidy publishers calling themselves traditional publishers and "self-published" confused with "subsidy published." Some identify print on demand with self-publishers, although many major publishers use POD printing. Many publishing terms are being used in different, often contradictory ways. I'll stick with the more generally accepted definitions, but the burden's on you to understand how any given publisher or printer is using the terms.

Publishing Option #1: Get Traditionally Published

Traditional publishers receive query letters and proposals from authors and/or literary agents, accepting only a small percentage of them. Why are they so picky? Because if they publish a book that doesn't sell thousands of copies, they typically lose money. The publisher takes a huge risk for each book it publishes, footing the bills for editing, designing, typesetting, printing, and marketing. They also pay the author an "advance" on royalties, meaning that if they pay a new author a $4,000 advance, the author gets paid nothing from book sales until sales have recouped the advance. **Traditional publishers are not paid by authors to either prepare books for publication or to publish them.** Traditional publishers typically (but not always) print offset runs of 5,000 or more copies in order to make the production cost per book low enough to make a profit after distributors, wholesalers, and bookstores take their cut.

Some Benefits to Getting Traditionally Published

I was delighted that Tyndale House, a respected traditional publisher, published my first book. They always dealt with me in a very kind and respectful way. I was thoroughly impressed with them and enjoyed the relationship.

Typical (but not assured!) advantages to traditional publication include:

1. **I get respect:**

- From other publishers, making it easier to get my next manuscript published.
- From bookstores, who are more likely to carry my books and allow me to do signings.
- From schools and libraries, who trust big publishers to carry quality products.
- From major book reviewers, who simply don't have time to review every book. They typically shorten their stacks of incoming books by first throwing out all the self-published and subsidy published books.

2. I get a professionally edited and designed book.

3. I'm much more likely to get it into bookstores. If your dream is to sell lots of copies in lots of bookstores, seek a traditional publisher that bookstores both respect and love to do business with. Often, self-published authors see bookstores as prejudiced and snooty toward them, as if they consider all self-published literature as trash. But authors need to understand life from a bookstore manager's perspective.

Imagine that you manage a large bookstore. You love books and love to sell them – that's why you're in the business. But you don't have time to read the one million plus books that were published in 2009 (2,750 per day!), to see which ones work for your store. Instead, you limit yourself to choosing from among the 288,000 traditionally published books, knowing that they're typically better edited, professionally designed, and often analyzed by book marketing experts.

But not having time to read the 789 books published by traditional publishers each day (33 each hour), you rely on the advice of respected distributors and the catalogues of major publishers. You also consult the recommendations of the major book reviewers.

"Sure," you might say to a self-published author, "I'll miss some great self-published works. But who's got time to read through each press kit and look over each book to make sure it's a quality book?"

4. I get to concentrate on writing while the publisher takes care of the publishing.

5. They will do some publicity. Tyndale House publicists had connections with radio and TV that I didn't have. They sent copies out for review. They arranged thirty or so radio interviews and a TV interview. They sent me copies of reviews from their clipping service. They also put my book in their catalogue, which went to bookstores and distributors.

6. They often have distributors who actually call on bookstores and the bookstores' corporate decision-makers, recommending your book. They offer your book to bookstores with an attractive return policy, through the major wholesalers, making it a low risk decision for booksellers.

7. There's no up-front monetary publishing risk on my part. Again, in traditional publishing, they pay me. I don't pay them.

Drawbacks to Traditional Publishers

1. They tend to spend their marketing dollars on their top authors, leaving very little for new and midlist authors.

2. It's difficult and discouraging to receive rejection after rejection. Yet, that's a part of the business.

3. If your book doesn't take off from the start (the first few months), they're not likely to do more marketing, other than continued inclusion in their catalogue. Understandably, they concentrate their efforts on newer books.

4. Great writing doesn't guarantee that you'll be accepted. Many books that became best sellers had great difficulty finding publishers.

5. Getting a publisher doesn't guarantee that bookstores will stock your book. They simply don't have room for every new book.

6. Getting into bookstores doesn't guarantee that the marketing campaign will be effective enough to bring people into bookstores to buy it.

7. Getting bought in bookstores doesn't guarantee that bookstores will automatically reorder.

Traditional publishing tends to work best for authors who:

1. Already have a following, particularly if you write fiction.

2. Have a high platform, particularly if you write nonfiction.

3. Write books that can be marketed to a large audience.

4. Demonstrate the willingness and ability to involve themselves in the marketing process.

5. Have the fortitude to endure rejection after rejection (from both literary agents and publishers) before getting accepted.

6. Can work with other people and have the flexibility to give up some control of final decisions concerning editing, title, and design.

If you want to shoot for a major publisher...

1. Browse the books most like yours (genre, topic, etc.) in your local bookstore. Write down the publishers and then look in their acknowledgements to find the names of their literary agents.

2. Look up those publishers and literary agents on the web to see what kinds of books they're looking for and how they like work submitted. Do they prefer e-mail? Snail mail? A query letter? Proposal?

3. Learn more about various publishers through Writer's Market (www.writersmarket.com). Libraries typically carry the latest copy.

4. Read a good book on traditional publishing, such as *The Essential Guide to Getting Your Book Published*, by Arielle Eckstut & David Henry Sterry, or *How to Get Happily Published*, by Judith Applebaum.

5. Put together a spotless query and proposal, according to the specifications of each publisher. Most authors don't. You've spent all this time and energy perfecting your manuscript. It's tempting to type up a query letter in a day and fling it out there.

Remember, your query is a publisher's first impression of your writing and your professionalism. Download Noah Lukeman's free e-book, *How to Write a Great Query Letter* (http://www.lukeman.com/greatquery). See also W. Terry Whalin's book, *Book Proposals That Sell.*

6. Remember, when seeking a publisher, it's not just about your book; it's about your marketing. In your proposal, convince the publisher that your book has a market and that you can and will actively market it.

In a publishers' forum, I read the following exchange with a literary agent:

> **Question:** "Which part of a formal book proposal do you feel is the absolute 'clincher' to make the sale to a major book publisher?"
>
> **Response:** "For nonfiction, it's the marketing section. This is assuming that the author is a legitimate expert, the subject is newsworthy and unique, and the writing is well crafted. The compelling description of a national platform from which an author can promote the book is hands down the (dare I say?) obsession of the major trade publishers."

Remember my quote from actor Johnny Depp, where he said he likes to add "that little something extra"? Apply that to your query and proposal. Describe, in detail, how you plan to market this book. Then say that you'll send them your 30-page marketing plan at their request.

Imagine yourself as an acquisitions editor at a major publisher. You've narrowed down that pile of 30 queries to five. But what's this? One author gives innovative ideas as to how he plans to market his book. He also offers his 30-page marketing plan that he will forward upon your request. That's "something extra." That shows initiative. That shows that this author plans to help market the book. It shows that he understands something about marketing. And that will be your answer to the marketing department's question of "Yes, but how will we market it?"

I don't think there's a standard format for a marketing plan. Mine is pretty informal, with a bunch of ideas divided into appropriate sections. One publisher told my agent that my marketing plan was "over the top."

Section One: Secure Blurbs

Section Two: Get Media Coverage

Section Three: Write Related Articles

Section Four: Partner with Organizations; Piggy-Back on Movements

Section Five: Utilize the Web

Section Six: Get It into Classrooms

Section Seven: Take Advantage of Gifts for Graduation

Section Eight: Use Other Proven Methods

Your sections will likely differ from mine. Where do you come up with marketing ideas? Read the second half of this book, indexing your ideas in the back. Then, read another book or two more on book marketing that specialize in listing hundreds of ways to market your books, indexing them as well for ideas. Formulate your plan from these ideas.

Three of my favorite books that list hundreds of ideas are:

1001 Ways to Market Your Books, by John Kremer.w

How to Make Real Money Selling Books, by Brian Jud.

Guerrilla Marketing for Writers, by Jay Conrad Levinson, Rick Frishman & Michael Larsen.

So show some initiative with your commitment to marketing. Every publisher's dream is to get writers with the motivation and savvy of Jack Canfield and Mark Victor Hansen.

7. Don't expect immediate results. And don't get discouraged by falsely assuming that rejection = poor writing. Michael Hyatt, now president of Thomas Nelson, the seventh largest publisher in the United States, had over 30 publishers reject his first book proposal. I'd say this is pretty standard. In Hyatt's case, it went on to be a *New York Times* bestseller.[1]

And what if you never get a traditional publisher? First of all, remember that publishers reject many good manuscripts for many different reasons, including:

- "You don't have a platform. Even if it's great, who's gonna buy it?"
- "Your marketing plan doesn't impress me."
- "New authors are risky. Our owners are limiting us to two new authors this year, which we already selected in January."
- "I just read six proposals for romance novels and they're all kind of blending together in my head right now."
- "Your book is on a subject I have absolutely no interest in."
- "We've already got a book on that topic and don't want to publish competition."
- "We don't know you. Meet us at a writers' conference."
- "I've got 60 proposals on my desk and my boss won't let me go on vacation until I've worked my way through all of them. I've got exactly four hours. I'll glance at your proposal while listening to voice messages and booking my hotel at the beach. Do you really think I've got time to sit down and get a good feel for your writing?"

If traditional publishers don't want to publish your book, consider other options.

Publishing Option #2: Self-Publish (or Publish Through Your Own Publishing Company)

In self-publishing, the author makes all the decisions, including editing, designing, printing, distribution and marketing. Some authors do their own design work. Others pay a professional to do the design. Some may choose to print copies through an offset or digital press. Others may choose a POD service. **The defining characteristic of the self-publisher is that she's at the helm, making all the final decisions.**

Self-publishing is a perfectly legitimate way to publish a book. Yet, prejudice persists. Just yesterday I heard of someone saying, disdainfully, "Self-publishing isn't publishing." I believe that this attitude is largely fueled by people who assume that:

> "If you write a good enough book, a publisher will recognize its greatness and publish it."

And its corollary:

> "If publishers fail to embrace your book, then it's not a good book."

Publishers are Far from Infallible

Yet, anyone active in the industry understands that these statements are patently false. Because of the overwhelming amount of submissions, acquisitions editors must make quick judgments about piles of book proposals, without even reading a significant portion of the sample chapters. Often, they toss manuscripts after reading the query. Even if they were able to read the sample chapters, their judgments would be accurate only insofar as their tastes match the tastes of a significant amount of the buying public.

This explains why 26 publishers rejected the now classic *A Wrinkle in Time*. Madeleine L'Engle's agent had given up and returned the manuscript to her, when L'Engle met someone at a Christmas tea party she'd thrown for her mom. He looked over the manuscript and insisted on passing it on to a publisher he knew. Although *Farrar, Straus & Giroux* didn't publish children's books at the time, they liked it enough to publish it. Once published, it won numerous awards and has been in print continually since 1962.[2]

Let's face it – gatekeepers in the creative sector don't possess an infallible sense of either great writing or marketable writing. We saw this in recent years when the top executives at Disney – drawing upon their years of experience in the entertainment industry – expressed their total disdain for a new series that their ABC underlings were pushing. They made such encouraging comments as:

- "This is a waste of time." (Robert Iger - past president of ABC and present CEO of Disney)
- "That's never going to work." (Michael Eisner – CEO of Disney at the time)

On a scale of 1-10, with 10 being the best, Eisner graded it a 2.[3]

But its creator, Lloyd Braun – against the recommendations of his superiors – moved forward with the pilot for "Lost," which became ABC's first breakout hit in years, topping all the ratings, capturing the imagination of millions of followers, and winning an Emmy Award for Outstanding Drama Series and a Golden Globe for Best Drama.

Yet, even after seeing the pilot, Eisner was singularly underwhelmed, saying, "'Lost' is terrible...Who cares about these people on a desert island?"[4] Although millions of viewers ended up caring, Lloyd Braun was fired before the series even started. Whether we're talking music, books, film, or television, the gatekeepers are very fallible with their subjective judgments on both programming and writing.

Great Books That Were Originally Self-Published

Richard Bolles self-published his first book, *What Color is Your Parachute? A Practical Manual for Job-Hunters and Career-Changers*, back in 1970. He wrote the book, designed it, and had his local printer make 100 copies at a time, as the market demanded (the earlier way to print on demand). After selling a couple thousand copies (proving the book had a market), he landed a traditional publisher. Currently, eight million copies are in print. It is still purchased by 20,000 people a month and has been on the New York Times Bestseller List for 288 total week.[5]

Personal finance radio personality Dave Ramsay didn't start out with his huge radio platform. He started with a personal story of how he overcame his own debt and a passion to help others who faced similar financial troubles. So he self-published his first book, *Financial Peace*, and took his first speaking engagements. Later, a publisher took it on and it became a best seller.[6]

William P. Young formed *Wind Blown Media* for the sole purpose of self-publishing his book, *The Shack,* after finding no success submitting it to 26 publishers. Published in 2007, it would claim the number one spot on the New York Times Bestseller List for 70 weeks. By May of 2010, over ten million copies were in print.[7]

> **Inspiration for Self-Published Authors**
>
> John Kremer inspires and instructs through his ever-growing collection of 500+ stories of self-published authors who made it big. Although the hard copy sells on Amazon, get the e-book version from his site, which contains many more stories than the hard copy. It's called *John Kremer's Self-Publishing Hall of Fame*, and is available at http://www.bookmarket.com.

And lest you think that these are rare counterexamples – curious flukes in an otherwise predictable world of publishing – John Kremer has collected over 500 examples of self-publishing successes, most of which sold hundreds of thousands or even millions of copies.

I suppose it's always been difficult to get published by major publishers. But over the past 20 years, with the consolidation of the book industry into a handful of large conglomerates and the emergence of bookstore chains, the emphasis has shifted toward getting sure, quick profits rather than betting on unknowns--even if the unknowns write remarkably well.

> *Under pressure from both their parent companies and booksellers, publishers became less and less willing to gamble on undiscovered talent and more inclined to hoard their resources for their most bankable authors.*[8]

Thus, for the low profile author – whether you're the literary author who's more dedicated to her craft than "making it in the industry," the scholar who yearns to display her research in the public arena, or the free spirit who wants to express himself – self-publishing provides a great option.

Understandably, since POD made self-publishing much easier and affordable, many self-published books are amateurish junk. But many authors turn out self-published books of excellent quality. Do it right and throw them on a table with 20 traditionally published books and I challenge anyone to tell me which were self-published.

Some Benefits of Self-publishing

1) I'm in control. I don't have to wrestle with the publisher about changing the story line, killing off a character, changing the title, or asking for a re-write that involves cutting the word count by one fourth. If you trust your own instincts better than the professionals at the publishing house, consider self-publishing.

2) I own the final product. I put it in any format I desire and sell it however I can, while controlling all rights. I can publish it digitally, publish separate chapters as pamphlets or white papers, or give away a chapter for marketing purposes, all without getting anyone's permission.

3) I can make a higher profit per book sold. (See chapter one.) By self-publishing a book that retails for $15, I can clear $6 or more per sale, compared to clearing $1.20 per sale of a traditionally published book (with a standard contract). So am I more likely to make more money total through self-publishing? I must ask myself, "How many more books is a traditional publisher likely to sell, leveraging his many advantages, such as superior distribution to bookstores?

"A book by the average author-that is, the average author who manages to find an agent and land a deal-sells just 11,800 copies, according to the Book Industry Study Group, a nonprofit research organization, and RR Bowker, a provider of bibliographic information."

4) I'm assured of getting published.

5) Speed. With traditional publishing, it might take six months to find an agent, another six months for the agent to find a publisher, and another year to publish it. That's a two-year process! These aren't extreme estimates. Although it might happen faster for you, it could also take a lot longer. With self-publishing, the process can move much more quickly, depending on your publishing schedule rather than the publisher's schedule.

6) Wisdom. Self-publishing is a great learning experience.

Drawbacks to Self-Publishing

1) There's a learning curve. Read a book or two on self-publishing and ask lots of questions to understand the process and your options.

2) If you're not a details person, find a friend who's already been through the process. There are a lot more details to take care of than you first think.

3) You'll probably find yourself hiring an editor, layout professional, and designer. You may have to fire some as well. Do you mind managing people?

4) You have little chance of selling many copies in bookstores, especially in the big chains. The bookstore industry is set up to work with traditional publishers, excelling with their best-selling authors. If you publish through Lightning Source or CreateSpace, your book will be *available for order* through bookstores. If you want bookstores to actually *carry* your book, arrange to have it available "with a return policy," so that bookstores can return unsold books for a refund. If you're with Lightning Source, make your terms attractive to bookstores by setting your "discount" to 50 percent so that bookstores can make their standard percentage on each sale.

Yet, since some authors have lost large sums of money with returns (printing thousands of copies to fill an order that later gets returned), many don't recommend establishing a return policy. (I don't have a return policy with my self-published books.) Unless you're doing some very effective marketing that's drawing hordes of people into bookstores to ask for your book, there's little chance that bookstores will carry your book, even if it's offered with a return policy.

Independent bookstores and specialty bookstores are often more open to carrying self-published books.

Which self-published books are most likely to be carried in large bookstores? Those that are selling so well outside of the bookstores that customers are starting to ask for them in bookstores.

Self-Publishing Tends to Work Best for Authors Who:

1) Have an entrepreneurial spirit. They relish the challenge of doing things themselves and making things happen.

2) Can handle details (or partner with a detail person).

3) Like to learn new things.

4) Are willing to market their own books.

5) Refuse to settle for a mediocre product.

Recommendations for Self-Publishers:

1. Don't appear self-published. Establish yourself as a publisher by registering your new business with your county/state and setting up a website with your publisher name in the url. It's neither costly nor difficult. Don't name the company after yourself. In this way, you're not immediately dismissed by reviewers, distributors, etc. Choose a general name that could encompass any type of book you might publish. Purchase your own ISBN numbers with your publisher name through Bowker. Now, look at yourself in the mirror and say, "I'm a publisher!" It's really that simple.

As a result, wherever your books are sold or marketed, the publishing company you created is listed as the publisher. Put your publishing company name and logo on the cover and early pages of your book. Now you look much more legitimate.

Take those few steps and you're no longer self-published. You're published through a press, albeit your own press. That's how Young formed Wind Blown Media to publish *The Shack*.

2. Decide between Print on Demand and Offset/Digital Printing

If you wish to print lots of copies and store them in your basement, digital printing is typically more cost effective for runs of 500 or less. For more copies, consider offset. With offset printing, authors print several thousand copies to save a couple of dollars per book. That's a big financial risk and a lot of books to store and ship, but if you can print a 250-page book for two dollars per book rather than four dollars per book, you can send out twice as many review copies for the same price and can price your books competitively through traditional channels.

For tips on hiring printers and a preferred list of those who specialize in books, see the Aeonix website(http://www.aeonix.com/bookprnt.htm).

I've been very pleased with using print on demand for my books. With the most popular POD companies, you risk very little up front (in some cases free to set it up), can get distribution through a large wholesaler (Ingram and/or Baker & Taylor), and can leave orders and shipping to your POD printer. Since books are printed as people order them, authors don't have to print thousands of copies, store them, take orders, and ship. Of course, if you own the copyright to your book, you can have your books available through POD and print special runs on digital or offset presses.

3. Understand the Services, Terms, and Charges of the Main POD Companies

During times of significant technological advance, people often have no idea how much time and effort services take and what is a reasonable price. If I wanted to purchase a practical, new family car, I know to expect a price of around $20,000. I'd consider $50,000 way out of line and $500 an indication that I'm buying a piece of junk. But since new writers aren't familiar with publishing costs, they're easily taken for a ride. You can spend from $200 to $20,000+ for editing, and from $150 to $2,000 for a cover design. How can you know if you're getting a quality service or product at a reasonable price?

One way is to compare with the major players. If you decide to go with print on demand, look first into the two biggest players, CreateSpace and Lightning Source International. As I write, they both have good reputations (although all large companies have their critics). I've been very happy with CreateSpace and I know many authors who publish through LSI and simply love them.

Even if you're pursuing a traditional or a subsidy publisher, you'd be wise to understand the costs of publishing after the revolutions, since many publishers use Lightning Source for printing and distribution to wholesalers.

Although both of these companies morph over time, I'll compare them as they exist today. I'm indebted to Pete Masterson, author of *Book Design and Production: A Guide for Authors and Publishers*, for helping me earlier with comparison figures.

Service Offered	Lightning Source	CreateSpace
Who can use this service?	publishers	authors and publishers
Cost to Print (If you come with a completed cover design and laid out book, in a digital format.)	$75 setup fee per title + $12 per year catalog fee per title to maintain the listing.	Free to publish through their Standard Plan. $39 fee per title to publish through their Pro Plan, plus $5 per year, per title, to maintain the listing.
Price author/publisher pays for personal copies (to give away, sell at speaking events, send for review, etc.) of a soft cover, 6"x9" book, black and white interior, color cover, 212 pp. (not including shipping).	$3.66 per copy (discounts apply for orders of 100 copies or more)	$5.74 per copy (Standard Plan) $3.39 per copy (Pro Plan)
Royalties (profits) on printed books. What the author receives per Amazon sale, if the book is priced at $16.00.	With Lightning Source, you can choose the wholesale discount. • With a 20% discount, the author receives $9.14 • With a 40% discount, the author receives $5.94 • With a 55% discount, the author receives $3.54	• With the Standard Plan, the author receives $3.86 • With the Pro Plan, the author receives $6.21
Distribution	The two largest wholesalers: Baker & Taylor and Ingram.	The two largest wholesalers: Baker & Taylor and Ingram. (Restrictions may apply for books of certain dimensions or if you use your own ISBN.)
Who holds the rights?	The author/publisher.	The author/publisher.

Publishing Option #3: Pay Someone to Publish Your Book

(Aka "Subsidy Publishing" or "Vanity Publishing")

Imagine that Arthur runs a successful small business, so successful that he's regularly asked to speak at business conferences. Often attendees say, "You have so much great advice; you should put it into a book." So one day he tells his secretary, "Let's do this book thing! Here are my last five seminars on video. Could you type them up for me and put them into a chapter format?"

She follows through and Arthur thinks that with some professional editing, it could indeed be a book. So Arthur considers his publishing options. Since conference leaders are currently interested in his speaking, he'd like to move quickly, in case interest wanes. So seeking a traditional publisher seems too much of a gamble. He'd hate to risk months and even years looking for an agent and a publisher. Besides, although his business is regionally respected, it's not nationally known. He doubts that traditional publishers would see a large enough market to interest them. Neither does he see bookstores as a big source of sales.

Should he self-publish? Arthur knows nothing about publishing, but enough about business to assume that the learning curve could be time consuming. And he doesn't want to take extra time away from either his business or his family.

His decision? Do the same thing he does in his business – outsource to specialists when it doesn't make sense to do something in-house. Arthur would rather pay a professional to take care of the details of editing, designing, and printing. Certainly it will cost more than doing it all himself, but he believes that his savings in time and effort would be worth it, resulting in a better product.

For Arthur, subsidy publishing may be his best choice, unless he can't stomach the thought of colleagues whispering behind his back at dinner parties, "He may be published, but it was a vanity press." But in that case, wouldn't his motive for *not* using subsidy publishing be his own vanity?

It's both unfortunate and unfair that "vanity publishing" has become the standard way to describe paying someone to publish your book. It perpetuates an often-undeserved stigma that's attached to every form of subsidy publishing. Although many "pay to publish" businesses prey on uninformed writers, taking way too much money for the paltry "services" they offer, and although many authors indeed publish their books out of vanity, knowing that no reputable publisher would ever consider their sloppy work, I believe that for some authors, such as Arthur, it is a legitimate option for getting published. This especially applies to publishing after the revolutions, since reductions in costs make possible all kinds of interesting publishing options.

But first, a disclaimer. I have no personal stake in this. Nobody has ever paid me to publish his or her books. Nor have I ever paid a subsidy publisher to publish my books. I simply know that authors differ greatly in their goals, their personalities, and their abilities.

Especially for those who are easily overwhelmed with a lot of details (which self-publishing involves), paying someone to take care of all the details can make sense. Calling this option "vain" doesn't lend itself to objective analysis. It's especially nonsensical when we compare publishing with other industries.

- If you're a filmmaker and you pay a company to help you produce your film, you're not labeled a "Vanity Filmmaker." You're "Indie," and are considered cool.
- If you pay someone to produce a CD for your garage band, you're not labeled a "vanity musician."

When people rant against vanity publishers, I think it's safe to say that what they're really against is publishing any crap as long as someone foots the bill. They're typically not against subsidy publishing as a matter of principle. To prove this, ask traditional publishers if they'd ever, under any circumstances, accept money to publish a book. Although it's not publicized, I'm told it happens all the time. A good manuscript comes along that they reject because it's too risky – there's not a big enough market. The author comes back and offers, "I believe in this project. If you publish it, I'll foot the bill to guarantee you don't take a loss."

That's the way Denmark's most famous author, Hans Christian Anderson, got his start. He paid a publisher to publish his first book. It did well enough for the publisher to keep publishing him for the rest of his life.

William Faulkner, esteemed by many critics the best American writer of the 20th century, paid (actually, a friend paid) to have his first book published – a book of his poetry titled *The Marble Faun*, in 1924.[5]

Many great writers of the past chose to subsidy publish or self-publish some of their works. Among them are Lewis Carroll, Mark Twain, Benjamin Franklin, E. Lynn Harris, Zane Grey, Upton Sinclair, Carl Sandburg, Edgar Rice Burroughs, George Bernard Shaw, Edgar Allen Poe, Rudyard Kipling, Henry David Thorough, and Walt Whitman.[6]

Example Subsidy Publisher Costs and Services

For purposes of comparison, here are some current prices and services from BookLocker, currently one of the most respected subsidy presses, which is very up front with its costs, services, and contract. These prices are for a black and white interior and color cover. (See the complete, updated list at http://www.booklocker.com.) BookLocker publishes through Lightning Source.

Set-up fee - $299 for your first book, $149 for subsequent books

Yearly Annual POD file hosting fee - $18

Royalties on POD books – 35 percent of list price

Royalties on bookstore/distributor orders – 15 percent of list price

Royalties on ebooks priced $8.95 or higher – 70 percent of list price

Pays royalties – Monthly

24-Hour online access to royalties? – Yes

List price – Author assigns (see minimum list prices below)

Minimum list prices for paperback books of

up to 108 pages – 11.95
109-150 pages – 12.95
151-200 pages – 13.95
201-250 pages – 14.95

DISTRIBUTION, ISBNs:

Are your print books listed on Amazon, Barnes & Noble, and other major online bookstores? Yes.
Can people special order your books from their local bookstores? Yes
Do you provide an ISBN at no additional charge? Yes
Can I use my own ISBN if I want? Yes
Can I print my company's name/logo instead of yours in/on the book? Yes
Paperback Cover Design - $150 (template); $200 (original design)
AUTHOR DISCOUNTS EXAMPLE – Assuming a 148-page paperback at minimum list price, these are the costs per book when authors purchase copies for their own use and/or sales:

1-24 copies – 35 percent off list price
25-49 copies – 8.17
50-74 copies – 7.92
75-99 copies – 7.52
100-149 copies – 6.62
150-499 copies – 6.42
500-999 copies – 6.17
1000+ copies – 5.77

Benefits of "Paying to Publish"

1) You don't have to spend time acquiring literary agents and publishers.

2) With some subsidy publishers, your book doesn't have to be great. With others, it doesn't even have to be good.

3) You don't have to find and hire and manage designers, editors, printers, etc. The subsidy publisher tends to do all that for you.

4) You don't have to be a detail person. Someone else takes care of ISBN's, Library of Congress numbers, and scores of other nitpicky details.

Drawbacks to "Paying to Publish"

1) If your book is published under the subsidy publisher's name, you're easily identified by reviewers, bookstores, and potential distributors as a vanity publisher. As a result, you're relegated to a literary leper colony that you'll find yourself constantly trying to escape from as you market your book. Especially if your publisher is known in the industry for publishing junk, many people will see the name of the publisher and look no further. So if you're going this route, find a publisher who allows you to publish under the name of your own press, using your own ISBN.

2) Many subsidy publishers charge exorbitant amounts for their services.

3) Some of them do less than quality editing and design.

4) Authors often get raw deals on royalties and inadequate reporting on sales.

5) You may have to pay so much for author copies that it hinders your marketing efforts.

Subsidy Publishing Tends to Work Best for Authors Who

1) Would rather spend money than time.

2) Need to publish quickly.

3) Have their own ways to market their books (through their blogs, sites, e-lists, and seminars) that don't require traditional bookstores.

Questions You Need To Ask

No Matter How Your Book is Published

Don't be afraid to ask lots of questions. If publishers and services are reputable and have nothing to hide, they'll be glad to help you understand the business and will be happy to give you straightforward answers. If they're reluctant or unclear, check further into their reputation.

1. **"Who will hold the rights to my book?"**

2. **"What percentage of your books make it into bookstores?"** (If your strategy involves bookstores.)

3. **"What percentage of your books are still in bookstores after two years?"**

4. **"If it doesn't sell well, do you give the rights back to me? In what time frame? Do you keep slow sellers in print as POD and e-books?"**

5. **"What percentage royalty do I get on each bookstore purchase? On each Amazon purchase? On each digital purchase?** Is the percentage based on the 'net' (what the publisher gets from a wholesaler or distributor) or the 'retail' (what it sells for in a store). I want to make sure I understand how these percentages work. If one of my books sells on Amazon for $15.00, exactly how much money do I get? If my book sells in a bookstore for $15.00, exactly how much money do I get?"

6. **"How often will I get sales reports for my books?"** This can be important for tracking which marketing campaigns are working and which are not. With CreateSpace, I can check direct Amazon sales daily.

7. **"Will my book be available through the major wholesalers? Which ones?"** (The major wholesalers are Ingram and Baker & Taylor.)

8. **"Will distributors be selling my book to bookstores? If so, who are the distributors?"**

9. **"Do you send out a catalogue to bookstores and book chain corporate offices?"**

10. **"How much will I pay for each copy that I purchase (to send out for review or to personally sell)."** Publishers don't tend to send many copies out for review. Thus it's critical, to be able to participate in many marketing initiatives, that you can get plenty (hundreds in some cases) of copies to send out for review. I typically buy them in orders of 50 over a period of time. If a publisher doesn't offer them at a reasonable price, consider negotiating that price in your contract. Purchasing 500 copies at $1.75 each would save you $1,000 over purchasing them at $3.75 each.

11. **"What does the wording of the contract mean?"** There are lots of ins and outs to book contracts. Since contracts tend toward legalese, and new

authors don't know what's standard and what's way out of line, it's safest to get an attorney or an informed friend in the industry to look over the contract with you.

12. "How often will I get paid?"

13. "Through what channels will I be allowed to sell my own books? Can I seek my own distribution channels and sell them in stores outside of bookstores?"

14. "What will you do to help market my book?"

Tips and Warnings for Publishing a Marketable Book

1. Beware of clever redefinitions.

- **Publisher Speak:** "We're a traditional publisher. We don't charge you to publish your book."

  Real Meaning: "We don't charge you to print it, but we'll charge you for editing, designing, etc. And we'll overcharge you for author copies and force you to charge retail prices that are out of line with other books of your type."

  (Refer back to the Abraham Lincoln quote under the chapter title.)

- **Publisher Speak:** "We'll make your book available in all the big bookstores."

  Real Meaning: "Hardly any of our books are sitting in bookstores. What we mean is that if someone comes into a bookstore and asks for your book, it's 'available' for the bookstore to order it through a wholesaler."

2. If the publisher's website has awkward sentences and misspelled words, why would you trust them to professionally edit your manuscript?

3. Track down other authors who have been published through this organization to get their frank assessment of their experience. Don't just talk to the authors they recommend.

4. Google the publishing company (or printer or service) to see what people are saying about them. Make sure to include searches such as (put company name first) "complaints," "sucks," "scam," etc. *Predators and Editors* (http://pred-ed.com) tracks complaints and make recommendations.

Do Something!

To put this chapter into action, I will...

1 –

2 –

3 –

Keep Learning!

- **See my free updates** to each chapter at www.sellmorebooks.org.
- **If you're seeking a traditional publisher, study *Writer's Market* at your library.**
- **If you're self-publishing, read Dan Poynter's *Self-Publishing Manual, Volumes 1 & 2.***
- **Whether you're self-publishing or seeking a traditional publisher, read *The Essential Guide to Getting Your Book Published*, by Arielle Eckstut & David Henry Sterry.** Great insider tips and insights on the industry.
- **If you're exploring publishing options, ask questions on an active, objective (not run by a publishing company) publishing forum or listserv.** Things change so quickly that books (including this chapter) are quickly dated. Get up-to-the-minute wisdom on what's happening now through listservs like the *Self-Publishing Group* at Yahoo, which I frequent.
- **To be encouraged and instructed concerning self-publishing successes, read *John Kremer's Self-Publishing Hall of Fame.*** The e-version is updated with many more stories than the hard copy. It's available at **http://www.bookmarket.com**.

Chapter 7

Get Lots of Blurbs from all Kinds of People

Let another praise you, and not your own mouth; someone else, and not your own lips.

- King Solomon

The Power of Blurbs

"Blurbs" is marketing speak for short, positive quotes about your book. Most books on publishing mention getting great blurbs as sort of a "duh" and quickly move on to the next point. But top-notch blurbs are critical and there's an art to acquiring them. They're particularly critical for those of us who don't have great platforms. They can grant us instant authority. In a very real sense, blurbers lift us up and allow us to share their platforms. Praise yourself and you're bragging. Let another praise you and it's authority.

I hold in my hand a *Chicken Soup* book. With over 30 books to the series and worldwide sales of 50 million copies in 30 languages, it's nothing less than a publishing phenomenon and worthy of any publisher's study. Why would they still need blurbs? Because authors Canfield and Hansen are book marketing geniuses and know the impact of blurbs. A third of the back cover is devoted to blurbs. Open the front cover and you'll find two full pages of blurbs.

If Jack Canfield and Mark Victor Hansen still need blurbs, even after establishing their highly effective brand, how much more do we? So let's camp out here for a time.

How many of you, when you're considering a book by an author you don't know, look seriously at the blurbs? Let's say you love Sue Grafton novels, but you just finished the last one. So you're browsing through novels at Barnes & Noble and notice a blurb by Sue Grafton on a front cover saying, "I wish I'd written this book!" Does this endorsement help sway you?

What are you more likely to trust, an author's word about his book, or a trusted, neutral source's word about a book?

I attended a recent library sale, looking particularly for books on "persuasion." I found one book that looked like it might fit the bill, but

1. I didn't know the author.

2. I found no bio telling me why this author was worth reading.

3. I found no blurbs, either by experts in the field or even just general readers. So I thought, "Come on author! You've written a book on persuasion for crying out loud. Persuade me to read your book!" Failing to establish her authority, I put it back, not even willing to pay $1.00. Even one enthusiastic blurb by someone I'd never heard of might have sold me.

To Impact Publishers as Well as Buyers

Blurbs impress audiences beyond potential buyers. Think earlier in the process, when you're trying to land an agent or publisher. Picture that acquisitions editor with thirty manuscripts piled on her desk, of which she's going to choose one. She's looking for reasons to narrow down the list. So in 1993 she sees some no-name author (Steve Miller) with no publishing record and no platform. She's ready to print out her standard rejection letter ("Doesn't meet our present publishing needs.") when she notices a blurb on my one page query from prolific author Josh McDowell saying that every mom, dad and child needs to read this book. So she reads further into the proposal and finds that Robertson McQuilkin, respected author and college president, calls it the best manuscript he's read on a much-needed subject. Barry St. Clair, a noted authority on youth work and prolific author, says it's critical for our times.

Now it's one thing for an author to try to convince a publisher that his manuscript is great. But when a respected authority in the field says it's good, the acquisitions folks just have to take it seriously. Also, it tells the publishing house that they just might be dealing with a savvy marketer – their dream come true.

On Getting Blurbs

How did I find Josh McDowell and get him to slow down long enough to look at my manuscript? I knew he was traveling with the rock band Petra and would be speaking at a music festival at an Atlanta theme park. I also knew he was getting flack from traditional pastors for traveling with a rock band. So

I volunteered to give him a ride from his Atlanta Hotel to Six Flags. I picked him up, gave him my elevator speech, and put the manuscript in his lap. He started reading it on the way to Six Flags and was hooked.

Robertson McQuilkin? I graduated from the school where he served as president. Barry St. Clair? I would soon be working for his organization, training youth leaders in Eastern Europe. I plopped it into Barry's lap as we were flying to Europe. By the time we landed in Vienna, he'd finished it and written a blurb.

Seek a Variety of Blurbs

"Variety" goes along with my emphasis on building *multiple* platforms. Too many authors think, "If I could just get a couple of household names from my field, I'd be set!" But that approach limits you. First of all, you may not be able to get those blurbs. Secondly, even if you get them, they may not be the best blurbs to reach certain audiences. Think instead of collecting blurbs to help you build multiple platforms to reach distinct market groups.

The Prevailing Paradigm of the Author Platform

A More Useful Paradigm: Multiple Platforms to Reach Multiple Groups

So let's look at my target audiences for my money book.

1) **Professional money managers**, who might write reviews and buy them in bulk to give to clients.

2) **Parents**, who are likely to read it themselves and give copies to their children.

3) **Educators**, who might use it as a text.

4) **College students and other young people**, who want to get started right with their finances.

Knowing that each of these groups might be more persuaded by different types of people, I collected blurbs that varied in both source and content.

Tip: Finding High Profile People to Give Blurbs

Some people are more apt to give blurbs than others. Perhaps they love to get free review copies of new books in their field. Perhaps they love the opportunity to get their names on the cover of a book (wise marketing). To discover who's willing to blurb, look through book after book in your field to see who wrote blurbs. Make your list, track them down, and ask if they'd be willing to review yours.

The household names in personal finance are the Donald Trumps and Warren Buffetts, but unless you've got a connection, what are your odds of getting them? (I did try, however. One of my early readers worked as a top executive for a company that was bought by Warren Buffett, and I asked him if he'd mind sending Buffett a copy. Although I've yet to get a call from Buffett over the past three years, I expect to hear from him any day now!)

Financial experts like John Bogle (of *The Vanguard Group*) and Burton Malkiel (Princeton professor) would impress serious economists, but they're not household names. So I shot for a variety of blurbs that would likely impress different segments of the population. A college student might resonate more with a blurb by another college student than an adult. An educator wants to know that other educators like the book. And don't just collect blurbs for use on your book. Collect them to use in your marketing campaigns.

Below, I've listed the blurbs I acquired. I put them together before I even sought a publisher. Study them. Take some notes. Circle something of interest. Note which is the most powerful to you personally. Which do you think would be the most powerful to a publisher? Note carefully the variety of takes on the book and how various audiences might respond.

- "A fast, fun read with practical and often remarkable insights. Should be required reading for every high school senior and every young adult who's landed his or her first full-time job. I'm incorporating parts of the book into my lectures." (Robert A. Martin, MBA, CPA, Lecturer of Accounting in the prestigious *Coles College of Business* at *Kennesaw State University*, founder of a tax and consulting firm.) **(Targets: CPAs and those who teach or counsel college students concerning finances.)**

- "Had I read this book in my 20s, I'd be financially independent today. It's a remarkable blend of fabulous research with clear and lively writing. You'd pay an expert quite a sum for this caliber of counsel. That's why I say that the best investment you make this year just might be this book. Your second best investment will be the copies you buy for your children." (Dr. Dwight "Ike" Reighard, Executive Vice President and Chief People Officer, HomeBanc – One of *Fortune's 100 Best Places to Work*, four years in a row.) **(Targets: Bankers, lenders, people who respect business leaders, and young people.)**

- "As a practicing CPA and financial counselor for the past 35 years, I've read scores of books and periodicals on personal finance. Just when you think you've heard it all, something like this comes along. It's rare and refreshing to find a book so enjoyable, so accurate, and so life changing. I'm purchasing hundreds of copies to give away to graduating seniors." (Larry Winter, *Winter & Scoggins CPAs*; Certified Valuation Analyst, Certified Fraud Examiner, Personal Financial Planning Specialist, serving on the Georgia State Board of Education) **(Targets: CPAs who**

might also purchase in bulk, government agencies, educators, and publishers.)

- "Financial responsibility has reached a state of crisis. This book attacks the problem in a common sense, refreshing manner that anyone can understand and apply to real life. It should be required reading for all young people, before they find themselves broke, deeply in debt, and miserable." (William C. Lusk, Jr., Senior Executive Vice President & Chief Financial Officer, Retired, *Shaw Industries*, a *Fortune 500* company and the world's largest manufacturer of carpet.) **(Target: All who respect business leaders.)**
- "A very entertaining, engaging book! The characters are appealing and aid the reader in interacting with the principles taught. Although especially geared to older teens and young adults, all ages will enjoy it and benefit. Meticulously researched and documented. Chock full of financial and lifestyle wisdom. I'll keep plenty of copies in my office to hand out to clients." (Dr. Ken Walker, Psychologist with the *Georgia Department of Juvenile Justice* and Director of *Dalton Counseling Service. Former regional credit manager*.) **(Target: Counselors and those who work with youth agencies.)**
- "A comprehensive look at managing your money. For me, the genius of this book is that it gathers wisdom from top financial gurus and uses it to explain clearly and practically how average folks can apply it to every-day living." (Alan Buckler, *Allstate Insurance*) **(Target: "Average folks" who just want solid information put in a way that's free from technical financial language.)**
- "I loved the story and the characters! Read this book and you'll get the practical tools and wisdom to chart your own course toward financial freedom." (Jamie Maddox, former Senior Business Analyst, *The Coca Cola Company*, present Pastor of Stewardship, *NorthStar Church*) **(Targets: Business leaders and church leaders.)**
- "For me, the section on savings was worth the price of the book, detailing scores of hidden ways to save a fortune over a lifetime. Then, unlike many books, it goes beyond '*having* more' to '*doing* more with what you have.' (Bryan McIntosh, Ph.D., Dalyn Corporation) **(Targets: Those who want to be successful without being materialistic; those who respect academic degrees.)**
- "I really liked the format! The dramatic layout used a totally different part of my brain when I read it...it's like watching a movie or reading a novel. The story line kept my interest so that I got through it quickly. The content was very inspiring. "Living differently" and "starting a financial counterculture" hits home to me. And it was SO PRACTICAL! I think it will also appeal to most of my generation and the one coming up behind

me." (Anthony Daniel, age 28, Chemist, *Tiarco Chemical*) **(Targets: Those who don't like dry financial books; young people.)**

- "Clever! The movie script format pulled me into the story and endeared me to the characters. Before I knew it, I found myself thinking about money strategies that I'd have never learned from traditional finance books. Teaching finance through people stories works for me. Rather than staring at obscure charts, I just followed the lives of successful people. Finally! A readable book on personal finance for people who don't want to read a book on personal finance...which of course is me and just about everybody else!" (Mark Hannah, Film Producer) **(Target: Creatives. I pulled my "elevator speech" sentence from this: "*the money book for people who hate money books.*")**
- "Teachers of financial management and life skills will be thrilled to discover this book! Miller uses people stories to breathe life into financial concepts, making lessons both memorable and enjoyable." (Phillip Page, Ph.D., Public School Principal) **(Target: Educators, particularly teachers of personal finance and life skills.)**

Observations on this Collection of Blurbs

1) Note that I didn't get any names that everybody knows. After all, not being very high profile myself, the biggest of the big are typically out of my league, unless I have a personal connection. But another problem is that, for the audience I'm trying to reach, many wouldn't recognize the top names in personal finance.

2) Since these are not household names, I give some information about each blurber, convincing the reader of the person's authority. Once they read the description, they may assume that they *should* know of the person!

3) In my opinion, the Larry Winter quote should be the most persuasive to publishers. Here's a person who believes in the book enough to put his money behind it. It's guaranteed money for the publisher and demonstrates a possible way to market the book (as a graduation gift). So I put his quote in my one page query letter and scattered other blurbs throughout my proposal.

Don't Stop, Even after Publication! Use Your Early Blurbs to Keep Leveraging More Blurbs

Remember, you're building your platforms. Once you've collected a set of blurbs like this, you can use them to get other people's attention. Once you've built a small platform, it's easier to reach out to people on higher platforms. The book review guys at *Money* magazine probably get wheelbarrows full of financial books that authors want them to review. But if I send my one page proposal to them with a quote from the CFO of Shaw Industries, they might actually take it seriously.

Brainstorm

1) How can you use your existing blurbs to leverage blurbs from higher profile people, or blurbs from other target groups?

2) Consider acquiring blurbs about your presentations and media appearances. Example: If you speak on a radio show and do a good job, ask if the host would mind writing a couple of sentences that you could put on your press page to attract other radio hosts.

Tips on Acquiring Persuasive Blurbs

After looking over these blurbs, you may assume that I'm unusually well connected. But I consider myself the opposite. I simply started thinking about people I've known, and those known to my family and friends.

1. Start by Asking for Honest Input on the Book

Beyond that, I asked myself who might be interested in the topic, and kept them on file. I thought through my various audiences and who might represent them: educators, CPAs, young people, senior citizens, businessmen, church leaders, etc. As I ran across people in these categories, I'd tell them about my book and ask if, when I got a manuscript together, they'd be willing to critique it and give me ideas. I'd assure them that it was nothing personal if they were simply too busy, but the great majority said that they'd love to look it over. I didn't have to lasso people and drag them in. They seemed honored to be asked for input.

Once I'd relentlessly self-edited and made changes based on my wife's and mother's input, but before I'd perfected my layout or put all my end notes in order, I sent it out to my readers. I gave them printed copies to look over. Some might prefer it sent digitally, but I felt that it was easier to get a feel for it and make notes on a physical manuscript. One read it on vacation at the beach. (I'm sending my present manuscript out for input and review primarily in digital format as a Word document.)

As they finished the manuscript, I'd typically invite each of them to lunch to get their input. It proved invaluable and led to significant changes. But I'd also ask the more general question: "What did you most like about it and how would you recommend it to others?" I took careful notes and then asked if they'd mind if I took what they said and try to write a blurb out of it. I promised to e-mail it to them for corrections and to make sure the blurb accurately expressed their feelings.

I offer to assist people in wording their blurbs for several reasons:

- Most of these readers aren't professional writers and they feel self-conscious writing something for a writer.
- Many people despise writing and it takes the burden off them. Hey, I already asked them to read something, and now I'm going to give them another responsibility?
- I know what unique angles have yet to be filled in my collection of blurbs.

Tip: You don't have to give the entire book to everyone. For some, the preface and first chapter might be a good start, since a full manuscript can overwhelm some people. If they read a portion and like it, you can give them more.

2. Write Your Own Blurbs as You'd Like People to Say Them

With your niche audiences in mind, write out your dream blurbs. I often work on this while I'm driving. Carry around a recorder to avoid wrecks. Think, "What would I like for someone to say about my book that would be unique and would likely intrigue someone in a target group?" I write these down (or speak them) and keep them on file.

Later, as early readers try to express what they feel about your book, I realize that parts of my pre-written blurbs express what they're saying. Simply say to a reader, "Are you trying to say...?"

As I got input from a high-profile person who'd read my manuscript, I looked over my pre-worded blurbs and said, "Does this express what you're saying?" He saw what I was doing, asked me for my list of dream blurbs, pointed to his favorite and said, "I want that one!"

You see, blurbs aren't just about me. They're about making the blurber look good as well. For some, it's free marketing for them as it gets their names in print. It helps them with their platform. No wonder it's not too difficult to get people to offer blurbs for an informative, interesting book.

Where to Find Blurbers

1. Preexisting Connections

The Lusks (Shaw Industries) were family friends when I was growing up. Ike Reighard (HomeBanc) was my former pastor. Bryan McIntosh (Ph.D., Dalyn Corporation) was a former member of my youth group. Alan Buckler sold us car insurance. His wife had a degree in journalism. (With seven boys and seven cars in our family, don't you think he was willing to do us a favor?)

2. Your High School Class

Among the people who graduated from my small town high school are lawyers, doctors, a missionary, a NASA engineer, film producers, a New York talk show host, etc. Attend alumni events and network with old friends. You'll be amazed at your connections!

3. Your Writers Group or Association

How did Arielle Eckstut & David Henry Sterry land the blurb from the author of *The Kite Runner*? They were in the same writing group together before *The Kite Runner* was published.

Exercise: Think through your current and past relationships. Who among them might be interested in your book?

4. Friends of Friends

We would be shocked to discover the connections we have, once we ask our friends, relatives, and acquaintances about *their* connections to high profile people.

A Good Habit to Acquire

I hear it all the time: It's who you know more than what you know. This especially applies to writers. So make it a habit to meet people wherever you go, take an interest in their lives, and find out a bit more about them every time you rub shoulders. (This should be standard behavior, but it's amazing how seldom people ask me about my life.) And I don't mean just the "big time" people that everybody's always trying to meet.

A rocket builder once shared that although the welders in his organization are on the bottom of the totem pole, he often gets his best contacts through them. A waitress I met at Waffle House had written seven historical novels. The guy who changes your oil might be a not-yet-famous musician or have a high-profile brother.

5. People Who Owe You One

Don't be afraid to ask for help. Others benefit from the joy of sharing when you give them the opportunity.

That's why a month ago I opened up a new file labeled "People Who Owe Me One." I thought, "I've given away free advice and free resources to hundreds of people over the years. Some of them would love the opportunity to give back. Why not keep up with them?" Now I do.

6. Social Networking via the Web

When you're searching for blurbs, look through your connections on Facebook and LinkedIn. These are powerful tools for connecting. LinkedIn is primarily a networking tool, especially for business/professional connections. Journalists use it to get introductions to experts for interviews; you can use it to find potential blurbers.

So let's say you'd like a blurb from somebody in PetSmart about your book on pets. If you have enough connections on LinkedIn, there's a good chance that one of their friends or friends of friends actually works there. I once needed to find a connection that worked for Sprint (the phone company). On the third level of my LinkedIn contacts, I found over 500 people! All I needed to do was to work on introductions through my contacts.

Blogs, forums, and other free social networking sites allow us to connect with many, many people who are already interested in the specific topics we're writing about. Some of them may read an advance copy and give you a blurb.

On Making Connections through Social Media

If you don't understand how to use these social networking tools, just find them on the Web (facebook.com, linkedin.com, etc.) and start fooling around. If they don't make sense to you, do a Google search for articles on "How to Use LinkedIn" or "How to Use Facebook." Better yet, ask your friends or children for help. I'll talk about these methods more in later chapters.

Got Blurbs? Use Them Everywhere!

My latest book has been published for well over a year and I'm still collecting blurbs and using them as I build new platforms and expand old ones. Any time I need the authority of another person, I employ one or more blurbs. Here are some places to use them:

1) In your query and proposal.
2) In your marketing plan (as presented to your publisher).
3) In your letters as you seek reviews and interviews.
4) In your e-mail signature.
5) Scattered throughout your author site.
6) Collected on your press page.
7) In the "Editorial Reviews" section of your Amazon page.

8) In your social networking bios (Facebook, LinkedIn, Twitter, etc.)
9) For targeted marketing.

Wrapping it Up

You're at a bookstore looking for a book on personal finance. You first notice the high platform authors.

"Ahhh...Dave Ramsey...I've heard him on the radio and have seen his billboards. Hmmm...Suze Orman...I've seen her on Oprah. Steve Miller...who the heck is Steve Miller? Hmmm...these business leaders say it's the most innovative, readable and accurate financial book on the market. That's exactly what I'm looking for. I wonder what others are saying? (You open the book to find two pages of enticing blurbs.) Wow! This is great!"

Don't underestimate the awesome power of the blurb. It's one of the most effective weapons in an author's arsenal.

Chapter 8

Optimize Your Amazon and Barnes & Noble Pages

Writing books is like an iceberg – ten percent is writing.
Ninety percent is marketing.

- Steve Harrison

It's difficult to overestimate the value of Amazon for authors. From the beginning, they've shown a commitment to constant improvement and expansion. If the last decade is any indication of the next, Amazon will only grow in its value to authors.

> **"Amazon" vs. "Amazon.com"**
>
> I'm well aware that Amazon is officially Amazon.com. But since it's popularly called Amazon and I relish cutting two syllables, I'll stick with "Amazon."

In many ways, Amazon has tried to level the playing field for authors, so that great books can rise to the top, whether they were written by a famous author with a top publisher, or by a self-published nobody. If your book looks great on the Amazon page and customers are buying it, Amazon allows it to rise to the top, so that customers looking for a book in your genre or on your topic will tend to find your book first.

But don't expect Amazon to optimize your listing. They expect authors and publishers to do that. As they say on their site:

> "At Amazon.com, it's up to you, the publisher or author, to make your titles stand out on our virtual bookshelves. You have the opportunity,

> using descriptive content and images, to personally hand-sell your titles to customers and persuade them to purchase."[1]

Fortunately, Amazon provides tools to help authors and publishers make their Amazon presence both findable and irresistible when customers arrive. Since these tools are free, we'd be foolish to ignore them. And don't be overwhelmed by the amount of information I'm about to give you. Once you get listed, it's not that difficult or time consuming to figure things out, put in your information, set up your profile, etc. Don't worry; you can optimize your Amazon pages pretty easily without becoming a geek or hiring an expert.

> Amazon isn't the only bookseller on the web. But since it has a very comfortable lead as I write, we'll look at it exclusively, knowing that we can apply what we learn to other web-based sellers as well. For optimizing your Barnes & Noble pages, like adding outside reviews, a publisher description, making corrections, etc., see their publisher Q & A page here:
>
> http://www.barnesandnoble.com/help/cds2.asp?PID=8153&cds2Pid=8153#9 .

Get Listed On Amazon

Your publisher should list you. If your listing is delayed, inaccurate, or needs improvement, start by working with your publisher. If you're printing through CreateSpace or Lightning Source, they should automatically set you up with Amazon. Follow their instructions for working with your Amazon page.

If you self-publish elsewhere, like having 2,000 copies printed offset, you'll need to set up your own Amazon Advantage account. Either Google "Amazon Advantage" or find it here:

https://www.amazon.com/gp/seller-account/mm-product-page.html?topic=200329780

Standard Terms of the Amazon Advantage Program

- "55% Purchase Discount (off the List Price, which you set)"
- "member-paid shipping to our warehouse"
- " a $29.95 annual program membership fee"
- Nonprofits can apply for a special "professional rate."
- "Amazon.com reserves the right to set the retail price to customers at our sole discretion. Amazon.com's decision to discount products is based on a number of considerations which can vary over time."
- "You must have a scannable ISBN/EAN/UPC barcode on every item."

Make Your Book Irresistible

Solicit Customer Reviews

When you're browsing Amazon for books, what feature is most likely to either persuade or dissuade you from purchasing? For me, I assume that the most objective assessment will come from customer reviews. Amazon apparently agrees, telling me the star rating right up top with the title. If I see five stars dangling below the title like a diamond necklace, I have my first indication that it's a classy book.

Beside the necklace is a diamond earring, telling me the total number of reviews. The more reviews, the more indication I have that this book is significant and the reviews are legitimate.

As a buyer, the title and publisher information are helpful, but a bit suspect, carefully chosen by the publisher/author to sell the book (although I also check the publisher section for reviews and a book description). Primarily, I look to customers to give me the real scoop. And unless I click to view the lowest reviews first (to see what people didn't like) I start with the first review.

I'm not alone in consulting customer reviews for my buying decisions. According to Shiv Singh, head of Digital for PepsiCo Beverages, customer reviews "invariably convince customers to purchase, and they lead to more sales." A Nielsen Online study found 81 percent of online shoppers reading online customer reviews. Research by Razorfish found 60.53 percent of respondents relying on user reviews, compared with 15.41 percent relying on editorial reviews.[2]

Thus, prioritize accumulating an abundance of great reviews, with the earliest reviews being the most compelling. Fortunately, if your book is truly great, we have ways to influence this.

First, don't assume that as customers read your book, they'll automatically begin posting reviews. I'm ashamed to admit that I review very few books, even if I absolutely love them. Unfortunately, most readers are review-averse ingrates like me. From the reviews of my money book, it appears that about one in 1,000 readers write a review without any prompting by me. If you don't do something to encourage people to leave reviews, you may have to sell thousands before someone reviews your book, making your Amazon presence give the impression that nobody's reading your book. The last words that you ever want to see on your Amazon page are: "Be the first reader to review this book."

Worse than no reviews is when only one person reviews it, giving it 2 stars. Now you're stuck with not only a two star review, but an *average* of two stars wherever Amazon posts them. (Search your book on Yahoo!. In the results, Yahoo! posts your number of reviews and star rating.) Obviously, two stars can destroy sales. You can't afford to leave your Amazon reviews to chance.

Get Early Reviews

If you followed my suggestion in chapter three, scores of people read your manuscript to give early input. Now that the book is out, getting early, positive reviews are a cinch. Send each of these people a free copy of your completed book, explaining in an accompanying note that you sent it out of appreciation for their early input. Thank them profusely, explaining how their input helped. End the note by asking,

> "If you really liked the manuscript, would you be willing to help me out one more time? To get this book into more people's hands, I desperately need early reviews on Amazon. If you could put up a review, it would mean the world to me. And don't worry about it being worded perfectly. People just want your sincere evaluation."

If even half of these respond, you may have twenty or so positive reviews to jumpstart your Amazon page. Since you got these up at the very start, those who read your book later and aren't as thrilled will find their negative reviews buried down in the list, less likely to influence customers.

What to do with Malicious, Unfair Reviews

If you write a great book, this is less likely to happen. Yet, many books are controversial by nature, provoking negative reviews. Some reviewers will write a one star review out of spite or to recommend their own book as the better choice.

First realize that reviews with a bit of negativism can produce more sales than a glowing review.[3] So don't sweat a four star review which gives mostly positives, but one or two drawbacks.

If the review is spiteful and misleading, try to contact the reviewer. If that doesn't work, contact Amazon. If Amazon sees it as someone who probably never read the book or another author trying to slam the competition, they may take it down. Consider asking friends to contact Amazon, since they may be perceived as having less self-interest. They can begin by clicking "report this" at the end of the review. If more than one report it as misrepresenting the book, Amazon may take more notice.

According to Amazon, "If you feel that a customer review falls outside of our guidelines, please contact us at community-help@amazon.com."

What if Your Worst Review Comes First?

I saw one book that had 90 percent great reviews. Unfortunately, the first review was very negative. Since that's the review that most people read first, I'm sure it took away a lot of sales. Now I don't want to unfairly manipulate things, but if the negative review didn't represent the typical reader's reaction, I wouldn't feel bad about trying to re-organize things a bit.

Amazon gives customers a way to influence the order of reviews by voting on the reviews that are the most helpful. (Note this feature at the end of each review.) The reviews with the most votes move to the front. Yet, this method doesn't always ensure that the earliest reviews best represent the book.

The problem is that people read the earliest reviews (those positioned first) more often than the more recent reviews. Thus, earlier reviews have an unfair advantage at being selected as "helpful." If your first review was unfairly critical, it may stay in pole position unless you take action. In this case, I'd not hesitate to contact my friends and say,

"To me, the first review on my Amazon page seems unfairly critical, not representing what most people think of my book. Can you do me a huge favor by looking over the reviews, picking several that you think most fairly represent my book and clicking "Yes" after the sentence 'Was this review helpful to you?'"

Keep Collecting Reviews

The more reviews customers see, the more peer pressure sets in and they think, "Everybody's reading it" and "Everybody thinks it's great."

Whenever people compliment your book, or whenever you give out free copies to people, ask them if they'd show their appreciation by putting up reviews. Emphasize that "it doesn't have to be expertly written. Just share your honest thoughts."

If people generally like your book, then contact top Amazon reviewers who review books like yours and tend to give positive reviews. To find them, look up other books in your genre and topic and find the top reviewers by looking for designations under their names such as "Top 1000 Reviewer," or "Top 500 Reviewer." Click on their names to see if they give contact information.

Make Sure Your Cover Image Looks Great

If you're with CreateSpace or Lightning Source, find their guidelines for uploading images and adding other content.

On the Importance of Relationships

When another author wrote a book criticizing the thesis of my music book, he blasted both me and my book in my review section. A friend took it upon himself (no prompting on my part) to e-mail the critic and said, in effect, "If you knew Steve Miller, you wouldn't say those kinds of things." The critic apologized and took down the comment.

This is common in social media. As companies develop loyal fans, the fans will speak up to defend their companies when detractors rant. This is often much more effective than the companies trying to defend themselves.

Are you noticing how many times the word "friends" keeps popping up in this book? You'll hear phrases like this over and over from marketing professionals:

- "It's not how much you know; it's who you know."
- "Social networking is primarily about cultivating relationships, not about selling stuff."
- "Publishing is as much about meeting people at conferences and getting along well with people as it is about great writing."

After the revolutions, your friends and enemies can make or break you more effectively than ever.

Do you want to do well at marketing your books? Remember your friends' birthdays. Call Mom. Meet your neighbors. Be nice and caring with no strings attached. Being kind to all and cultivating friendships is the best investment we can make in our future.

If you use your own Amazon Advantage account, use the Advantage update form. Otherwise, you can use the Books Content Update Form:

http://www.amazon.com/gp/help/customer/display.html/ref=hp_rel_topic?ie=UTF8&nodeId=14101911

Submit your image according to Amazon's Specifications. (I searched "Amazon Specifications for Images" in Google to find this.)

http://www.amazon.com/gp/help/customer/display.html?ie=UTF8&nodeId=200109520

Note that they offer a special section for troubleshooting.

After it's up, view it on several computers, other devices (iPhones, etc.) in several browsers (Internet Explorer, Firefox, etc.).

Optimize Your Editorial Section

You can include a product description, blurbs, and/or a high-level review. I like to include my best blurbs here, rather than just information from the publisher. Again, "let another praise you..." Perfect the wording. Take it through the editorial process, getting input from your friends. Ask,

- Do you see any mistakes?
- Is it helpful in describing the book?
- Is it compelling?

Make sure the book information ("Product Details") is complete and accurate. If there are inaccuracies or typographical errors, here's how to fix them:

> "Propose corrections using our Online Catalog Update Form which is accessible through a section called 'Product Details' and found midway down each book's detail page. This form will allow you to correct errors or omissions for many bibliographic fields. For more information, please see the Corrections page."

http://www.amazon.com/gp/help/customer/display.html/ref=hp_rel_topic?ie=UTF8&nodeId=14101911

Complete Your Author Profile Page

Many people like to know more about authors. By completing your Author Profile Page, customers can click through from your book page to get to know you better, read your blog, find your author site, etc.

But more than a "get to know you" area, it also functions as sort of a command central from where you can generate "Listmania" lists, "So you'd like to..." guides, edit your reviews of other books, start a blog (or set up your existing author blog to feed into Amazon), etc.

Some like to identify themselves with their real name, while others are more guarded about their identity, choosing a pseudonym like "Book Lover," since this is the name that will be shown on their reviews, how-to guides, etc.

Amazon encourages people to use their real names, as identified by their credit card, in reviewing books, submitting lists and guides, interacting on their forums, etc. They believe that using real names leads to better quality content, since people build or lose their reputations based upon the quality, sincerity, and helpfulness of their writing. Thus, they reward using real names by putting "Real Name" beside the name and giving your information a bit of priority over others. You can still become a top-ranked reviewer if you review under a pseudonym, but in certain ways they prioritize those who use real names.

If you want to use your real name for some functions and a pseudonym for others, you can establish two Amazon accounts, using different credit cards and different e-mail addresses, allowing you to set up two author profiles, one using your real name and one using a pseudonym.

Amazon also lets you choose whether certain information will be available to everyone, to just your friends, or to yourself only.

- http://www.amazon.com/gp/help/customer/display.html/ref=hp_rel_topic?ie=UTF8&nodeId=14279641 – on real names.
- http://www.amazon.com/gp/help/customer/display.html/ref=hp_rel_topic?ie=UTF8&nodeId=16465241 – on setting up and using your profile.

Make Your Book Findable

If you've taken the above steps, your book will look appealing when people find it on Amazon. But how can you ensure that lots of people find it?

Imagine that you're walking through the world's largest brick and mortar bookstore, looking for Dave Barry's *Babies and Other Hazards of Sex*. Enter the store and ask for the book by name and the manager will walk back to the well-stocked humor section, find it alphabetized by the author's last name, and bring it to the checkout counter for purchase.

On Amazon, that's the equivalent of typing the name of the book into the search box. The search engine should have no problem finding it, since Amazon prioritizes titles in searches.

But let's say you enter the brick and mortar bookstore without a specific title in mind. You tell the manager that you want a funny book for expectant parents. The manager could show you the humor section, containing one hundred thousand funny books, or he could show you the childbirth section, which contains tens of thousands of books. You settle for a humor book that has nothing to do with babies, since you ran out of time and never ran across the Dave Barry book, which would have been perfect.

The beauty of Amazon is that it allows people to search by key words. Search "baby humor" and you'll find book after book on that topic, eventually leading you to Dave Barry's book.

But how does the search engine know to pull up these books, if "baby humor" isn't in the title or subtitle?

Fortunately, the author or publisher optimized the page for Dave Barry's book so that Amazon's search engine "knew" that the book contained "baby humor." If no one had optimized the page for that phrase, customers couldn't have found it by searching that phrase.

So here's how to be more easily found on Amazon.

> To find the latest Amazon instructions on how authors can optimize their Amazon pages, see the *Amazon.com Publishers and Booksellers Guide:*
>
> http://www.amazon.com/gp/help/customer/display.html/ref=hp_lnav_dyn?ie=UTF8&nodeId=13685551

Optimize Your Title and Subtitle

Refer back to chapter four for a discussion of this. Remember, Amazon prioritizes helping searchers find book titles over subjects. By including popular key phrases in your titles and subtitles, more searchers can find your book.

Allow for "Search Inside the Book"

Don't worry, Amazon doesn't allow people to read the entire book. But Search Inside allows Amazon to do three very important things to help market your book:

1) It allows customers to browse your book much as they would in a bookstore to get a feel for how it's written and what it's all about.

2) It allows Amazon to collect key words and phrases from the book that might help people searching for a book like yours. Example: Let's say that someone read *Enjoy Your Money* in a high school personal finance class. Years later, she wants to purchase a copy, but can't remember the title or author. She does, however, remember a phrase from the book that might be unique enough to search in Amazon. So she searches "The Counterculture Club." My book comes up in that Amazon search because "Search Inside," allowed Amazon to search the book for "statistically improbable" phrases that people might search.

3) It allows your book to be found through Amazon's personalization and merchandising features. If you've ordered from Amazon, you've probably noticed that they occasionally recommend other books you might like. How do they come up with these recommendations? If you've set up "Search Inside," Amazon uses the information in your book to try to match it with similar books. As a result, Amazon might recommend your book.

As Amazon puts it, "If Chris Customer views *The World is Flat* by Thomas Friedman and later returns to Amazon, he may see recommendations for other books that discuss the concept of 'triple convergence.'"[3]

To enable Search Inside, either contact your publisher or start here: www.amazon.com/searchinside.

Add Tags and Search Terms

Besides grabbing terms from your title and utilizing Search Inside, Amazon allows authors and readers to suggest search terms (tags) and rate other people's suggested terms. This especially helps if neither your title nor book content mentions certain much-searched phrases. Let's say you wrote a book on character education, but never used the phrase (in your title or text) "values education" – the most popular term for the subject in certain countries. Here's how you could add these tags:

1. Find popular terms that people use to search for your topic. Use Google's Keyword Tool (https://adwords.google.com/select/KeywordToolExternal) and compare the tags people have assigned to other books of your genre and on your topic.

2. Type the most important phrases into the Tag section of your Amazon page. You can type up to 15 tags through your Amazon Account. Use your friend's Amazon accounts (or ask them to add tags to your book) if you need more words and phrases.

3. Check the box next to each tag you deem most relevant.[4]

Gray Area Warning: Using Tag Groups

You can find sites and forums where authors help each other by putting checks next to the tags they want to target. Presumably, the higher the number of checks by a given tag, the more positively an Amazon search for that term is influenced.

But I've got a moral problem with asking people I don't know and who've never read my book to check which tags they feel are most relevant to my book. They don't know which tags are most relevant, unless they trust me – a person they don't even know. Even if you're asking strangers to check only phrases that are truly relevant, realize that some people will abuse this practice by trying to get positioned for phrases that aren't truly relevant. If Amazon decides to penalize people who do this, you might get penalized as well.

Learn a bit from history. People used to try to trick search engines by putting highly searched words like "sex" in the background of their sites, matching the color of their font to the color as their background, so that the words were invisible to human eyes. But search engines could identify sites that used that trick and penalized sites that tried it. Amazon "knows" what tags you've chosen for other people's books. It's quite possible that it "knows" when the same 50 people go to the same 50 book pages and all click the same few terms on each page, all within a month's time. Isn't it quite possible that one day they'll penalize these authors?

Link to Your Amazon Page from Everywhere

Whether I'm commenting on a blog post or sending an e-mail, I always link to my book on Amazon. I also link from all my blogs and sites and articles. That allows people to purchase it immediately, whenever they see a link. Moreover since Amazon pages are spidered by Google, more incoming links should help the page's positioning when people search for your book, or your book's topic, on Google.

Utilize "So You'd Like To..." Guides

These are written by customers, not Amazon, to help other customers know more about a topic of interest. If you write European travel guides, you could write a "So You'd Like to Travel" guide, recommending up to 50 travel guides, including some of your own. Link to each product using either the 10-digit Amazon Standard Identification Number (ASIN) or 13-digit International Standard Book Number (ISBN).

After it's completed, you can edit it through your Author Profile Page. Note that only your top three suggestions will appear when your guide is displayed on

Amazon. The other recommendations become visible when someone clicks on the guide.

Benefits of "So You'd Like To..." Guides

1) It's another way for people to find your book on Amazon from a Google or Yahoo! search. Search "Yankee Trivia" in Google and you'll see a "So you'd like to impress your friends with Yankee trivia" Amazon guide.

2) If customers like to consult the guides, they can search for a guide on your topic using Amazon's search box. (See "So You'd Like to" on the dropdown list by the search box.)

> **Tip:** Search for guides on your topic. If your book would make a good addition, click on the guide author to see if she provides contact information. If so, e-mail her to ask if she'd like to receive a free copy of your book and consider adding it to her guide. If so, you just got a third party to recommend your book – much more effective than recommending your own book.

3) When a customer looks at a book on your topic or in your genre, she may see your guide listed at the bottom of the page. If she clicks on it, she will find your book.

To learn more about "So You'd Like To..." guides:

http://www.amazon.com/gp/help/customer/display.html?nodeId=14279691

To learn how to set one up:

http://www.amazon.com/gp/richpub/syltguides/create

Create (or offer your book to) "Listmania" Lists

A "Listmania" page is simply a list of recommended books that people can create on a topic. These lists can be found in searches for your subject matter. For example, if I search "best dog books" in Google, the first result I see is someone's "Listmania" list, which they titled, you guessed it, "Best Dog Books." Last month, 2,400 people searched the term "Best Dog Books" and found this list in pole position. Since they're probably all searching for a book to buy, targeting these 2,400 searchers is probably very effective.

So when choosing a title for your list, look back over the most-searched key words that you found for your topic. Your title could draw some significant searches.

In this case, the author didn't use his/her name for the profile (some want to remain anonymous, fearing people might look for them), so you don't know if some of the recommended books are his/her own.

To learn more about "Listmania" lists and how to set them up, see:

http://www.amazon.com/gp/help/customer/display.html/
ref=cm_lm_create_help?ie=UTF8&nodeId=14279651

Participate in Amazon's "Customer Communities"

Here you can participate in forums and view listmania lists. You can also peruse Amazon's "Tag Cloud" to find the most popular topics:

http://www.amazon.com/gp/tagging/cloud .

If you find a particularly active forum, you may wish to participate, answering people's questions and recommending your book when appropriate. But I see no reason to prioritize an Amazon forum over any other forum. If you want to participate in forums – a good place to interact with other people who are interested in your topic – why not choose from among the most active forums on your topic anywhere on the web? If that happens to be an Amazon forum, then go for it! For a larger discussion of forums and social media, see Chapter 16.

Find Amazon's "Customer Communities" here:

http://www.amazon.com/communities

See also their "starting place" for "Customer Communities" here:

http://www.amazon.com/gp/help/customer/display.html/ref=hp_rel_
topic?ie=UTF8&nodeId=200280960

Recommend a "Browse Path."

Over time, Amazon assesses your book, your tags, etc. to determine if it belongs in a certain category in its directory.

On the Product Details section of your book's Amazon page, find your Amazon Bestsellers Rank. There you'll find your rank (recalculated every hour) compared to all other books on Amazon. Just below that, if you've been assigned a category, you'll see something like:

"#6 in Books > Business & Investing > Personal Finance > **Money Management for Young People**"

Is it good to be assigned a category and browse path? Well, I have mixed feelings.

Positives include:

- **You're put in Amazon's book directory, which some customers browse** (but I'm not sure how many use it). To find Amazon's directory, look in the search boxes at the top of the page, choosing "books" as the category. Click "Go." You'll see a new list of links below the search boxes called "Browse Subjects." Click it to look for books by subject.
- **On your book's Amazon page, customers can see the browse path to your niche in the directory, with your ranking in that category.**
- **If you sell a lot of books in one day, putting you number one in your category, you can brag that your book has been #1 in Amazon sales in that category.**

Negatives include:

- **The possibility that these categories turn some customers away by making them think a book is too niche.** I don't want my money book to be pegged as exclusively "for young people," yet seeing this category designation could make adult customers conclude that it's not for them.
- **Customers might decide to go for the most popular books in that category instead.** So they click on the category and choose another book.
- **If you've sold no books in a couple of days, (Amazon reevaluates sales every hour), you may be telling the world how badly you rank in a category.**

So if you want your book put in a category and you don't see yourself in a category, contact Amazon through Author Central (https://authorcentral.amazon.com) and recommend a category or two that you think best fits your book and that you could potentially dominate. CreateSpace (contact through your CreateSpace account section) allows their authors to request up to two categories.

Get Input from Others

I have a strange tendency to obsessively edit my books but to write my Amazon author bio as a reluctant afterthought, without getting even one outside opinion. How absurd! Get plenty of input on your Amazon presence. Something may come across pushy or obnoxious or with a wholly different meaning than you intended.

You get only one chance to make your first impression. Make it impressive.

Closing Thoughts on Amazon

For most authors, just being on Amazon and Barnes & Noble doesn't guarantee sales. Unless you make your pages attractive and findable, your book will be as hard to find as a novel in a humongous book stack (a stack of 14 million books, at present count). Even when you implement these strategies, some say that many optimization techniques don't show significant results until a year or more later.[5] Typically, even after optimizing your pages, you still need to find ways to tell customers about your book, so that they'll go to an online bookstore to order. But driving people to bookstores, online or off, is the topic of the second section of this book. For now, we're just setting things up to make those efforts more fruitful.

Online bookstores are a force in book sales that we can't afford to ignore. And they will likely become even bigger players over the years. Since they're ever evaluating present tools and tinkering with new tools, some of this chapter will inevitably be dated the day it comes off the press. So find ways to keep up as they continue to morph and provide exciting new opportunities for authors to sell their books.

Do Something!

To put this chapter into action, I will...

1 –

2 –

3 –

Keep Learning!

- **See my free updates** to each chapter at www.sellmorebooks.org .
- **Observe how other successful books present themselves on platforms such as Amazon and Barnes & Noble.** Look specifically at newer marketing books such as *Sell Your Books on Amazon*, *Aiming at Amazon*, and *Plug Your Book* to see what they're up to. These authors are experts at making the most of these platforms and should give us great examples of how to use them. Check back every six months or so to see if they're using new methods.
- **Study Amazon's Booksellers' Guide** to learn how to use each of the features they currently offer:

http://www.amazon.com/gp/help/customer/display.html?nodeId=13685551

- **Since CreateSpace is a subsidiary of Amazon.com, check their forum** to see what their members are discussing about creative ways to present their books:

  https://www.createspace.com/en/community/index.jspa

- **Read Barnes & Noble's suggestions to publishers here:**

http://www.barnesandnoble.com/help/cds2.asp?PID=8153&cds2Pid=8153#9

Chapter 9

Build a Professional Online Presence

"I'm so Much Cooler Online"

In Brad Paisley's song, "I'm So Much Cooler Online," a socially backward loser gets online and projects the image of a confident, mysterious world-shaker. If you're not familiar with it, go ahead; indulge yourself for a few minutes. You just might learn something important about marketing.

http://www.youtube.com/watch?v=UE6iAjEv9dQ

I suppose Paisley's point is that this nerd should occasionally turn off his computer and get a life in the real world. But I say, let's give the nerd a break. At least he's accomplished coolness online. Many of us authors are nerds in real life *and* online.

Here in the cul-de-sac I do nothing that strikes awe in my neighbors. I'm small of stature, clueless about fashion, dress a notch above your average homeless person, and drive an old, scarred minivan. Unfortunately, that persona doesn't sell books.

I'm so much cooler online.

My author site (www.jstevemiller.com) presents a slightly debonair world traveler who's becoming known as a thought leader in several fields. I'm not lying when I project that image. Like most folks, I'm multi-faceted. If you want to sell more books, it's a good idea to get in touch with your debonair, respectable side, and put it forward online. Let's call it "building your personal platform."

The Need for a Professional Online Presence

Everyone from publishers to the media wants to check you out, to see how you present yourself and to decide if your book is worthy of their attention. Especially after the revolutions, they *expect* to find you online, using that presence to make quick judgments as to whether you're worthy of their representation or a fit for their news column or blog or radio show. If you have no web presence, or if your web presence fails to inspire them, don't be surprised if you find the media reluctant to take a chance on you.

Over and over and over, as I seek reviews, pursue top bloggers, and contact radio, I find myself e-mailing a brief introduction, with a link to my press page for more information.

Identify the Audiences Who Want to Know More about You and Your Book

Don't start by looking around at what other authors are doing; we'll get to that soon enough. They may be targeting different audiences from you. Instead, start by thinking about *your* potential audiences and how you can best meet *their* needs. Think about not only your present book, but future books as well.

- If you plan to publish traditionally, you need a place that **publishers** can check you out after they read your query. They'll want to know how you present yourself as an author.
- If you're targeting **the media** – seeking reviews and interviews – you'll want a press page to link to from your brief, introductory e-mail. The page may contain (or link to) a book summary, example chapters, reviews, sample media questions, blurbs, links to former media events, etc.
- If you're targeting **present readers**, set up a web page or blog to give more information about your book and offer discussion questions for book clubs. Provide a way to keep in touch, like signing up to receive blog posts or a newsletter.
- If you're gathering new people, in hopes that they'll be your **future readers**, why not start an information center such as a blog and/or website to try to gather a following by giving them regular information in an area where you're establishing yourself as a thought leader? Provide a schedule of upcoming appearances.

As you can see, depending upon what you're trying to accomplish, your online presence can take on many different forms. In this chapter, we'll talk about author sites and the many forms they can take. In chapters 14 and 16, I'll suggest other ways to make your presence known on the web.

* * *

Don't start an author site because everyone says that you should have one. First decide what you want to accomplish online and whom you're targeting.

* * *

Don't Try to Do Everything – Big Things Can Happen with Simple Solutions

Start with meeting your present needs. You can always develop more over time. What you choose *not* to do can be as significant as what you choose to do. In my opinion, many authors waste huge amounts of time and money pursuing things that have a negligible payoff in book sales.

For many authors, their online presence can be very simple. One local author, Danny Kofke, author of *How to Survive on a Teacher's Salary*, pursues primarily radio (see him highlighted in chapter 20), but also some TV and print media as he markets his book. To aid him in this effort, he put up a single, simple blog page that introduces himself and his book and provides links to his many interviews. As he e-mails the media, he links them to this page, which immediately lets them see that he's experienced in their medium and comes across well. I think his web presence is wonderful in its simplicity and functionality. Take a moment to look it over:

http://dannykofke.blogspot.com

Notice that he doesn't do a lot of things that "everybody" says you must do.

- He didn't buy a special URL for his name or the name of his book.
- He doesn't do new posts on his blog. He uses one static page.
- He didn't hire a professional designer.

It's free and takes minimal time to maintain. But I can almost hear some zealous marketing experts complaining, "You need to post a blog every day, or at least a few times a week. You need to get links from other prominent sites. You need to post on other people's blogs." To which I'd respond, "Danny doesn't have unlimited time. He's got something that works for him, and he's selling lots of books. Why ruin it?"

By not doing a lot of things, he saves both money and time. As a full-time middle school teacher, a husband, and father of young children, he wants to spend what little marketing time he has contacting radio stations. If he has an hour in the morning before school, he could choose to either write a blog post or contact 20 radio stations. For him, using that hour to pursue the media makes more sense. By not doing 1,000 other things, he averages contacting

100 radio stations, TV shows, and print media per week. That's using your time and resources wisely.

The author site serves many functions. Some use it to connect with their readers, collect e-mail addresses for a newsletter, or to provide information for the media. If you plan to publish future books with traditional publishers, consider building a place on the web where publishers can easily find you and be impressed when they arrive. Consider what publishers look for in authors (serious about your craft, willing to market your books, past successes, a nice person to work with) and present yourself as such.

How to Build an Author Site

First, brainstorm elements you'd like to include in the site to meet your specific goals for your specific audiences.

Second, study other author sites to see what they include. Make a list of what you like and dislike about their design and content.

Third, decide the best host for your site. A few years ago, everyone would have recommended building a traditional website. But think creatively here, because today there are many viable options.

Author Site Option #1 – A Facebook Page (Formerly a Fan Page)

We don't traditionally think of this as an author site, but if your main purpose is to connect with your readers and your main concern is ease of use, it can be a good choice. Especially if you're on Facebook, enjoy Facebook, and already have a following there, it makes sense to start a page for your book, or for you as an author, or for the topic you write about (or all three).

Cherie works as an admin in a Masters program at Kennesaw State University. For her, Facebook has become a primary way to keep up with her present students and to recruit new students, roughly paralleling many authors' concern to keep up with present readers and recruit new readers. For this purpose, she set up a Facebook page that allows prospective students to find out more about the program and meet students, faculty, and administrators. It's very effective. With a fan page, you can carry on conversations with your readers, send them notices when you have a new book coming out, and link to your Amazon page and press page.

Founded in 2004, in a mere six years Facebook has dominated the social networking scene with over 400 million active users (more than the entire population of the United States). But it's not the sheer numbers that are astounding from a marketing perspective. These users are connected and continue to connect, allowing word of mouth to spread at unprecedented rates. The average user has 130 friends and is connected to 60 pages, groups, and events.[1] It makes sense to harness that power. It's also free – the magic word for starving artists.

To set up a page (assuming you're already on Facebook), **first look over some other pages** to see how they're set up and how they function. So open up your Facebook account, type "writer fan pages" or "writer pages" in the search box, and click "pages" on the left side (to specify that you want to search "pages").

http://raisingceokids.com/2010/07/14/how-to-create-custom-tabs-on-facebook

Rather than detail here how to set up a Page (the details of which morph over time), I'll refer you to a short tutorial by an author who walks you through setting up a Page in the "Writer" category. She also recommends other fan pages to study:

http://www.goodreads.com/topic/show/165875-how-to-create-a-facebook-fan-page

If you need more help, Google "how to set up a Facebook fan page" or "Facebook fan page tutorial." We'll talk more about using Facebook and fan pages in chapter 16.

A Facebook page may not work for someone who doesn't enjoy meeting new people and interacting with them, or doesn't have time to fool with it. If you set one up and then fail to respond to people, you'll disappoint them. Social networking should be 80 percent social, not selling, so you'll need to interact.

Caution: Realize that Facebook is just one of many social media platforms and these platforms may or may not exist in their present form five years from now. For this reason, many authors prefer to have a hub that's not tied into any one social media group. For some, a blog serves as a good alternative.

Author Site Option #2 – A Blog

Many people don't think of a blog as an author site, but this has emerged as the first choice for many. A blog has many advantages.

- It can be set up to appear virtually indistinguishable from a traditional website, with a home page, subpages, etc.
- In some ways, it is more easily searched and ranked by search engines than traditional websites.
- It is typically easier for authors to update than a traditional site, without having to use complicated tools like DreamWeaver or ExpressionWeb.
- One of the pages can function as a traditional blog, where you make regular posts and get feedback.

- You can include a press page.
- With several functions all in one place (blog, site, press page, etc.), it's easier to get incoming links, thus making you more visible with search engines.
- It's cheap – free, if you don't mind having ads on your site. (In the early days of the web, there was a stigma associated with having ads on your site – suggesting that you were using a free, cheapo host. Today, people may think you're so popular that you're selling ads!)
- With WordPress, you can either let them host it or have it hosted on another server.

Blog Tips:

1. Consider Blogger and Wordpress. I have a couple of blogs with Googles' blog platform, Blogger (blogspot.com). I love Blogger's simplicity and intuitiveness. Some authors may prefer starting there. Danny Kofke, whom I mentioned earlier, has a Blogger blog. It seems to work fine for him.

WordPress has several advantages, especially if you want to expand your blog. As today's reigning industry standard blog platform,

- people write helpful tutorials on whatever you want to accomplish
- programmers continually develop new applications/plugins for it
- new templates are constantly being designed
- you'll likely have friends and acquaintances who can help you when you get frustrated
- plenty of professional designers and programmers know how to work with Wordpress, when you need help from someone geekier than you.

2. Purchase your own domain name (url or web address). Your domain will travel with you if you decide to move your site to a different location, so that your followers can still find you. My author site is www.jstevemiller.com. One of my blogs is www.enjoyyourwriting.com. Even if they're just separate pages on the same site/blog, you can purchase different domains for each section.

The ".com" ending is preferable, although if the wording you need isn't available for ".com," you have many other choices, starting with ".org". One very popular place to purchase domains is http://www.godaddy.com, where you pay an $11.50 per year registration fee. I buy mine from www.000domains.com and have been very pleased with their service.

3. In choosing a domain name, think through how you want to brand yourself throughout your web presence. If you name your home page after your book, won't things get confusing when you publish your second and third books? If you plan to write several books, perhaps branding your name should trump branding each book. Seen in this way, your home page might be www.(yourname).com, linking from your menu to your book page www.(my book name).com and your blog www.(my blog's name).com.

Since Cherie and I have common names, we add our initials to brand ourselves as J. Steve Miller and Cherie K. Miller.

4. Consider doing it yourself to save money and to be able to update it yourself. This is what I typically do. First, I set up a blog or site as well as I can, setting up my individual pages, writing what I want to say on each page, choosing some stock photos if I don't like any of the templates, and writing the content.

Then, if it looks rather amateurish (I ask others for their candid opinions), I pay a good designer about $200 to go over the site and make it look nice. (You might get this for less. Find several designers that others recommend. Do their former projects appeal to you? Tell them you've already put the site together, but you just need them to go over it and make it look good. Tell them you're shopping around and ask how much they'd charge.) That's how Cherie and I designed our author sites and publisher site:

www.cheriekmiller.com
www.jstevemiller.com
www.wisdomcreekpress.com

5. If you need professional-looking images, look at online stock photo companies. I personally use www.istockphoto.com. Browse through this superb collection of over 6 million photographs, vector illustrations, videos, audio tracks and Flash files, offered by over 70,000 artists worldwide. You can purchase the rights to a 3.9" x 5.9" (283 pixels x 424 pixels) web-ready image for $5.

I find that if I can come to a designer with some images I like for different pages, this helps her to see what I like and saves her time. I can copy watermarked images (marked to prevent stealing) to show the designer before deciding whether to purchase them or not.

Tip for Starving Artists

Contact web design teachers at your local technical school or university. Ask if any of their most talented students would take on a simple project for low or no cost to give them something on their resumes.

6. Get a professional photo of yourself. A photographer's job is to make you look better than you really look, and more interesting. In my case, I'm glad I paid a professional.

Author Site Option #3 – A Traditional Website

If you're already comfortable with web-building programs such as Expression Web or Dreamweaver, it might be easiest for you to build a traditional website. Even if you don't know these programs (both of which require quite a learning curve), most big hosts offer free templates and free web-based tools to help you build your site. Many of them are fairly easy to use. Also, most big hosts, like Host Gator (which I use for several sites), allow you to attach a Wordpress blog to your site at no extra charge. That's what I did, since I was already paying a host for a traditional site.

To find the best rated web hosts and compare their features, go to www.cnet.com and click Reviews/All Categories/Web Hosting. After building it, if you don't think it looks professional enough, pay a professional designer a "spiff up" fee.

To build your site, apply the above blog tips 2-6.

Should Authors Learn a Web Design Program like Dreamweaver or Expression Web?

If you're really excited about web design and want to pursue it, go for it! But in my opinion, if you're not already comfortable using either of these programs, they take way too long to learn for the average writer who wants to spend his time writing rather than designing websites. With some programs, like using PhotoShop for manipulating images and doing basic design, you can learn the 1/10,000th of the program you need to size images, crop, etc., and do fine with it. With Expression Web and Dreamweaver, however, from my experience, even after you think you've learned the fundamentals, you run into one frustrating complexity after another.

That's why I recommend using either a site host's web-based tools or a blog's web-based tools, trying out the templates they provide, and hiring a professional to make it look better if you're not pleased with the result.

Author Site Option #4 – A Special Section of an Existing Site

If you're known for something else more than your books and you already have a strong web presence, consider just adding a few author pages to your existing site. Example: You run a great company and wrote a book about it. Why not start out by adding some author pages to your company site and linking to them from your company's "About Us" page? Since your company site already has incoming links, visitors, and search engine positioning for key words (like your name, the company's name, etc.), why not start your presence on this site? And if you like your company's webmaster, she can help you as well.

If you later sell the company or write other books unrelated to the company, you can always move your author pages to another host. Just make sure to purchase a domain name with your name and your book's name, so that your followers can find you easily if you move.

Author Site Option #5 – A Subject Site with an Author Site Component

Let's say you write primarily about vampires and you want to attract audiences that are interested in vampires. So you purchase the web address, www.allaboutvampires.com (sorry, it's already taken), collect scores of articles on vampires, do interviews with famous vampires, offer reviews of vampire movies and books, and blog about which devastatingly beautiful girls are now dating vampires. Your object is to attract people who are already searching for vampire information, interact with them on your blog (attached to your site), and hope that they'll notice your author information and book information on your site.

This is typically easier if you write nonfiction in a specific subject area. For a good example of this web presence, visit http://www.bookmarket.com. It's the primary web presence of book marketing author John Kremer.

Note that his site isn't primarily an author site introducing John Kremer to the world. Instead, it's all about helping authors market their books. His web address is about book marketing rather than John Kremer. In this way, he attracts tons of visitors, who come to find out how to market their books. His author information and book information are available through the navigation on the left.

Obviously, this draws hordes of people to his site. By focusing on helping others and providing scads of free information on his site to help them, he gets plenty of attention in return. Whether you search "book marketing" or "John Kremer," his site comes up first.

For other examples of authors using topical sites, see Brian Jud at www.bookmarketingworks.com, or Dan Poynter at www.parapublishing.com. Darren Rowse uses a blog for his subject site at http://www.problogger.net.

In some cases, a subject site built on a traditional platform might get more traffic than one built on a blog platform (e.g., Wordpress). For example, let's say you don't want to commit yourself to blogging several times a week or adding content several times a week – you want it to be as passive as possible. In this case, if Google were to spider your site and "see" that you were on a Wordpress platform, it might penalize your ranking for not regularly posting, since regular posting should characterize a popular blog. This theory was tested and found to be true with Google's current algorithm:

http://www.angelseo.co.uk/seo/general-seo/wordpress-vs-pure-html-css-web-sites-which-is-better-for-seo

Reality Check: Subject-specific sites work better for certain subject areas than others. The above examples are on marketing-related topics. Visitors come to these sites searching for marketing information, **which is information they are willing to pay for**. On the other hand, if you develop a successful reptile site, trying to sell your books on Geckos and Snakes, I'd suggest that most of your site visitors are simply looking for free web information and might be reluctant to buy your books. Besides, you'd be competing with many authoritative, established animal sites. (But then again, who knows? I'm just guessing here.)

I have a site dedicated to helping educators teach life skills. I assumed that many of these visitors (around 800 unique visitors per day) would be interested in purchasing my book on personal money management, which is a life skill. But neither my mentions on the site nor my e-mails to members (about 6,000 members) have produced, as far as I can tell, more than a handful of purchases over the last year. So don't let people tell you that it's simple to build a successful subject site and that it's assured to sell tons of books as a result. For some topics it works, for others it won't.

For more information on using sites and blogs to sell books, see chapters 14 and 16.

Author Site Option #6 – A Site Provided by Your Publisher

If it's easy to update and customize and it's free, go for it. But think ahead. If you write other books with other publishers, will you need to build your own site to avoid a conflict of interest? Again, purchase your own url and attach it to the site in case you need to move later.

What Elements Should You Include on Your Author Site?

That will differ according to your purposes, your audiences, and the strengths you want to project. If this is the only book you've written, and your only other writing was an article in a small, local newspaper, then don't include a section that highlights your lack of publishing.

Here are some areas that some authors include on their sites:

1. A press (media) page. This page typically replaces the expensive "**media kit**" that authors and publishers formerly mailed to the media. Here's my press page for *Enjoy Your Money*:

http://wisdomcreekpress.com/press_kits.html

Offer everything the media wants to know:

- Blurbs
- Reviews
- Author interview
- Links to audio interviews and TV appearances
- Calendar of book-related activities
- Link to sample chapters
- Sample interview questions
- Link to Amazon for purchasing
- Link to other full reviews
- Contact information

2. Your author photo and book cover. Offer it in a high enough resolution and large enough size so that the press can use it in print publications. The professional standard is 300 pixels per inch, although 240 pixels per inch might work in some cases. To allow someone to print a sharp 4 x 6 picture, you'd need a web image of 1200 pixels x 1800 pixels.

3. Biographical information. Go beyond the bio on your book by telling, not only why you wrote the book and what qualified you to write it, but any interesting material about yourself. Often these interesting personal items can connect with an interviewer, or give her ideas for using your background to connect with her audience. If you're raising an autistic child, build houses with Habitat for Humanity, breed horses, or play the accordion, why not mention it? People are interested in people's lives, as we see from the popularity of such magazines as *People*.

4. A speaker page. If you want to give presentations, design a specific page to impress event organizers. Include recommendations from those who've heard you speak. Include video clips of your speaking. At the end of each speaking engagement, get input on how you did, how you could do better, and a blurb you can use on this page to advertise future speaking. This is your place to build your speaking platform.

5. A description of other services you provide. Do you speak at author gatherings or book clubs or libraries? Consider putting together a free discussion guide on your site. Do you write articles for magazines? Consider a page that lists your credentials, with links to your published articles. This builds your freelance writer platform, helping you to land future articles.

6. Consider separate pages targeting specific media. Examples: a specific page targeting radio, another page for educators (including a teachers' guide).

7. Your blog. If it's hosted elsewhere, you can have still have it appear on your site.

8. Links to your favorite sites.

9. An annotated list of recommended books in your field.

10. A list of purchasing options, including how to save money by purchasing your books in bulk.

11. A way to keep in touch, by signing up for your newsletter or blog. (You might want to offer a free gift as an incentive, like a white paper or e-book.)

Make It Easy for People to Find You

> **Snoozer Alert:** If the above discussion convinces you that all you need to set up is a one page, Danny Kofke look-alike blog, then the following is overkill – way too much information. If you're not into optimizing your site for search engines, feel free to skim or skip. Seriously, it's okay.

If your sole goal is to give media folks a place to check you out when you link to them from your introductory e-mail, then you don't have to worry so much about search engine optimization. Danny Kofke's author blog functions beautifully as he sends e-mails to TV and radio hosts and links them to his blog. They don't have to randomly find him through a search engine.

But it's important to note that if they lost his web address, they could search "Danny Kofke" in Google and find his blog ranked first. Why? For one, he's blessed with an unusual name. But additionally, he set up his site so that his name's in the web address: http://dannykofke.blogspot.com. Which brings us to our first principle of Search Engine Optimization (SEO):

Activity: Think Like a Search Engine.

When I teach on search engine optimization, I encourage students to try to think like a search engine. Why? Because if they simply put themselves in Google's shoes, certain tactics become intuitively obvious and others can be invented. This activity led me to a couple of innovations that increased my traffic significantly.

Basically, Google's "spiders" crawl the web, bringing back data from every site to determine how they should be ranked when people search for their subject matter. So think, if you were Google, what site content would be most important to determine if a site should rank high for a certain search term? Hint: "spiders" can't see your beautiful pictures and graphics, so aesthetics don't count. "Spiders" can, however, tabulate how many times you use certain phrases, and how they are used (As links? In bold? At the top of the page? As a title?).

SEO Do's

1. Choose your web address to attract key searches. Danny didn't purchase this url. He just set it up in Blogger to where his name would be a part of the Blogger address. (I'd advise him to purchase his own url, so that in case he moves his blog, at a later date, any media who already link to him would be able to continue to find him. If he did this, his url might read: www.dannykofke.com. Then again, Danny may never want to move and would rather save his money.)

So take the one term or phrase you most want to attract and put it in your web address. If it's primarily an author site that that's all about you, then you'll probably want your name in the url. If you have a popular name, add an initial, or put in your full name. For branding, try to keep your web address name consistent with the author name on your book covers. If it's already been taken for .com, try .org or another ending. If those are all taken, try separating your name with hyphens (www.j-steve-miller.com) or adding a relevant word (www.jstevemillerauthor.com). This should be balanced with choosing a web address that's easy to say (dashes can be a problem here) and easy to remember.

It's also handy for people to be able to find your site when they search your book title. Your Amazon page will probably grab pole position, which should be no problem. But if you want people to be able to find your media page when they search the name of your book, you could purchase a url with your book name in it, and have it as your press page.

If you have a subject site, you'll want to determine which phrase you most want to capture. That's why John Kremer's site is called www.bookmarket.com – the web address itself attracts searches for "book marketing." Since you already searched key phrases in Google's Key Word Tool (see chapter 4) you already know which phrases you want to target.

Caution! If you're targeting a topic, be realistic. If you wrote a book on personal money management, don't imagine that you can optimize your site to capture searches for the single word "money." Do you really think Google will prioritize your author site over such established behemoths as MSN's *Money Central*? Narrow down a niche market (and related key phrases) that you could realistically capture.

2. Brainstorm all the words and phrases people might use to look for your material.

3. Use Google's Key Word Tool to discover which terms are searched the most.

4. Use key words/phrases generously throughout your site. Caution: Don't go crazy with this! Using a phrase eight times in a page might look good to Google; fifty times may look like you're trying to spam the system. Google penalizes people who try to unfairly manipulate search engine rankings.

5. Use your key words in different ways and on different parts of the page (top and bottom, in naming links, in naming images, as a "heading," in bold).

6. Use key words in "meta tags." (They're invisible to site visitors, but visible to search engine spiders.) Since they're always placed at the top of a page, they can be very important for search engines. Use your "title" to describe the page, using appropriate key words. Search engines might use part of your "description" tags to describe your page on their search results.[2]

How to Add Meta Tags

On a traditional site, you can add them with Web programs such as DreamWeaver or Expression Web, or perhaps with handy tools provided by your host. To add meta tags to your posts on a Wordpress Blog, follow the instructions in their "codex" entry on meta tags here:

http://codex.wordpress.org/Meta_Tags_in_WordPress

To make it easier, you'll probably want to download one of their plugins from here:

http://wordpress.org/extend/plugins

where you can search the word "meta tags."

7. Use a good host.

8. OFFER GREAT CONTENT! This is of utmost importance. Look at John Kremer's or Brian Jud's or Dan Poynter's sites. They offer tons of free content. If the key words for real estate are "location, location, location," the key words to search engine optimization are "content, content, content." People return for great content. People tell their friends about great content. People link to great content.

9. Put up fresh content regularly. Search engines prioritize new content. If you're trying to get your blog noticed, blog several times per week.

10. Optimize each page for the searches you want to attract. Remember, many will enter your site from pages other than the home page.

11. Put appropriate tags below your blog entries. If you're writing a post about rats, type in related tags such as pests, rodents, mice, etc.

12. GET INBOUND LINKS (from other sites and blogs). This is extremely important. Try to word inbound links with appropriate key words. Google assumes that if lots of people link to you, you must be pretty important. A link from a popular site in your field counts more than a link from a site that few people visit or link to. Find sites that link to sites like yours, and ask if they'd consider linking to you. (If they ask for a reciprocal link, and their site makes sense to link to, then do it. Optimization often involves trading favors with other popular sites.)

13. If all else fails, experiment with "pay per click" with Google AdWords and Yahoo Marketing Solutions. Search a phrase in Google and you'll notice that the top couple of results have a colored background. They're ads. Also, you'll find results on the right side of search results called "sponsored links." They're also ads. If you click on one of those links, the sponsor will pay for that click.

Generally, pay per click won't be cost effective for authors. But in some cases, it might be worth a try. You can always set it up for a period of time and see if you sell enough books to be cost effective. I use them effectively to advertise my web-based character education resources.

SEO Don'ts

1. Don't use your key words exclusively in images. Search engines can't "see" the name of your book in your book cover image. So when you add an image to a page, name the file (using "image alt tags") with your key words. If your home page is one big image, the spider doesn't see the words at all.

2. Don't build your site with frames. Again, search engines can't "see" your words.

3. Don't attempt gray area SEO tricks like hiding key words from human eyes by putting them in the same color as your background. (Google knows that trick.) There are many tricks out there, but search engine managers typically discover them and penalize sites that try them.

4. Don't submit your site to services that claim, "We submit your site to 100 search engines." Studies show it doesn't work and they will probably sell your e-mail address to spammers.

Only a few search engines really count, and they should be able to find you. According to StatCounter GlobalStats, in the 12-month period through January 2011, 90 percent of all searchers used Google, four percent used Yahoo, four percent Bing, and the remaining two percent were divided among all the other hundreds of search engines. But this can differ from country to country. Eighty-four percent of searchers in China used Baidu in the last quarter of 2010.

5. Beware of companies who guarantee that they'll position you at the top for the key words you're targeting. They simply can't guarantee this. To prove it, Google the key phrase that all SEO companies would love to capture: "search engine optimization." Where does the SEO company you're checking out appear in the search? Obviously, only one SEO company can capture pole position for that spot!

We don't know all the factors that Google considers in ranking sites; neither do we know how each factor is weighed. They guard their algorithm so that people can't abuse it. Add to this incomprehensible mix that once a month or so, Google "dances," making changes to its algorithm. So how could anyone legitimately claim with certainty that he can put you at the top of a search?

Again, beyond the basics of SEO, I encourage you to occasionally look at your site from a search engine's perspective. Ask yourself, "If I were Google, would I prioritize this page in a search for this phrase? What can I do to make it more appealing to Google?" Or better, "How can I offer the best information available on this topic?"

Cautions about Building an Author Site

1. Don't get discouraged thinking that you have to do everything. Start somewhere. Do something. Take one step at a time and you can eventually grow an effective Web presence.

Tip: To see your web page as a search engine spider "sees" it, bring the page up in your browser and click "View/Page Source" on the top menu of your browser. There, you'll see the "hidden" meta tags, names of images, etc. Find the sites that rank highest for the search terms you want to capture. Go to those sites and click "View/Page Source" to see how they place their key words, etc.

2. Don't overpay for a blog/site. You may be able to do it all yourself. The professional photographer I chose for my author photo worked from her home to keep costs down. My programmers and web designers work from their homes. Especially beware of large monthly fees. Remember, a starter Wordpress site is free to start and has no monthly fees. A site with a host like HostGator gives you more space than you'll likely ever need, with a cost of between $5 and $10 per month. (This continues to get cheaper over time and can cost a couple of bucks per month per site if HostGator hosts several of your sites.) Hosts may also offer inexpensive e-commerce solutions, if you need to sell books/products from your site.

When you talk to web designers or webmasters, don't commit to anything immediately. Tell them you're just checking out many options. Explore widely before making a decision.

3. Beware of webmasters who want to host your site/blog on their own server or their small company's server. If the server (and thus your site) goes down when they're on vacation, or if they take up another interest besides web design, you might be in trouble. Larger, top-rated hosts must keep their servers running, up to date and have good backup plans in case of emergencies.

4. Don't commit yourself exclusively to one webmaster or group of webmasters. I typically end up with one person I love for design and another for programming, but we're in no way contractually bound. Especially in times of rapid change, I like to leave my options open.

5. Don't get into a situation where you're dependent upon (and paying) someone else to do all your updates. If someone is designing your author site for you, tell her to set things up so that you can easily update it yourself. If you decide later to hire out the maintenance of your site, you can choose whom to hire rather than being stuck with one person.

Conclusion and Summary

A professional web presence makes book marketing so much easier. The press will view you as a professional. Media moguls will interview you as an expert. You will have a central place to collect your reviews, interviews, and media events. Some authors use their web presence to connect with present readers, find new ones, and build a following. Since a web presence is very affordable and easy to maintain, it makes sense to start somewhere and continue to develop it throughout your lifetime.

Do Something!

To put this chapter into action, I will...

1 –

2 –

3 –

Keep Learning!

- **See my free updates** to each chapter at www.sellmorebooks.org.
- **Visit many different author sites, book sites, and subject sites** to learn from their strengths and weaknesses.
- **Visit and learn from press pages for products both inside and outside of the book industry.**
- **Learn more about optimizing your site for search engines here:** www.searchenginewatch.com.
- **For Google's suggestions and warnings about search engine optimization, see:**

http://www.google.com/support/webmasters/bin/answer.py?answer=35769

Chapter 10

Submit Your Book to Contests

Writing is rewriting; publishing is marketing.

- Georgia author

Enjoy Your Money won a National Best Books Award in the Personal Finance category. I didn't notice a jump in sales, leading me to believe that an award, unless it's a Pulitzer, should be thought of more as a platform than a direct source of sales. But I've found it to be a very useful platform.

- **I ordered a set of gold stars**, which paste nicely on my cover. When I took my book to a local bookstore, the manager took one glance at the star, pointed to it, and said, "This helps," and asked for several books to sell on consignment. The star singled out my book as special. It was no longer "just another book."
- **I sent out a press release concerning the award**, one through an organization that recommends books to libraries. Within a month, a book distributer contacted me, saying that they were receiving orders for my book. We signed a contract and they began distributing the book to libraries. The timing suggests that these orders resulted from the press release.
- **Every time I mention the book – on my press page, in a press release, in an e-mail to a columnist or radio host or blogger or anyone in the media – I refer to the book as an award-winning book.** Not every book can claim that. That differentiates it from most other books received by the media; thus, it gets special attention.

Now a Best Books Award isn't a Pulitzer by a long shot, but it's a legitimate award. Judges read and determine the top books. Each category has only one winner. If they declared every book received as "nominated," even those that were terribly written and produced, their reputation would suffer.

Winning an award bestows special honor upon my book, separating it from millions of other books in print. Especially for low-profile authors who can't separate themselves out by their very names, a gold or silver star can help many of your publicity efforts.

Other Benefits of Book Awards

Winners of awards may:

- have their books displayed at ceremonies in major book conventions.
- be offered special promotions.
- have their books considered by distributors and booksellers.
- receive cash awards.

Do Your Odds of Winning Make It a Worthwhile Gamble?

I'm not the type to enter contests. I hardly ever put my name in for drawings. I've never played the lottery. In my mind, the odds are so overwhelmingly against me that they're not worth my time.

But book awards are different. Your odds are better than you might first think.

First of all, for most of the awards I researched, you're seldom competing with best-selling authors. They apparently don't feel the need to compete for "small time" awards. Moreover, major publishers focus their marketing efforts on their best-selling authors when the book first comes out – not a year later when contest winners are announced.

Second, the odds for winning a specific category aren't that bad. Let's estimate the odds of winning an award from "the largest independent book awards contest in the world" – The Independent Publisher Book Awards. They claimed to have 4,000 entries in 2009. Having so many entries, I assumed that it was one of my longest shots for winning. But those 4,000 entries are divided into 67 categories, narrowing down my competition to an average of 60 books per category. But each category offers three awards, giving me even better odds. So if you've written a great book and submit it to 12 contests, those aren't bad odds.

To make the odds even better, if you fit into a specialized category, like "multicultural nonfiction adult," it is entirely possible that you'll find yourself competing with five other books, three of which are titled "How to Get Rich on the Internet," written in broken English by telephone company support personnel.

Even if you don't win a category, if the judges deem your book worthy, some contests will declare your book "nominated" for the prize. That distinguishes your book from books that were not worthy of the contest and allows you to order a star of a different color (perhaps silver?) that says "Nominated for...."

David Cady, author of *The Handler*, submitted his book for a Georgia Author of the Year award (the longest-running book award in the Southeast). Although he didn't win his category, he was nominated for an award, giving him the right to put a "Georgia Author of the Year Nominee" sticker on his book. The sticker helped with his marketing.

If your book is well written, well edited, and well designed, these are decent odds, with a handsome enough payoff to make awards worth pursuing.

Caution: There will be much more competition in the broader categories. But a first, second, or third place in one of these categories says a lot about the quality of the winners.

Narrowing Down Appropriate Contests

I started by hitting the library to peruse the latest editions of both Literary Market Place (LMP) and Writers Market, both of which have sections listing book awards. (There's also a section of the Christian Writers Market dedicated to contests.) Don't be overwhelmed by the huge number of awards. You can narrow down pretty quickly which ones apply to your book.

> **Tip:** Some great contests don't list themselves in Writers Market or Literary Market Place. So search Google for other awards that might be an even better fit for your book. There may be specialized contests for textbooks or pet books or picture books or cookbooks. New contests are announced regularly in writers' publications. Being new, they may have less competition. Even if they lack prestige, does the average book-buyer know a prestigious contest from a non-prestigious one?

Since my book is a nonfiction personal finance book by a Georgia author, written in a story form, published by a small publisher, targeting people 16-32 years of age, I can ignore all awards that:

1) Don't accept submissions. (Some contests do their own searching.)

2) Accept submissions only from Canada or Ohio or people born in Texas.

3) Cater to big-name authors and big publishers. (Determine this by browsing last year's winners.)

4) Take only fiction or poetry or books about orchids (yes, there's an orchid book contest).

5) Accept only non-published manuscripts.

After making my list at the library, I took it home to study each award on the web. I wanted to know:

- Do they require a nomination fee? If so, is it within my budget?
- What are my odds of winning or at least getting a nomination?
- Do they subdivide into categories, or is it me against hundreds of others for one or two big prizes?
- How prestigious is the award?
- Do I think the name of the award and the look of the sticker (digital and/or physical) will work with my marketing strategy?

Important! Note Differing Deadlines for Entry! I errantly assumed that all awards would be for books published in the previous calendar year, thus having deadlines of a couple of months into the next year following publication. But some work on different schedules. Check each contest to find its schedule.

My Resulting List

Here's my narrowed down list, with notes intact, in alphabetical order. I sent my book to five of these.

800CEORead.com Best Business Books – http://800ceoread.com/page/show/book_awards – (11 categories) Each book is judged on the originality of its ideas and content. Submit two copies. Deadline: October 15. No entrance fee.

Benjamin Franklin Awards – www.ibpa-online.org – (54 categories) Sponsored by "the largest non-profit trade association representing independent publishers": The Independent Book Publishers Association. "Regarded as one of the highest national honors in small and independent book publishing." Deadlines: Sept. 30 for books published through August; Dec. 31 for the rest of the books published during the year. $80 entrance fee for IBPA members, $180 for non-members, which includes a membership.

Best Books Awards – http://www.usabooknews.com/2009bestbooksawards.html – (100+ categories) Benefits: special promotions. Deadline: Sept. 30. $69 entrance fee per book, per category.

The Christopher Awards – www.christophers.org – Few categories (less chances to win) and winners seem weighted to big presses. No entrance fees.

Eric Hoffer Award for Independent Books – www.writersnotes.com – (15 categories) "Each category will be awarded a winner, runner-up, and multiple honorable mentions." Deadline: Jan. 21. $45 entrance fee.

Foreword Magazine Book of the Year – www.forewordmagazine.com – (61 categories) "*ForeWord* is the only review trade journal devoted exclusively to books from independent houses." *Foreword* is respected by libraries, distributors, and booksellers. With 61 categories, first, second and third places in each category, plus an announcement of finalists, there's a decent chance to get some recognition. Even to say your book was "a finalist in the Foreword Book of the Year Awards" could be a huge boost. Deadline: Jan. 15. $75 entrance fee per title, per category.

Georgia Author of the Year (GAYA) Awards – http://georgiawriters.org – The oldest literary award in the Southeastern United States. Both fiction and nonfiction. $45 entrance fee per title.

The Independent Publisher Book Awards http://www.independentpublisher.com/ipland/LearnMore.php – (67 categories) "Gold, silver, and bronze medals will be awarded in each category." Over 4,000 entries..."the largest independent book awards contest in the world." Deadline: March 20. $85 entry fee per category with discounts for earlier submission.

Michael L. Printz Award – http://www.ala.org/ala/mgrps/divs/yalsa/booklistsawards/printzaward/Printz.cfm – "An award for a book that exemplifies literary excellence in young adult literature." Sponsored by Booklist, a publication of the American Library Association. Most of these awards require submission by someone other than the author/publisher/editor, e.g., a librarian. If librarians are raving about your book, see if a librarian will submit it for you. Note also their category for Outstanding Books for the College Bound.

Mom's Choice Awards – http://www.momschoiceawards.com/enter.php – (100+ categories) Benefits: book reviews, special promotions, etc. Deadline: Oct. 1. $300 entrance fee per book, per category.

National Indie Excellence Awards – http://www.indieexcellence.com/ – (100+ categories) Benefits: promotions, etc. Deadline: March 31. $65 entrance fee per book, per category.

Nautilus Award – www.marilynmcguire.com – (28 categories) *"Recognizing books...that promote spiritual growth, conscious living, and positive social change as they stimulate the imagination and inspire the reader to new possibilities for a better world."* Deadline: Submit August to January 15. $165 entrance fee, but discounts for submitting earlier.

Patterson Prize for Books for Young People – www.pccc.edu/poetry.

The Writer's Digest International Self-Published Book Awards – http://www.writersdigest.com/competitions.

The Result

> **It won the personal finance category of the National Best Books Award.**
> **It won an Honorable Mention award in the Young Adult Category for the Eric Hoffer Award.**
> **It was nominated for a Georgia Author of the Year Award.**

As a result, I can call Enjoy Your Money a "multiple-award winning" book!

Using Awards to Sell Books

As I mentioned, don't expect a spike in sales to follow each win. Instead, use it as a platform for special publicity (announcing your award) or to enhance other publicity. Send out a press release (see chapter 24). Put a digital image of the award in your press page and on your brochures. When courting media, always call it an "award-winning" book. Order a roll of stickers from the contest company and put it on your books.

Best wishes as you seek recognition for your book!

Do Something!

To put this chapter into action, I will...

1 –

2 –

3 –

Keep Learning!

- **See my free updates** to each chapter at www.sellmorebooks.org .
- **Study each of the contest sites that I reference in this chapter**, to better understand how they work and to see if your book is a match.
- Go to your library, pen and legal pad in hand, to **find awards that fit your book** in Literary Market Place (LMP), Writers Market, and (if appropriate) Christian Writers Market.

Part II

Let the World Know About Your Book

Chapter 11

Check Your Attitudes toward Marketing

(And Keep Productive During Discouragement and Failure)

The two secrets to book sales are: 1) to produce a good product that has a market and 2) to let people know about it.[1]

- Dan Poynter

When you're going through hell, keep going.

- Winston Churchill

An author's underlying beliefs and attitudes can make the difference between selling one book and selling millions. So do a bit of soul-searching to see if you harbor any of these sales-quenching attitudes.

Sales-Quenching Attitude #1: "Promoting my own books demands a huge ego that I personally despise."

The Problem: A Skewed Image

I'm turned off by shameless self promoters.

Cherie and I recently sat in bed, pen and paper in hand, listening to a pod-cast from a book-marketing conference. The speaker told story after story of his great successes, often mentioning famous people as his "good friends" and shamelessly promoting his own products. At the end of the presentation, my paper was blank. He told me nothing practical about how to market my books. It was all about *him*. I looked at Cherie and said, "If you EVER hear me give a talk like that, shoot me."

If the image to the right is what authors envision when their publishers say, "Get out and market your books!" no wonder they resist.

A Solution: View Marketing as Helping

I read Debbie Allen's *Confessions of Shameless Self Promoters*, thinking that it might help to push me a bit out of the "humble author who never mentions his own books" mentality. I was pleasantly surprised that the advice was far from the image that the title had brought to my mind. The collection of successful promoters repeatedly extolled the virtues of giving, caring, learning, and joining hands with others to promote each other's products. Here are a couple of quotes from Debbie's book:

> "People hate pushy, loud, obnoxious people who only talk about themselves." (Rick Segel, speaker, author, and director of the Retail Association of Massachusetts).[2]
>
> "Networking has been the way of the world. We just gave it a new term. It used to be called...helping!" (Susan RoAne, keynote speaker and bestselling author of *How to Work a Room* and *The Secrets of Savvy Networking*).[3]

Jack Canfield and Mark Victor Hansen have sold over 115 million of their *Chicken Soup* books in over 40 languages. But like many of us, they started out with a low profile and no funding (they were both in debt and couldn't afford a publicist.) Nearly 150 publishers rejected them.

In an interview with Steve Harrison, they told about a critical change of attitude that revolutionized their marketing. Here's a snippet of the interview (italics mine):

Harrison: Did you just get lucky? What made the difference?

Hansen: We make our own luck. *We started thinking differently*, thinking like a marketer. *It took several years to get beyond the stigma of marketing – thinking that it was something less than legitimate for an author. It took a shift in attitude*, a learning of techniques and strategies.

Harrison: Many authors have passion to serve and make a difference but feel awkward about self-promotion. What would you say to them?

Canfield: *If you had a cure for cancer, would you have a fear of being a self-promoter? Believe that what you have is extremely valuable. To not share it hurts people.* If you have food for the hungry but don't tell the starving you have it, you've done them a disservice. *You're not an egoist; you're simply helping people.* We have over 2,000 people who've said they didn't commit suicide because of a *Chicken Soup* book.[4]

Selling Books with a Giving Attitude

Most of the authors I know write books to help people. But if they never get out into the marketplace and if nobody buys their books, they don't help anyone. The more I view my marketing as helping people, the more motivated I become to engage people and sell my books.

- You wrote a children's book. When you do a reading in a fifth-grade class, you're not promoting yourself; you're inspiring the next generation to fall in love with books.
- You wrote a financial book. When you do a radio interview, you're not trying to impress people with your greatness; you're giving people hope and the tools to survive in difficult times.
- You wrote a novel. When you participate in a writers' forum, you aren't selling books; you're helping writers at their point of need.

The giving, helping attitude also helps me to emotionally deal with a big effort that doesn't pay off in sales. I've had some great TV opportunities that resulted in no sales at all. But if my motive to get onto TV was more to help people than to sell books, I can feel great about the initiative. And in the end, of course, we find that deeds done out of a heart of service come back to reward us in many ways. Producers, viewers, and listeners love sincere people with a giving heart. Producers ask givers back a second time. Audiences enthusiastically recommend givers' products. As the Good Book says, "Give and it will be given to you."

Sales-Quenching Attitude #2: "My publisher will do all the marketing."

Publishers know different. That's why they ask authors to include a marketing plan with their proposals.

I'm not putting down publishers here. Some do a fantastic job of mailing review copies, sending out a press release, and setting up radio interviews. But typically they've got so many books to push that if word of mouth hasn't taken over within three months of publication, your book becomes ancient history in light of the newer books they need to promote. The experience of many successful low profile authors shows that it takes much longer than three months to get the word out.

Besides, nobody knows your book like you do. You are the best person to find niche markets, contact influential thought leaders in your field, and answer people's questions on relevant forums. The publicists at your publishing company simply don't have time to adequately search out niche markets and make hundreds of personal contacts. Here's what the experts say:

- "No matter how you choose to sell your books – whether through bookstores, to libraries, via mail order direct to the reader, or however else – one thing you will always have to do: you will have to sell your books. No one else can do that for you." (Book marketing expert John Kremer)[5]
- "If you don't promote it, no one will." (Seth Godin, author and internet-marketing guru)[6]

Sales-Quenching Attitude #3: "If I make a couple of attempts, that should be enough to get word of mouth going."

It's easy to sink into self-doubt when you mail your book to fifty reviewers, speak at the Rotary Club, and do a local book signing, but see no significant sales as a result. Yet, your failure may not reflect at all upon the quality of your writing. More likely it's due to your failure to grasp one of the most significant characteristics of the publishing industry: *the winners separate themselves out by the scale of their marketing efforts*. Not understanding this, many authors do very little marketing, while hoping that the same magic may visit them that visit other authors – the magic that offers a review on national radio or distribution to Wal-Mart. But it's likely that if you were to speak with these "fortunate" authors, you'd be surprised at the context in which the magic occurred.

When Marketing and Magic Meet

I'm sure some low profile authors, by some inexplicable stroke of fortune, publish their books, get a phone call from Oprah within the first month, become instant media darlings, and watch their books quickly climb to best-seller status. It's like magic, but a magic that graces far less than one in a million authors.

The more typical magic comes in the midst of the daily, mundane tasks that authors do to get their books noticed. Sadly, the great majority of authors will never experience the tap of the fairy's wand, not because their books suck, but because they failed to create the context frequented by fairies. You see, fairies quickly lose interest in authors who hope that their mother and brother will read their books and start an unstoppable word-of-mouth campaign. Instead they flutter off to visit a more worthy author – like the one passionately speaking to half-interested students at an obscure school, wondering how in the world her life came to this. But then, quite unexpectedly, the fairy arrives with her wand. A teacher recommends the presentation on a popular teachers' forum, and the author arrives home to find school after school begging her to speak at their schools and sell her books.

In broad strokes, that's how high school author Christopher Paolini was touched by the magic. He tried traditional bookstore signings for his self-published novel, *Eragon*, but soon discovered that it didn't work very well for an unknown, first-time author. So he tried school presentations. He called school librarians in Houston and several of them allowed him to speak. Then the first fairy appeared, in the form of a librarian who posted an enthusiastic recommendation on a teachers' forum. That one recommendation allowed him to book a solid month of school talks in Houston.

Paolini went on to do over 135 presentations. In the summer of 2002, the second fairy appeared, in the form of novelist Carl Hiaasen, who was vacationing in a city where Paolini was speaking. Hiaasen's stepson showed the book to him and he recommended it to his publishing house. They signed Paolini and his book appeared on the New York Times bestseller list for 121 weeks.[7]

You might wonder, "How lucky was it that one of those librarians frequented such a forum?" Or, "What are the odds that a novelist with connections just happened to find Paolini's book?" Well, I'd argue that, although the odds of either of those specific events happening may be quite remote, the odds of *something* happening, given his 135 presentations, was almost certain. Paolini took his marketing to a far greater scale than most authors, creating the very atmosphere that fairies love to visit.

At first, I didn't understand the magic. I thought that if one of my marketing efforts didn't produce immediate sales, it was just one more failure. But just getting out there and trying stirs things up. Fairies notice when authors shut down Microsoft Word and begin connecting with real people. Eventually, their wands come out tapping and truly extraordinary stuff happens.

During my first few months of marketing *Enjoy Your Money*, I felt much like the pastor who went to watch the train go by every day. When someone inquired about his unusual habit, he said, "I enjoy watching something that moves without my having to push it." My book sold only when I was out there doing something. If I let up for a day, nothing happened. And 90 percent of what I tried seemed to have no impact at all.

But somehow, all that publicity made things start to happen. Was word of mouth taking over? Had I reached a tipping point? Was I touched by an angel? Whatever the cause, it certainly looked magical.

- A book reviewer to school libraries wrote a positive review.
- A respected distributor to school libraries started getting orders and requested a contract. Then a second distributor picked me up.
- Twice as many sold on Amazon the next month, and three times as many the following month, without any promotion on my part at all.

Some may call them lucky breaks, but from my experience luck tends to fall upon those who've been doing the daily, mundane stuff for nine months straight.

Thomas Edison was one of the most prolific inventors in history, with about 2,000 patents to his name. He used to say, "Good things happen to those who hustle while they wait." Authors should take notice. While you're waiting to hear back from a potential reviewer, contact 100 other potential reviewers. While you're waiting to hear back from an influential blogger, find 200 other influential bloggers and e-mail them about your book.

One day I was rather discouraged with my marketing efforts and Cherie e-mailed me this thought by Robert Louis Stevenson:

> "Judge each day, not by the harvest you reap, but by the seeds you plant."

So much of publicity is sowing rather than reaping. Often I find myself putting time and effort into initiatives that make no immediate sales at all. But don't count them wasted. They're all a part of getting the word out. So take your marketing to a scale that makes success more likely. From my experience and that of many others, when you sow long enough and broadly enough, exciting things begin to happen.

Sales-Quenching Attitude #4: "Don't involve others."

Network with Fellow Authors

I think it's significant that the incredibly successful *Chicken Soup* series was co-authored. Two rabid marketers working on the same book produces more drive and ideas than any two people working separately. Business gurus call it synergy.

As Jack Canfield said, "Mark Victor Hansen was more outgoing than me. You might need to team up with a person who's more out there."[8]

For my last book, I connected regularly with two people who were on the same publishing schedule with me. We shared ideas and kept each other motivated. Cherie is always significant in my marketing efforts. Since my responsibilities keep me close to home, she helps me with local networking. She's also a whiz at social networking.

Use Quality Publicists

Publishing companies hire publicists because they know they can sell enough books to more than pay for their salaries and business expenses. If you're self-published or your publisher doesn't do enough publicity, consider hiring one or more good publicists. Here are the reasons I hired Blythe Daniel and Stephanie Richards:

1) Publicists can leverage relationships I don't have. Good publicists have relationships with key players in the media, who have learned to trust their judgment. When a trusted publicist recommends an expert for an interview, producers and editors listen and respond.

2) Publicists have expertise I lack. Stephanie helped me to put together my first press release in a format that's most likely to get a response. She also knew which press release companies to use. Good publicists excel at pulling together updated lists of media contacts in niche areas. Paying a publicist to spend an hour or two pulling together a list of key media contacts can often save an author weeks of research.

3) Publicists often have tools I can't access on my own. Blythe subscribes to Profnet (www.profnet.com), a paid service that many reporters use to request expert comments for their articles. Blythe regularly forwards relevant requests to me, one of which landed me on the Microsoft Network (MSN), bringing tens of thousands of people to my site.

Choose publicists who have expertise and contacts in the geographic and niche areas you want to use them. One author had lived in three metropolitan areas and wanted to get publicity in each of them. To do this most effectively, he hired a publicist who lived in each geographic area. Stephanie has strong mainstream media contacts in metro Atlanta. She got me booked on two of Atlanta's largest TV stations. Blythe lives in Colorado and has a strong background in the Christian marketplace, so I hired her to help me with an initiative targeting Christian media.

On Finding Book Publicists

Always talk to some of their former clients about their results and their overall satisfaction with the publicist. John Kremer provides a free annotated list of over 150 book publicists here:

http://www.bookmarket.com/101pr.htm

Trust in God's Wisdom and Power

In the spirit of candor, I should mention that I take my spiritual life seriously and wouldn't feel right without giving God credit for motivating me, carrying me through discouraging times, and intervening to make things happen. I mention this in part because many of the authors I meet tell me that they believe God prompted them to write their books. If that's you, just remember that if God helped you in the writing phase, I doubt He plans to dump you in the marketing phase. So call out to Him and trust Him, even when things look bleak. Even when it seems like nothing's working and nobody's buying, trust that God will help you to get your book into the hands of those who need it most. Trust Him for guidance. Trust Him for strength.

Benjamin Franklin – one of America's most famous and successful writers, printers, and publishers – prayed to God daily for wisdom.

> "And conceiving God to be the fountain of wisdom, I thought it right and necessary to solicit his assistance for obtaining it...."[9]

I'd suggest that his prayers to God for wisdom impacted his life and helped to make his life story become the world's most read autobiography.[9]

I personally attribute the "magic" I spoke of above to interventions by God. Here are a few events in my publishing and marketing career that are so improbable in a purely naturalistic world that I think they're more reasonably described as God-directed than happenstance:

- The acquisitions editor at Tyndale House had the manuscript for my music book on his desk when he met his daughter for lunch. She'd recently attended a seminar that she enjoyed, but disagreed with the seminar leader's teaching concerning popular music. Those were the very issues I addressed in my manuscript. They offered me a contract. What were the odds?

- It had been a discouraging month for sales of *Enjoy Your Money*. I wanted to start moving toward radio interviews and had on my desk a note to try to get in touch with the Moody radio station out of Chicago, with a closer presence in Chattanooga, about an hour from us. As I went to the gym to work out that week I thought, "I've been working out here for a year and have met hardly anyone. I think I'll meet somebody today." So I started a conversation with the man on the stationary bike next to mine. I asked him where he worked and he said that he worked for Moody. He took a copy of my book to look over. What were the odds?

- I reluctantly attended a Kennesaw State networking meeting with Cherie. I thought, "What are the odds of meeting anyone important to my book marketing there? It's just a general alumni gathering and I'm not even a graduate of KSU."

But I went anyway.

I talked to three people, the first two of whom I gave important information to. (Perhaps I was the answer to *their* prayers.) The third one said that his wife worked with a company that distributes textbooks to schools. One of my priorities that very month was to get my money book into classrooms. He took a book for his wife's review.

Driving home that evening I looked at the lights in neighborhood after neighborhood and thought, "Of the 700,000 people in Cobb County, how few (perhaps one?) work for a book distributor targeting schools? And what are the odds that her husband would be at this networking event? And what are the odds that, out of the eighty or so attending, that he would be one of the three that I met?"

I admit, these aren't miracles of the caliber of raising the dead, but they're miraculous enough to keep me praying and trusting during the times when I'm tempted to get discouraged at the lack of visible fruit from my efforts.

What Attitudes Hinder *Your* Marketing?

Perhaps you have no problems with the attitudes I've discussed. But I challenge you to examine your attitudes, since they greatly impact your ability to sell books.

- What attitudes hold you back? How could you overcome them?
- What attitudes motivate you to sell your books? Are there ways to fuel these attitudes and make them more dominant?

Harvard professor and prolific writer William James once said,

> "The greatest revolution of our generation is the discovery that human beings, by changing the inner attitudes of their minds, can change the outer aspects of their lives."

Do Something!

To put this chapter into action, I will...

1 –

2 –

3 –

Keep Learning!

- **See my free updates** to each chapter at www.sellmorebooks.org.
- **Find some other authors who are on your same publishing schedule.** Learn from each other and encourage one another as you move toward publication.
- **Meet regularly with a writers' group and/or a regional or statewide writers' organization.** Authors face many of the same fears and frustrations. It helps to be able to share.
- **Interact online with other authors in a forum, listserv, or writers' community.** Participate by asking questions, sharing your experiences, and encouraging other writers.
- **Subscribe to a writers' magazine or two.** Again, you'll find helpful hints and inspiration during your down times.

Chapter 12

Use Guiding Principles to Prioritize Initiatives

"Think simple" as my old master used to say - meaning reduce the whole of its parts into the simplest terms, getting back to first principles.

- Frank Lloyd Wright – Noted architect, writer, designer, educator

In the early days of Microsoft, Bill Gates knew that to lead the software industry, he'd have to squeeze every last minute out of his waking hours. So he disconnected his car radio to free up more time for thinking. At home, he refused to hook up a TV, although he'd later consent to hook up a VCR (but no cable) to watch movies with his girlfriend.[1]

In a world limited by time, deciding what *not* to do can be as important as what *to* do. In promoting our books, we can't do everything. Yet, as I interact with authors, I find many who are busily promoting their books from discussion group to discussion group, breathlessly tweeting and blogging, but seem to have no idea whether or not these initiatives will pay off in sales.

I promised to help you prioritize which marketing strategies would most likely pay off for you. At www.sellmorebooks.org I'll cull many more principles from my experience and research. Here I'll introduce a few that especially come into play in the following chapters.

What are Priority Principles?

As "principles," they're *not* absolute truths or inviolable laws that apply to every situation. You can always find counterexamples. Sometimes, breaking these rules will be your wisest course. Yet they are based on common sense and input from behavioral and marketing studies, and should prove useful as you strategize about selling your books.

As "priority," I consider these principles to give

- low profile authors
- the best odds
- for effectively selling books
- with a reasonable investment of time and money.

Again, I don't mean that their opposites should never be tried.

Three Guiding Principles

#1

The Optimal Recommender Principle
"Let others praise you, rather than praising yourself."

The Evidence: It's at least as old as King Solomon, who recommended,

> *"Let another praise you, and not your own mouth; someone else, and not your own lips."*

Prove it by asking yourself, "What would influence me most about trying a new brand of toothpaste – a recommendation from my trusted dentist, or an ad from the toothpaste manufacturer telling me 'We're the best!'" Manufacturer's advertisements are suspect. Thus, we trust *Consumer Reports* over car salesmen and customer reviews over publishers' claims.

As I mentioned earlier, a Nielsen Online study found 81 percent of online shoppers reading online customer reviews. Research by Razorfish found 60.53 percent of respondents relying on user reviews, compared with 15.41 percent relying on editorial reviews. In *The Tipping Point*, Malcomb Gladwell well argued that harnessing the power of influencers such as connectors and mavens and salesmen is key to successful marketing. In other words, get others recommending your books, especially the optimal recommenders – those who wield the greatest influence.[2]

Applications

- For short-term (one to two year) sales, prioritize getting reviews from trusted authorities rather than setting up platforms to promote yourself.
- Prioritize getting journalists to write about you, rather than writing articles about yourself.

Exceptions

- You'll probably have to "praise yourself" a bit to the trusted authorities in order to land their endorsements. But even then, use blurbs to let them see that others recommend you.
- If you've established yourself as a trusted thought leader, people are more likely to trust your recommendations. But you'll still want to use the endorsements of others.

#2

The Optimal Setting Principle "Go where people are already gathered, rather than gathering a crowd around you."

In the film, *Butch Cassidy and the Sundance Kid*, a local sheriff stood on a wooden platform in the middle of town, gathering a crowd to try to raise a posse to hunt down Butch and Sundance. As it became apparent that nobody was interested, an enterprising salesman stepped onto the platform to try to sell his goods. As he explained to the sheriff, *"Well, you got the crowd together...so I just thought I'd do a little selling."*

This mental picture helps me to recognize the benefits of going where people are already gathered, rather than trying to gather my own crowd. To make the image more accurate, picture the sheriff welcoming the salesman as an asset to his agenda, perhaps offering faster horses and high quality pistols at reduced prices to coax the townspeople into joining the posse.

The Evidence: This would appear intuitively obvious, and it explains why low profile authors typically find bookstore author signings rather disappointing. Your name doesn't draw a crowd. Unless you received decent local news coverage about the valuable insider information you're giving out (e.g., who's hiring and how to get jobs during a dismal economy) why would anyone show up?

On the other hand, some bookstores host Saturday evening author events that the community has come to recognize as valuable, so that a crowd gathers no matter who the author is. That's called going where people already gather. Civic organizations and chambers of commerce often host regular events that are well advertised and well attended. Pitch a popular topic related to your book and you'll likely sell some.

Applications:

- **Prioritize speaking engagements where publicity is already in place and people are used to coming, rather than trying to create and publicize your own events.**
- **Prioritize getting on busy radio stations rather than starting your own Internet radio station.** I'm not here to dampen dreams. If you've always

dreamed of being a radio personality, go for it! I'm just saying don't try to start an Internet radio station *with the sole goal of selling your books*. Even if you manage to draw a crowd, your listeners will likely tire of your sales pitch. If it's solely to sell books, that's a tremendous amount of time to spend on a long shot.

Wouldn't it be wiser to spend your time trying to get interviewed on 20 established radio stations – with the chance of becoming a regular guest on one of them – rather than starting from scratch trying to draw a crowd to your own station?

- **Prioritize getting recommended on busy blogs and contributing guest posts to busy blogs rather than trying to gather a following around your blog.** Wouldn't you likely get more sales over a twelve-month period by getting reviewed on the top fifty blogs in your field, than by trying to start a blog from scratch and hope to gather a significant following? I know this goes against much popular advice, but I'm not alone in my opinion. Book reviewer David J. Montgomery said:

> "Blogging is a colossal waste of time for 90 percent of authors. Any author who launches yet another blog at this point without some unique, exciting and valuable angle is just spinning his wheels."

With hundreds of millions of existing blogs, and with the number of blogs doubling every six months, you can see Montgomery's point.[3] Thus, it makes sense to prioritize finding the bloggers who already have the ear of your niche audience, and getting them to spread the word about your books.

> As PepsiCo's Shiv Singh states:
> "The holy grail of social influence marketing is increasingly considered the ability to identify which referent influencers are most powerful and have the highest impact on brand affinity and purchasing decisions. After you've identified them, the next question is, how does a marketer reach these referent influencers that surround their customers?"[4]

Exceptions: Who Should Consider Gathering a Blog Following?

- **You're already a high profile thought leader.** Thus Michael Hyatt, successful CEO of Thomas Nelson Publishers, can start a blog about books and publishing that crowds will quickly follow and interact on. I want to hear what Michael Hyatt says about publishing. If I see one of his books listed on the blog, I might buy it.

- **You have a unique approach (idea or angle or talent or expertise) that's appealing to the media and could go viral.** Cherie got a great idea for a blog where people would share their frustrations with their pets. Rather than sharing endearing stories of cuddly animals doing cute things, people could vent about their cats ruling their lives and their dogs destroying their homes. She knew it could potentially be lots of fun (not a place for animal haters) and pet experts could share their solutions to common pet problems.

So she started www.pet-peeves.org – "My pets annoy me. Tell me about yours."

Within a month, her blog was featured on MSNBC, the Chicago Tribune, The Atlanta Journal-Constitution, Redbook Magazine, and more. If she had an animal book for sale, it would be a great place to sell it! But note that "just another pet blog" wouldn't garner that kind of publicity.

- **You're low profile now, but envision building a high-traffic site in the years to come.** You don't have expectations of selling a lot of books from your blog in the next year or two, but you're building toward the future. For you, taking the time to post several times a week on your blog makes sense. Others may start filling their website with useful resources so that in years to come, Google will rank it as a top site in its field. Example: John Kremer, Brian Jud, and Dan Poynter have websites that provide many useful resources for book marketing. Today their sites are easily found by people searching for book publishing and marketing solutions. By taking a long view and providing authors with many quality resources (many of them free), they can sell books from their high-traffic sites.

#3

The Optimal Recipients Principle
"Address the interested, rather than interrupt the disinterested."

The Evidence: We're typically annoyed by TV ads and try to ignore them by muting them, talking over them, or popping popcorn.[5]New digital tools allow us to target those who are already looking for our information. This has resulted in a culture of people on the web who don't appreciate being interrupted with pop up ads when they're searching for something entirely different. It's an example of the profound shift from "interruption advertising" to "allow me to help you" positioning.

Applications:

- **Find where the people congregate who are looking for your information. Offer them what they're looking for.**
- **Don't invade social networking conversations (e.g., on forums or blogs or Facebook) and obnoxiously advertise your books.** It's considered a faux pas and will likely result in a verbal face slap. On some platforms you could be shunned or even banned. It's typically okay to answer someone's question and, if your book would truly provide more help, to mention it. It's also typically okay to answer a question and leave a link to your book in your signature.
- **Optimize your web presences to attract people who are searching for your information.**

Exceptions

Interruption marketing through TV commercials and radio ads still work for certain products, like showing us a trailer to introduce a new movie or to help make a brand ubiquitous – think: Coca Cola. In book selling, best-selling author James Patterson (he worked as an advertiser before becoming a writer) created an effective TV ad to launch his novel, *Along Came a Spider*, which became his most successful book to date. His prior books had sold unremarkably. But advertisements like this come at a high price and may or may not pay off in sales.[6]

Conclusion

I'll suggest more principles at www.sellmorebooks.org. But I've found these to be particularly helpful in maximizing my use of the newest technologies. I'll refer back to them in the following chapters as I lay out practical marketing strategies. They also help you see why I put such a priority in the following chapters on contacting influencers, finding niche audiences, and getting reviews.

Do Something!

To put this chapter into action, I will...

1 –

2 –

3 –

Keep Learning!

- **See my free updates** to each chapter at www.sellmorebooks.org.
- **As you find tactics that work in selling your books, compare them to tactics that work for other authors.** Can you discern some common, basic principles that can help you in predicting what other marketing methods may work?
- **The more author experiences you read and hear, the more likely you are to see patterns.** So share and read authors' success stories at places like The Book Marketing Network (http://thebookmarketingnetwork.com).

Chapter 13

Seek Early Reviews from Respected Book Review Sources

Librarians and decision-makers at Barnes & Noble can't read every new book, so they rely upon the recommendations of the most highly respected book review organizations. A great review in one of these can easily result in thousands of sales.

In this chapter I discuss the early reviewers who accept only prepublication copies – typically galley proofs or advance reading copies (ARCs). Since they want their reviews available either before or during your book's month of publication, they typically require your book three to four months prior to its release date.

If your publishing team thinks that your book has a shot at getting reviewed, they might print and mail the galleys for you. Make sure that you have an understanding about this. If your publisher has no intention of sending copies to these reviewers, but you want them sent, perhaps they'll provide you with early copies

Tips for Small-Time Authors and Small Publishers

The organizations I discuss in this chapter receive many more titles than they can possibly review, so they're eager to lighten their load from the moment the day's mail arrives. If your book looks self-published, subsidy published, or rinky-dink, your book may be discarded before it's ever opened.

To increase your odds of making it past the first round:

1. The finished book should exhibit top quality cover art, layout, and editing.

2. Read the latest specifications on their sites and follow them precisely.

or allow you to take it upon yourself to make it happen.

What Books are Eligible for Review?

Typically, the review organizations won't review self-published or subsidy published books (except for *ForeWord*, who targets independently published books and tries to judge each book without regard to who published it). Many of them additionally review titles published in audio, video, and eBook format.

Just what are the odds of an author getting reviewed? *Foreword Magazine* reviews five percent of the books they receive. *Booklist* reviews about seven percent. For the math-challenged, that means they reject 93-95 percent of the books they receive.

Although the odds seem slim, if you think your book has qualities that distinguish it from the herd, the potential payoff just might make it worth a try.

3. Make sure it's available through major distributors/ wholesalers like Baker & Taylor and Ingram. They don't recommend books that libraries and bookstores can't easily order. **4. If you self-publish**, establish your own publishing company; don't name it after yourself; create a sharp publisher website; use your company's ISBN, and have someone other than yourself (e.g., your publicist, etc.) mail the galleys.

I'm *not* suggesting that you fool the companies into thinking you were traditionally published. I *am* recommending that you take the necessary steps to establish yourself as a reputable publisher.

What are Galleys and ARCs?

Although I often see these terms used interchangeably, galleys are typically less finished than ARCs. While a galley has been edited, it often needs a final edit and is thus referred to as an "advance, uncorrected reader's proof."

Galleys typically have a plain paper cover with information about the book, but no fancy artwork or colors. Endnotes and indexes don't have to include page numbers. ARCs may be close to or in final form with full color covers and a special note printed on the cover specifying, "Advance Reader Copy: Not for Resale."

Sending Galleys: Estimated Costs

I had a local printer print 15 galleys (250 pp., b/w interior, b/w cover) for $10.00 each. I mailed them to 10 organizations for review (some require more than one copy). To mail them Priority Flat Rate (USPS, envelope or box) costs ≈ $5.00 each. To follow up with a finished copy cost me $4.00 for each book, plus $2.58 shipping (media mail), plus .50 for each bubble mailer.

Total cost ≈ $275.00

Put a good bit of information on the cover itself, assuming that the accompanying information sheet might become separated from the galley.

As an example, these are Publishers Weekly's specs:

"All galleys should have the following information on the cover:

- Title

- Author

- Price

- Publisher and imprint

- Format

- Number of pages in the finished book

- 13-digit ISBN

- Month and day of publication

- Distribution arrangements

- Publicity contact information"

What additional information should I include?

Include a separate sheet, customized for each review company, with additional information. Consider noting the company's target audience and explaining why they would be interested in your book. Example: tell *Library Journal* why libraries would want your book. Tailor the information to each organization's specifications, since they vary.

Here's the information that *Library Journal* requests:

> "Author, title; name, address, and telephone number of publisher; date of publication; price; number of pages; and ISBN and LC numbers if available. Please indicate whether any illustrations, an index, or bibliography will be included; also include a brief description of the book, its intended audience, and information on the author's background."

How Early Should I Send Titles?

Unless they specify otherwise, shoot for at least four months prior to publication. For this reason, since you may not be able to predict precisely when your title will be available, choose a publication date at the far end of your estimate to give yourself plenty of time.

Which Organizations Might Review My Book?

Consult each website for the latest information on exactly how and where to send your book. This is especially important during these revolutionary times, with review organizations reinventing themselves and rethinking the types of books they solicit.

Some are creating digital options for disseminating reviews, enabling them to do more reviews and offering paid reviews for worthy books that aren't selected on the first round. Here are the basics, up-to-date as I write (November, 2010), with information gleaned from their websites and personal interviews with several of the organizations.

***Booklist* - http:www.ala.org/booklist**

Published by: *The American Library Association*

What they review: Books appropriate for libraries.

What they don't review: "Periodicals, pamphlets, vanity publications, and highly technical, specialized, sectarian, and free materials are outside the scope of the regular reviewing program."

Number of reviews: About 4,000 per year (seven percent of the 60,000 submitted for review each year).

How to Submit: Send galleys or completed books at least 15 weeks prior to publication. "Many publishers depend on United Parcel Service, Express Mail, or Federal Express to reduce the number of lost or late materials."[1]

Address and contact information: Booklist, American Library Association, 50 E. Huron, Chicago, IL 60611. Phone: 1-800-545-2433.

> **Tip: Finding Shifty Web Pages**
>
> Often, when organizations move their sites or reorganize them, their web addresses change. If I suggested a url that no longer works, place your cursor after the final letter or symbol and backspace, deleting section after section until you come upon something searchable. If they changed their entire web address, search Google with the name of the organization.

***BookPage* –** http://www.bookpage.com/infopage.php?type=guide

Who they target: Distributed to consumers by bookstores and libraries.

What they review: "...almost every category of new books."

Number of reviews: Publication sent monthly. The July 2010 edition contained 63 new reviews.

What they don't review: "We rarely review poetry or scholarly books, and we do not give review consideration to self-published books, print-on-demand titles or books from presses that lack major distribution."

How to Submit: Send an advance reading copy at least three months before the publication date. "Along with your galley, include a letter with the name, phone number and e-mail address of a publicity contact for the book. The letter should also include the book's publication date, price, number of pages and ISBN number."

Addresses: Adult titles: Lynn Green, Editor, BookPage, 2143 Belcourt Ave., Nashville, TN 37212. Children's titles: Children's Editor, BookPage, 2143 Belcourt Ave., Nashville, TN 37212.

ForeWord Reviews – http://www.forewordreviews.com/get-reviewed/submission -guidelines

Who they target: "Librarians, booksellers, publishing professionals, and other book lovers who require a reliable source of reviews of independent and university presses."

How many get reviewed: They publish their print edition every two months, limiting them to review only five percent of the 800 books they receive each month. But all good books (deemed worthy by *ForeWord*) can get a digital review (see below).

ForeWord's Tips for Getting Reviewed

ForeWord lists nine tips for beating the odds in getting reviewed. Note especially these:

- Pay attention to their editorial calendar. Each issue has a theme. If your book relates to one of these themes, time your submission to coincide with the theme.
- If you're sending an ARC, "an unprofessional cover or layout will guarantee a trip to the recycling bin. A professional design for your book is well worth the cost."

What they review: Eighty percent nonfiction. They review books by small and independent publishers (not major publishers), including university presses and self-published books.

How to submit: Send galley or ARC four months before publication with a fact sheet.

The *Digital Review* option: Because of space limitations in their print publication, they must reject many worthy titles. So if your title doesn't get reviewed, but *ForeWord* deems your title worthy of review, you may pay for a digital review. It's also a good option if you're beyond the "four months in advance" deadline. For $99 (you don't pay if they decide it's not up to their standards for review), "it will be featured on our website and licensed for publication in the top title information databases used by booksellers and librarians: Baker & Taylor's TitleSource III, Ingram's iPage, Bowker's Books in Print, and Gale's licensed databases."

I chose this option for *Enjoy Your Money* and was pleased with the review they provided. You can view it here: http://wisdomcreekpress.com/press_kits_full_reviews.html. Because of other promotions I had going on at the time, I'm not sure if it resulted in immediate sales. If it did, it wasn't dramatic. But it makes sense to get reviews out permanently on prominent, respected sites.

The *Clarion Review* option: If *ForeWord* doesn't offer you a digital review, you can be guaranteed to get a review by paying $305 for a *Clarion Review*. "With your permission, the review will also be archived with the top three title information databases used by booksellers and librarians who make purchasing decisions: Bowker's Books-In-Print online, Baker & Taylor's Titlesource III, and Ingram's iPage, in addition to our Website."

Address: Book Review Editor, *ForeWord Reviews*, 129 ½ East Front Street, Traverse City, Michigan 49684.

Kirkus Reviews – http://www.kirkusreviews.com/about/submission-l

Who they target – "Booksellers, libraries, online retailers, and library-service companies rely on our reviews to help determine which books to sell, stock or include in their databases."

What they review – They look for "books of particular literary merit or popular appeal, and these we acclaim as they deserve. If they're captivating, capable, and interesting, we'll applaud them. If they're not, we'll say so." Applicable categories are "fiction, mysteries, science fiction and fantasy, translations, nonfiction and children's and young adult books." They review "traditional, mainstream trade titles from traditional, mainstream and other established publishers." The company has a database of publishers they deal with, so they'll likely know if you self-published and set up your own publishing company to make it look more professional. A *Kirkus* employee told me that if the introductory letter is addressed from the author and they're not familiar with the publishing company, they may assume it's self-published and throw it out.[2]

What they don't review – *Kirkus* is very specific. Do not send already published books, reprints, mass-market titles, self-published titles, print-on-demand titles, e-books, poetry, most anthologies, journal entries or diaries, textbooks, specialized technical or professional or academic works, reference books, compendiums of information (e.g., travel guides, puzzles and games), instruction manuals, guidebooks of any kind, photography, arts and crafts, self-help, screenplays, parenting, home improvement, business, personal finance, health and fitness, cooking and entertaining, dating and relationships, religion and spirituality (other than general history or memoir), comic books, computer and technology handbooks, or books of regional interest.

How many get reviewed – They receive between 100 and 300 titles per day and review 4,000-5,000 books per year – an average of four to 12 percent.

How to submit – Send two galleys (preferred) or completed manuscripts three to four months before publication. If you send galleys, send two copies of completed titles when they are available.

The *Kirkus Discoveries* option – Pay *Kirkus* $425 (standard) or $575 (express) and you're guaranteed to get a *Kirkus Discoveries* review. They'll review any type book, not limited by the categories that *Kirkus Reviews* does not review. They will distribute eight to ten select reviews to "key book-buying and filmmaking professionals and representatives" in their monthly *Discoveries* newsletter. (A *Discoveries* editor told me that they include about 50 reviews per month in their newsletter – 16-20 percent of their total *Discoveries* reviews.)[3]

At your request, they'll include your review on www.kirkusdiscoveries.com. You can use the review anywhere, but you must refer to it as *Kirkus Discoveries* to distinguish it from *Kirkus Reviews*.

Caveat emptor! A *Discoveries* review may be positive or negative, or a combination of both. You don't get your money back if they don't like your book. But it won't be published anywhere without your permission and a glowing *Kirkus* review may get more respect from informed book enthusiasts.

Addresses: Adult fiction: Elaine Szewczyk, Kirkus Reviews, 1133 Broadway, Suite 406, New York, NY 10010. Adult nonfiction: Eric Liebetrau, Kirkus Reviews, 479 Old Carolina Court, Mt. Pleasant, SC 29464. Children's and young adult materials: Vicky Smith, Kirkus Reviews, 99 Mitchell Rd., South Portland, ME 04106.

***Library Journal* – http://www.libraryjournal.com/csp/cms/sites/LJ/SubmitToLJ/TitlesForReview.csp**

Who they target: "…a broad spectrum of libraries."

What they review: Titles of interest to libraries, with the exception of "textbooks, children's books, very technical or specialized works (particularly those directed at a professional audience), and books in languages other than English or Spanish."

How many get reviewed: 7,000 annually.

How to submit: Three to four months prior to publication, send one copy of your galley, page proofs, or manuscript. If you submit a finished book, send it "as early as possible with the words 'In lieu of galleys' and the publication date affixed to the cover." Some specialty books, such as reference works or heavily illustrated works, may be reviewed up to three months after publication. In addition to sending them a manuscript, send a finished copy when it's available.

Address and contact information: Book Review Editor, Library Journal, 160 Varick Street, 11th Floor, New York, New York 10013. Phone: 646-380-0700. For special concerns, contact the proper editor via e-mail addresses listed here: http://www.libraryjournal.com/lj/reviews/book/885142421/library_journal_book_review_editors.html.csp .

***Publishers Weekly* – http://www.publishersweekly.com/pw/corp/submission-guidelines.html**

Who they target: Booksellers and librarians.

What they review: Books and audio books, including "Nonfiction, Fiction, Mystery, Science Fiction/Fantasy/Horror, Poetry, Comics, Lifestyles (cooking, gardening & home, health & fitness, or parenting), Mass Market," and children's books.

What they do not review: Self-published books (see paid exception below), with the exception of self-published children's books (rarely). How do they know if a book is self-published? When I spoke to PW associate editor Mike Harvkey, he said that they pretty much know from their experience which publishers are legitimate. When they see a book from an unfamiliar publisher, they may check the publisher website or call an editor for more information. But Harvkey suggested that since the industry is changing, their policies are being discussed and could change at any time.[4]

How many get reviewed: Over 8,000 books, audiobooks, and e-books – 26 percent of the 31,000 titles they receive.[5]

How to submit: Mail two copies of galleys, finished books, or bound manuscripts, with an accompanying letter, three to four (preferred) months "prior to the 1st day of the month of publication."

Paid option for self-published books: In August of 2010, PW announced their PW Select program, whereby self-publishers pay a $149 processing fee that guarantees the listing of their title in a quarterly supplement. At least 25 of the books will be selected for review.

Addresses: Mail to Publishers Weekly, Nonfiction Reviews [or "Poetry Reviews" or other relevant category], 71 West 23 St. #1608, New York, NY 10010. Send Religion titles to: Marcia Z. Nelson, Publishers Weekly Religion Reviews, 1118 Garfield St., Aurora, IL 60506.

wwSchool Library Journal **– http://www.schoollibraryjournal.com/csp/cms/sites/SLJ/Info/submissions.csp**

Who they target – Librarians who serve preschool through 12th graders in schools and public libraries. They publish their reviews in their monthly magazine and on their website.

What they review – "New children's and young adult general trade books, original paperbacks, and reference books from established publishers." Titles must be "of national interest" and "readily available from national distributors at an institutional discount." (They told me that distribution through wholesalers *Ingram* and *Baker & Taylor* is adequate.)

What they do not review – "Books for parents or teachers, reissues, textbooks, books that have blanks to be filled in by readers, direct submissions from authors, or books that are self-published."[6]

How many get reviewed – 5,000+ per year.

How to submit – Two copies at least two months before publication, along with a publisher's catalogue, to SLJ Book Review, *School Library Journal*, 160 Varick Street, 11th Floor, New York, NY 10013. If you send a galley, follow it up with two copies of the finished book.

Address – SLJ Book Review, *School Library Journal*, 160 Varick Street, 11th Floor, New York, NY 10013.

Choice **– http://www.ala.org/ala/mgrps/divs/acrl/publications/choice/selctionpolicy/selctionpolicy.cfm**

Who they target – "*Choice*'s primary mission is to assist librarians who build collections at the undergraduate level by providing concise, critical reviews.... In addition, *Choice* serves faculty and students selecting resources that support work in the classroom."

What they review – "Current scholarly books and electronic resources." Titles should be "authoritative, well presented, and well organized; should include appropriate supporting apparatus, e.g., index, illustrations, bibliography, notes, and appendixes."

"We give special attention to university presses.... We give serious consideration to the works of small and alternative presses because their titles may never be reviewed elsewhere. We review self-published works very selectively. We review popular works only if we judge the work authoritative and sufficiently documented."

How many get reviewed – 7,000 annually (25 to 30 percent of titles submitted).

How to submit – Send finished works only (no galleys or arcs), ideally within six months of publication.

Address and contact information – Choice, 575 Main Street, Suite 300 Middletown, CT 06457. Phone: 860-347-6933.

***Horn Book Magazine* – http://www.hbook.com/aboutus/publications/submissions.asp**

Who they target – "Most of our subscribers are professionals who work with younger readers: librarians and educators. We are also read by artists and writers, scholars, graduate students, and parents."

What they review – "Children's and young adult books and audio books published in the United States."

What they don't review – "Books produced by publishers that are not listed in *Literary Market Place* are not considered."

How many get reviewed – Over 4,000 per year.

How to submit – Send two copies of either a galley or finished book as soon as available, with an accompanying sheet of complete publication information.

Address – Review Editors, The Horn Book, Inc., 56 Roland Street, Suite 200, Boston, MA 02129.

Early Review Newspapers

The digital revolutions allow us to find free news online, leaving newspapers with declining readerships and struggling to find paid advertisers. Book reviews have been hit particularly hard, with some papers eliminating their special book review sections and others cutting back on reviews. They're experimenting with putting reviews in appropriate topical sections (like "Lifestyle" or "Business") and putting some reviews exclusively in digital format.[7] When sending review copies, study each paper to see if they're reviewing your type of book and how they want to receive it. A call to their main phone number might be appropriate, since few papers currently have web pages dedicated to telling publishers how to send books.

Even with all the changes, a good review in any of the following papers grants credibility and national exposure that's hard to rival. And to be able to say in your publicity, "As reviewed in the *New York Times*" can grant instant credibility, even if the review was scathing.

Are They Worth Pursuing?

If you think the lottery's odds are worth playing, then you'll be delighted to know that the *New York Times Book Review* selects 20-30 books each week from the 750+ books they receive for review (a rejection rate of 97 percent) – much better odds than winning the lottery.[8] As they say on their site:

> "Please be aware that we review only a very small percentage of the books we receive and the odds against a given book receiving a review are long indeed."

Further, you should ask yourself, "Am I confident enough about my writing to risk a public critique by a brilliant connoisseur of literature who mentally compares me with the best writers of all time?"

I'm not trying to discourage you – just reminding you that you're dealing with the gold standard of book reviews. Set your expectations accordingly.

To better your odds, browse each paper's archived book reviews to judge whether or not your book would be a likely candidate. Each paper and each column exhibits distinct preferences, and these change over time. If you've written a biography of a well-known entertainer, with up-to-date research and exclusive interviews, consider the *LA Times*. If you've written a significant cultural history of Savannah, Georgia, consider the *Atlanta Journal*. Since New York City is the publishing center of the universe, I just might (gulp) send the *New York Times* a galley of this manuscript.

If you decide that your book isn't likely to land a newspaper book review column, consider pursuing other columnists who write about your subject. That's how I landed a glowing review of *Enjoy Your Money* in a personal finance column of the *Oakland* (California) *Tribune*. In chapter 15 I detail how I accomplished this.

How to Submit

Although other publications may not receive the volume of books as the *New York Times*, neither do they have as many reviewers to divide them between. So assume they're overwhelmed with books and e-mails. That explains why one person e-mailed 65 newspaper book reviewers and got no response atall.[9]

Busy editors read e-mail titles and decide if they want to read further. If your e-mail title reads "New Book for Review," like 50 other e-mails the reviewer receives each day, don't be shocked that you never receive a reply. At some point, the reviewer must decide, "Do I want to spend my morning reading and responding to e-mails, or actually reviewing a book?" The latter pays better. So if you send an e-mail, title it something intriguing, like "New Marlon Brando Bio Reveals Shocking Insights from Personal Letters."

Typically, they want galleys or ARCs six to 12 weeks before publication. Mail it to the newspaper address or the reviewer's address, with a press release, to the attention of the senior reviewer (or the one who reviews your genre). Include a personal note thanking the reviewer for her reviews and explaining why she might find your book interesting.

Newspapers that Review Books

Here is a list of big-time newspapers that review books:

http://www.angelfire.com/ca4/tela

Below I give some specific information on the top book review papers, gleaned primarily from their websites and personal calls to their editorial staff.

New York Times Book Review – http://www.nytimes.com/membercenter/faq/books.html#booksqa2

According to the New York Times, send galleys or finished books three or four months before publication to:

Editor

The New York Times Book Review

620 Eighth Avenue, 5th Floor

New York, NY 10018

Relational Tip

When dealing with major book reviewers, avoid firing off increasingly agitating e-mails pushing them to read your book. Remember, they're book lovers like us, not likely making a lucrative living from their trade. They're our friends – not enemies – so treat them with respect.

Direct children's books to the attention of the "Children's Book Editor." Please note: "...we cannot respond to queries regarding the status of a galley or book sent for review consideration." You'll face less competition if you time it for review in January, February, July, and August. They only review books "available through general-interest bookstores." Self-published books are generally not reviewed.[10]

Here's a tip from an interview with the Editor in Chief:

> "If a writer is not bringing something new to the conversation or is not very well-established with a following...or [lacks] really superb narrative or analytical skills, there's a good chance the book won't get reviewed."[11]

***New York Review of Books* – http://www.nybooks.com**

"It is the journal where the most important issues are discussed by writers who are themselves a major force in world literature and thought." Send galleys or finished books as soon as they are available to: *The New York Review of Books*, 435 Hudson Street, Suite 300, New York, NY 10014. Phone: 212-757-8070.

***LA Times* –** http://www.latimes.com/features/books

They currently offer six monthly book review columns, each covering a different genre. They also offer about ten book reviews each Sunday in their *Living* section. Los Angeles Times, 202 W. 1st St., Los Angeles, CA 90012. Phone: 213-237-5000.[12]

***Los Angeles Review of Books* –** http://lareviewofbooks.org

This online book review venture is scheduled to launch in 2011. Dr. Tom Lutz, who chairs the department of creative writing at the University of California at Riverside will serve as senior editor. According to Dr. Lutz,

- "...if two, or for that matter ten of our contributing editors want to review a book, we will post all ten."
- "I want the discussion not to be relegated to a "letters to the editor" page, but to have the discussion to be what we offer."
- "I, personally, consider the novel to be the queen of the sciences...so we may have a somewhat disproportionate emphasis there. But I want to have very vibrant pages dedicated to all fields of nonfiction, and we have a very fine group of poets and poetry critics involved as well."
- In answer to the question: "University presses have noted the difficulty of getting their books reviewed in mainstream media. Care to comment?" Lutz responds, "Bring 'em on."
- "...we hope to be of national and international interest, and to cover the national and international book scene."[13]

***USA Today* –** http://www.usatoday.com/life/books/default.htm

If you find a reviewer who reviews books like yours, either mail a book to the *USA Today* address, to her attention, or try to contact her through e-mail to find where to send the book, in case she doesn't work in the main office. You can find some e-mail addresses through their Reporter Index http://www.usatoday.

com/community/tags/reporter-index.aspx. If she has a profile, click it. If there's no profile, Google the name to see if she also writes for a blog or can be contacted through social networking. If all else fails, try the paper's typical e-mail format: first-initial-last-name@usatoday.com, or just mail it to the main address to the attention of the reviewer: USA TODAY, 7950 Jones Branch Drive, McLean, VA 22108-0605.

The Village Voice – http://www.villagevoice.com/books

Wide ranging, but specializing in literary fiction. Send books to Brian Parks, The Village Voice, 36 Cooper Square, New York, NY 10003. Phone: 212-475-3300.

Wall Street Journal – http://online.wsj.com/public/page/news-books-best-sellers.html

Wide ranging, but specializing in business and finance. Send books to the *Wall Street Journal*, 1211 Avenue of the Americas, New York, NY 10036. Phone: 212-416-2000.

The Washington Post – http://www.washingtonpost.com/wp-dyn/content/print/bookworld/index.html

In 2009, they closed their book review section and currently have book reviews in various sections of their paper.[14] On their site, click the tab for Arts & Living/Books to find their reviews all in one place. They do not review self-published books. Send galleys or finished books to Book World, c/o *The Washington Post*, 1150 15th Street NW, Washington, DC 20071. Phone number for book review information: 202-334-7882. Email - bookworld@washpost.com or bwletters@washpost.com.

The San Francisco Chronicle **–** http://www.sfgate.com/books

One of the few papers that still publishes a weekly book review pullout, inserted into their Sunday edition. Phone: 415-777-8464. John McMurtrie, Editorial, Book Review Books Editor, jmcmurtrie@sfchronicle.com.

More Newspapers that Review Books

Beyond the above nationally recognized reviewers, John Kremer provides a free, updated list of 65 newspapers that offer book reviews: http://www.bookmarket.com/newspapers.ht.

Tips from a Professional Book Reviewer

By Teresa Weaver, *Atlanta Magazine* book editor, former *Atlanta Journal-Constitution* book editor

I asked Teresa to tell me what she'd like authors and publishers to know from the book reviewer's perspective – from preferences to pet peeves. Here's her advice for those seeking reviews from newspapers and magazines.

- My number one tip is not to waste one minute of a reviewer's time!
- No cutesy gimmicks, no fancy packaging, no press releases that go on for pages and pages.
- Be direct and clear!
- One sheet of paper is better than 100 pages of biographical background, blurbs, reviews of previous books, etc.
- These days, it's all about a local connection. If there's any local connection whatsoever, state it clearly upfront – if the author lives in town, went to college in town, grew up in town, whatever. Or if the book is about a topic of local interest, state it clearly and concisely.
- Editors have less and less time to cope with the volume of books being published. Every press release needs to make the case quickly and cleanly.
- The reality is, all the fancy packaging and voluminous background most often gets thrown directly in the trash. Nobody has time to sift through that.
- It's my experience that the harder a package is to open, the less likely anything of value is inside.

Keep it simple and smart. That's my best advice!

Do Something!

To put this chapter into action, I will…

1 –

2 –

3 –

Keep Learning!

- **If you're presently seeking early reviewers, you'll need to visit each site to make sure what each is currently looking for.** Policies and submission requirements change.
- **See my free updates** to each chapter at www.sellmorebooks.org.

Chapter 14

Seek Reviews and Endorsements from Busy Blogs

A year after publishing *Enjoy Your Money*, I experienced a couple of slack sales months. I was discouraged. My book needed a push, so I pushed with a new campaign. By the next month, my daily sales had doubled; by June, they had tripled. More importantly, I believe that this campaign will continue to show results over the life of the book. What did I do to achieve these results?

* * *

I found the top personal finance bloggers and offered them a free copy of my book for review.

* * *

Bloggers as Influencers

Blogs have come a long way from their humble beginnings, when one pundit observed that they were largely written by "computer geeks who'd never French-kissed a girl." Today about 150 million blogs exist. Bloggers provide respected sources of cutting edge information in a dizzying array of fields. Many have enough followers to make a decent living off their ads, exclusive members' content, and related products and services. Some have followings the size of entire countries.[1]

More importantly, top bloggers wield vast influence. In *The Tipping Point*, Malcomb Gladwell wrote of the importance "Connectors" (people who have lots of acquaintances), "Mavens" ("people we rely upon to connect us with new information") and "Salesmen" (people who easily persuade others to adopt their opinions). In their own unique ways, these three personality types are effective in spreading new ideas.[2]

Popular bloggers seem to possess all of these characteristics to some extent, making them extremely valuable allies for authors. For example, Gladwell states that, "Mavens are really information brokers, sharing and trading what they know." Although Gladwell wrote years before blogs became popular, doesn't this describe serious bloggers?

The Benefits of Blog Exposure

When successful bloggers rave about a product, people listen – not only their regular followers, who often receive posts through RSS feeds and e-mail, but people searching the web for information. Search engines love to direct people to popular blogs, since significant sites link to them (giving them authority) and they provide more up-to-date information than most traditional websites.

With traditional newspapers struggling, bloggers are becoming the new journalists. (And, we should say, many great journalists are becoming bloggers.) Mix in the fact that top newspapers and magazines now have blogs of their own, and we've simply got to take them seriously.

Get mentioned in a top blog, and you get more than a day of fame. The post stays there permanently and may be found years later by people searching on your topic. Also, you get a permanent link back to your press page, author site, blog, Amazon page, or whatever page is important to you. Incoming links from popular blogs make search engines rank you higher, giving you more traffic.

> **"RSS Feed" Definition**
>
> RSS stands for "really simple syndication." In the present context, I'm speaking of people who use RSS to receive blog posts from their favorite blogs, automatically, when they're posted. This is easier than having to go to each blog to find recent posts.
>
> People subscribe by clicking on a link from the blog that might appear something like this:
>
> - Subscribe to the RSS Feed

Just How Much Exposure Can You Get?

Imagine that you're promoting a personal finance book that gets reviewed by "Wise Bread," (www.wisebread.com) one of the top personal finance blogs. How many people are likely to hear about your book? Here are some indicators:

- On average, 400,000 people visit *Wise Bread* each month ("unique visitors").
- Additionally, over 29,000 people will get your review delivered to their computers via RSS feed.
- If *Wise Bread* "tweets" about your book, their 12,000 Twitter followers can read about it.
- Many readers might "re-tweet" to their lists or repost the information to their blogs and networks, giving further exposure.
- Many others may find your review years later when they search your topic in Google. With over 150,000 incoming links, *Wise Bread* posts are considered priority content by Google.

How Many "Visitors" Actually Read Your Review?

To be more realistic with these stats, let's admit that not all of those "unique visitors" will see your post. Many visit the blog to see other specific pages. And many who receive RSS feeds don't read them regularly. As with baseball stats, it's easier to track how many attended than how many actually saw a given play. Some were buying hotdogs when the winning home run sailed by their seats.

Is This an Extreme Example?

Writers love to use the most dramatic illustrations, which, unfortunately, don't often apply broadly. Thus, I should point out that *Wise Bread* isn't atypical among popular personal finance blogs. It's actually ranked second in the category, with an Alexa Rank of 8768. The number one personal finance blog ranks 3,855 (lower is better). The third blog ranks neck and neck with *Wise Bread* at 8,777.

Neither did I choose an unusually popular playing field. Personal finance blogs are not the most popular blogs. If you write about technology, consider http://www.boingboing.net, which has millions of unique monthly visitors and over 600,000 RSS subscribers.[3]

Obviously, blogs have wonderful potential for getting the word out about our books. How can we harness their vast influence?

Blog Priority #1: Solicit Reviews

Why I Prioritized Reviews

There are several ways to get noticed on blogs. You can start your own blog, comment on other's posts, do guest posts, or solicit reviews from established blogs. I prioritize getting reviews because the blogger – the one who already has the readers' ears and respect – will be recommending my book. This wields much more influence than anything I'd say about my own book.

When *Not* to Use this Tactic

If your book doesn't tend to get good reviews, consider a different tactic. You can always do radio interviews or something else that doesn't require reviews.

Revisiting our "Priority Principles"

Here's how I applied our "Priority Principles" to decide the most effective way to use blogs in publicizing my books. Let's use the analogy of a speaking event at a packed football stadium, the largest of which hold around 100,000 fans, far less than the millions of monthly visitors to the *Boing Boing* blog.

- **"Let others praise you, rather than praising yourself."**

  Recommendations by trusted authorities are typically more effective than authors pushing their own books. The popular blogger writing a post about your books is analogous to a respected thought leader recommending your book to the stadium crowd.

- **"Go where people are already gathered, rather than gathering a crowd around you."**

  It takes a lot of time and effort to gather your own crowd via a blog or Twitter following. So why not go where people already gather?

- **"Address the interested, rather than interrupting the disinterested."**

  The stadium is packed with people who came to hear about your topic. You don't have to interrupt them with an annoying advertisement.

The Overview: What I Did

So I found the top 200 personal finance blogs and offered each of them a copy of my book for review and another copy for a giveaway. Their response:

- Forty-five bloggers requested a copy. That's almost one out of four. Not bad.
- Eighteen wrote a review so far and/or did the giveaway. Although eighteen doesn't seem like a lot, you've got to remember that these are popular bloggers. A review by one of them might be more influential than 100 reviews on blogs with small followings.
- Nobody acted like I was bothering them. In fact, they seemed truly appreciative and some expressed a lot of excitement about getting the book. After all, they are passionate about the subject, love fresh ideas, and understand the appeal of giveaways to their audiences.

The Boring Details: How I Did It

This campaign is as easy as finding busy, relevant blogs and asking them to review your book. If you're the type who likes to wing it, don't let the following details discourage you and lead you to think it's more complicated than it really is. But if you can endure details, some of these tips can set you way ahead and help you to be much more effective.

1. Find the Most Influential Blogs in your Subject Area.

a. Search for previously compiled lists. Why compile your own list if someone else has compiled it for you? Search your subject area in Google in various ways. I searched: "Top Financial Blogs," "Popular Money Blogs," "Top Personal Finance Blogs." Eventually, I found an invaluable list of over 500 personal finance blogs, listed in order of Alexa popularity, updated daily.

> **Caveat**
>
> Compilations of top blogs in a specific subject area aren't typically comprehensive. Often, bloggers must submit their blogs to be included.

(http://www.wisebread.com/top-100-most-popular-personal-finance-blogs).

Obviously, this made my campaign much easier.

> **Technorati "Authority"**
>
> This number tells the number of sites that have linked to a given blog in the past six months. The higher the number, the better.

Note: The University of California at Berkeley recommends searching with more than one search engine, since each searches different materials from different perspectives. They recommend Google, Yahoo, and Exalead.[4]

b. Search www.technorati.com. Beside the search box, click "blogs," instead of the default "posts." Search your subject and its synonyms to find top blogs according to Technorati "authority."

c. If you're searching a large, popular subject area, click "Blog Directory" on Technorati's home page to see what they've compiled for subjects such as "pets," "home," "religion," etc.

d. Once you've found some popular blogs in your subject area, note which blogs each of them recommend and link to. They typically link to the most helpful, popular, authoritative blogs in their field. Add them to your list.

2. Keep good records.

First, I collect the names of the blogs in a word processing file. I use a Microsoft Word file, listing each blog, its rank, and other pertinent information. If you're like me, after contacting ten blogs, you can't remember who responded and who didn't. After you've contacted scores of blogs, you may need to search ("ctrl f" on your keyboard) the document to make sure you're not duplicating your efforts. I plan to keep using and adding to this file over the years as I build relationships with the bloggers, comment on their blogs, do guest posts, and add new blogs. Think of it like a salesman's contact list.

Second, I record which blogs I sent books to in a three-ring notebook, with copies of my e-mail correspondence. This helps me track all the books I've mailed out, whether sent to bloggers, radio stations, newspaper columnists, etc. For some reason, I like opening a physical notebook for this part of my record keeping. (My apologies to trees. I promise; I'm green in other ways!)

3. For optimum learning and tweaking, start by contacting twenty or so blogs. You'll likely learn something from the experience that will make your next 20 more effective.

4. Study each blog and make notes.

- Is the blog really compatible with your book? A relationship blog which explores customer/business relationships would not likely review your book on husband/wife relationships.
- In the "About Us" section, find out what they're trying to accomplish with their blog and how they like to be contacted. You may also discover that you have something in common that you can mention in your e-mail (common roots, location, schooling, interests, business background, number and age of children, etc.).
- Do they maintain a list of recommended books? If they do a positive review, ask them to consider adding your book to the recommended book list.
- Do they also write for a magazine or newspaper? If so, consider offering expert advice that could help them with an article.
- Do they belong to organizations or associations that need to know about your book?
- Do they do book reviews?
- Do they welcome guest posts?

Think beyond trying to get them to do a review. How can you add value to their blog? How can connecting with them be a win/win? Cultivate a relationship that may pay off handsomely years from now.

5. E-mail them or contact them through their contact page.

Make the e-mail title appealing. It may be all they read of your e-mail. Since they may have a stack of unread books by their beds, they may not be enticed with a generic title like "New Book for Review." Make the title appeal to the blogger's needs. What's in this deal for the blogger? Since she always needs fresh ideas for posts and some love giveaways (you'll find this by exploring the blog), I entitled one of my e-mails, "Idea for Timely Post and Giveaway." (The "timely" aspect was that we were a couple of months from graduation season. Since my book targets graduates, a review of it in their blog would make a timely graduation season post for their blog.)

- **Make the opening sentences grab them.** Your book isn't just another book; it's special. Tell them why. According to blogging guru Darren Rowse of www.problogger.net, successful bloggers get so much e-mail that they decide within a couple of lines whether to keep reading.[5]

- **Let others praise you through a blurb or two.** They're used to hearing authors trying to convince them that their books are great. Give a quote by another source saying that it's great.

- **Link them to further reviews and information.** If your Amazon reviews are compelling, include a link to your Amazon page. Also include a link to your press page, so that they can read more reviews, get an overview of your book, and read example chapters. This keeps your e-mail brief. You don't have to say it all. Some blog reviewers told me that they asked for my book because they were impressed with previous reviews. They don't want to waste their time reading a book that other readers have already declared second rate.

- **Make it personal.** I try to tie the message into something about the blog, so that the recipient knows I took time to read it. I often open with a note of appreciation for something specific about the blog. Later in the e-mail, I may mention another specific: "Since you recommend conservative investors like John Bogle, I can tell that we're on the same page."

  I often find a connection in their "About Us" section. "Since you're raising children, you'd be interested in my chapters on...." That separates me out from authors and publicists sending mass, impersonal e-mails. I've had bloggers say, "Thanks for taking the time to read my blog and make sure we were compatible."

- **Make it easy on them.** Remember, successful bloggers are very busy. They must write substantive, unique posts every day or two. They search far and wide for great content. Publishers send them piles of books. Women throw themselves at successful male bloggers at bars. Then there's the constant harassing by the paparazzi. But hey, you're an author. You know these problems well.

  So lighten their load: 1) Offer to mail the second copy directly to the giveaway winner. (Side benefit: you're alerted that they came through with the giveaway.) 2) Offer to write a unique review, tailored to the blog's style. For many, that solves their time issue. Others are self-conscious about their ability to write a decent review. I assure them that they can use all, some, or none of it, depending upon how they really feel about the book. Several asked for me to write the review. Almost all personalized it.

6. Allow for a giveaway. The negative of giveaways is that some who would have bought the book after reading the review will delay purchasing and wait to see if they win the free copy. Also, you take on the time and expense of mailing a copy to the winner. The positive is that people love giveaways and may tell their friends. Savvy bloggers encourage social networking about the giveaway by saying, "to sign up for this giveaway, write about it on your blog, a forum, or Facebook; or you can tweet about it." In this way, the word spreads about the giveaway and excitement builds. You wouldn't likely get this amount of publicity without the giveaway.

When you send the winning book to the contest winners, consider writing a note saying, "Congratulations! Here's your signed copy! Hey, I'm finding book marketing to be quite a challenge. If you like it, would you consider doing an Amazon review?" (That's not being pushy; you just sent them a free book! I'd say they owe you one!)

At the end of the giveaway, especially if several people replied to the post(s), consider posting your own reply, expressing appreciation to all who participated and to the blogger for so generously reading and recommending your book. Then, put a link to your Amazon page. My rationale for doing this? Those who were waiting to buy my book until after the contest may have forgotten their initial intent. But if they signed up to receive posts of responses to that blog post, then they'll see your reply and have the opportunity to click on your link and purchase it.

How Blog Recommendations Can Spread

This blogger came through with a great review, but notice additionally how she encouraged more exposure by encouraging readers to tweet about the book and mention it on Facebook, with the incentive of increasing their odds of winning a free book. It's easy to see how news of the review can spread. Plus, she's a member of a national network, which allows for even more exposure. http://inexpensively.com/articles/finance/debt-management/enjoy-your-money-how-to-make-it-save-it-invest-it-give-it-book-review

7. Make the most of the review. Help get the word out by tweeting about it (including a link to the review). Link to it from your press page. Take a couple of key sentences from the review to add to your collection of blurbs. Remember, you're continuing to build a platform to other bloggers. When potential blog reviewers check out your press page, you want them to see that other bloggers loved your book.

8. Establish more good will. Even if they mentioned some negatives in their reviews, don't express disappointment. Popular blogger Darren Rowse of ProBlogger.net found that often his product reviews that include negative comments will sell more products than exclusively positive reviews.[6] Apparently, negative comments make the review appear more believable and objective. If they read and reviewed your book, they've done a huge favor that took a lot of time and effort. Thank them. Let them know you're linking to them. (Bloggers live for incoming links!) Ask if there's anything you can do to help them, now or in the future. Mention their most useful posts in your blog and link back to those posts.

Mailing Tips

1) I ordered 100 bubble mailers at about 30 cents each from http://valuemailers.com . (Compare $1.00 each @ brick and mortar discount stores. I saved $70 for each $100 spent on mailers!)

2) Write "Requested Material" on the front of the mailer, to distinguish it from unsolicited materials.

9. Set up a *Google Alert* for your name and the name of your book, so that when someone reviews your book, you're alerted so that you can update your records. If a blogger fails to let me know she's posted a review or comment, I generally receive an alert by Google (although it doesn't catch every review). To set one up, you need a Google Account. Search "Google Alerts" in Google to find how to set it up.

10. Follow up with:

- **those who requested a book, but failed to come through with a review.** (Record in your notebook each time you make a contact.) I usually give them a few months before e-mailing a reminder. A onetime reminder shouldn't be considered nagging. After all, they asked for the book and you mailed a free copy at your expense. I don't say that in my e-mail, however. I just use those thoughts to motivate me to follow up. In the follow-up e-mail, I ask to make sure they received the book and ask if they need a new copy. I let them know of an upcoming event or newsy item (an award, a recent review, graduation season, a recent study) that makes the review more pertinent to their readers. Mention a couple of his/her posts you especially appreciated. This approach makes the reminder less pushy and more encouraging.

- **those who did a review.** If you need Amazon reviews, tell them your need and ask if they'd be willing to post their review on Amazon. Ask, "Do you have any other ideas as to how I can get the word out about my book?" Ask if there's any way you might serve them. I can also volunteer to do guest posts, ending with my signature and a link to my book. One of these reviewers became a particularly "raving fan," letting me know that she wanted to push the book as much as possible. She volunteered to bring a free chapter to a blogging convention and put it in the conference handbags.

Look over the reviewer's blog one more time. Is there anything else she could do to get the word out? Search her blog for any "best books" lists. When someone Googles "The best knitting books," Google often brings up lists that people have posted on their blogs. It doesn't matter that they posted it two years ago on their blog. Google still takes people there. So remind them of their list. "If you think mine is one of the top books you'd recommend, would you mind adding it to your recommended books post?" Typically, she would have wanted to do this anyway, to keep the page updated, but it's the kind of thing that a busy blogger might forget to do.

- **those who never replied at all.** John Kremer reminded me of this. Don't write them off. Often, they simply missed your e-mail. Or you e-mailed on an exceptionally busy day. By the time you follow up, they may have seen other reviews and now want a copy of their own. Remember, as your platform builds, you become more desirable. Several bloggers mentioned that they'd seen my book talked about on other blogs.

  Re-contacting is typical in the publishing industry. Successful freelance journalists contact the same magazines repeatedly with different ideas. They don't take their silence to mean, "don't inquire again."[7]

Make Long-Term Plans

- If you contacted the top 100 bloggers and it worked (sold enough books to offset the costs, got the word out), why stop? If you've found something that works, keep contacting smaller blogs until you're no longer getting results.
- Every six months or so, contact new blogs that are becoming popular in your subject or genre.
- Expand beyond your primary topic to broader topics that could easily include yours. If you write on gardening, check out blogs on home life or hobbies. Find related themes by checking tags in posts or running some terms through the Google Keyword tool.
- Carry on a mutually beneficial relationship.
- Offer guest posts on appropriate topics and at appropriate times. Is your book appropriate as a Valentine's, graduation, or wedding gift? Offer special posts and giveaways during the appropriate seasons from year to year.

What *Not* to Say in a Comment on a Blog Post

I see comments like this all the time:

"Wow! Great Post! But why don't you read Elmer Gantry's latest book, *How to Become a Millionaire by Working only Holidays* to get the REAL scoop."

It's obvious that the author's just trying to get seen, rather than contribute meaningfully to the conversation. Do this and people will slam you.

The Happiness Factor

Some types of book publicity can be a royal pain. I thoroughly enjoyed this one. And for me, the delay in bloggers coming out with reviews (I originally hoped for all May reviews) meant that most weeks during the summer a blogger would e-mail me to say that his/her review was coming out. Since my hard work was done by the end of April, I got this week-by-week reward that spread itself throughout my summer.

Blog Priority #2: Comment on Influential Blogs and Do Guest Posts

This isn't my first priority, since it involves me talking about my own books, rather than allowing a trusted expert to recommend my book. Yet, it's another way to get the word out. Not only do people see your comments, noting in your signature that you've written a book on a related topic, but you can typically leave a link back to whatever site/blog you're trying to popularize. And since incoming links from popular blogs and articles are so powerful to search engine optimization, successful bloggers tend to spend a good bit of time commenting on other popular blogs and linking back.

Think Outside of the Blog

Popular newspaper sites, (*The New York Times* ranks 91st on Alexa), news sites (MSN ranks 9th) and magazines (*People* ranks 467th) often allow comments on their articles. Talk about an opportunity to get seen and acquire a powerful incoming link! Imagine the visibility obtained by posting an intelligent first comment on a relevant *Wall Street Journal* article?

How to Do It

1. Target some of the most popular and most relevant blogs/sites in your field. You could visit them regularly to check for new posts, but you may find yourself consistently posting toward the end of the pack, which less people read. By setting up an RSS feed from significant blogs to your browser, or signing up to receive their latest posts via e-mail, you could quickly post a reply in a highly visible position. If competition motivates you, think of getting "pole position" (the racing term for front starting position) in the replies section.

Time Saver Tip: Don't Manually Type Your Signature Every Time

It takes too much time to type a four-line signature after each post. So download a free program that allows you to save often-used texts permanently in a clipboard, so that it's ready to paste at any time, with the click of a few keys.

I use "Clippings," which I downloaded as an "Ad On" through my browser, Firefox. (In Firefox, click Tools/Ad-Ons/Get Ad-Ons/ Browse all Ad-Ons.) Or, find an application by Googling such terms as "multi clipboard" or "free clippings manager."

2. Set up your browser to receive alerts when articles are posted on your topic. Again, search "Google Alerts" in Google and set up alerts for terms related to your topic. If you write novels about horses, get alerts for the terms "horses," "ponies," "stables," "ranches," etc. When the *Wall Street Journal* posts an article about profitable ranches, you'll be one of the first to know so that you can leave an insightful comment.

3. Be real and insightful. Human eyes review comments to screen for spammers. They'll reject your comment if it reeks of self-promotion. You're making a comment to add to the conversation. Leaving a link to your book must stay unobnoxious and entirely secondary.

Typically, it's acceptable to leave a meaningful comment, and then put a book name and link in your signature. Here's how I typically sign off:

> J. Steve Miller
>
> Author of *Enjoy Your Money! How to Make It, Save It, Invest It and Give It*
>
> "The money book for people who hate money books"
>
> http://wisdomcreekpress.com/press_kits.html

Blog Priority #3: Consider Starting Your Own Blog

We discussed setting up your own blog in chapter 9, in the context of setting up your author site. Here I'll speak of it in relation to its potential to sell books. Some marketers advise all authors to start blogs to market their books. If you gain followers and become known as a thought leader in your field, surely some of your followers will buy your books.

By all means, if you have a blog, advertise your book from the blog through a permanent ad that everyone sees, no matter what page they're reading on the blog. Also, feel free to mention the book occasionally on the blog.

But there's a reason I put "start your own blog" last in this discussion of blogs. **If your sole interest in building your blog is to promote your books, you'll probably be disappointed.** To gain and retain a significant following, much of your book-writing time will be deflected toward blogging, and since constantly pushing your books tends to turn off your regular followers, don't expect big results.

In brief, people who create busy, influential blogs love putting a lot of time into substantive posts, several times per week, on a topic that lends itself to regular followers and interaction. They also spend significant amounts of time writing posts for other busy blogs, cultivating incoming links, commenting on others posts and networking with other bloggers. In other words, to build a successful blog, you typically must publicize that blog, which takes time from writing books and publicizing books.[8]

If you're not already a celebrity or recognized thought leader, your blog needs to have a unique angle or provide the most helpful information for a niche audience. Why? Because you're probably not the first person to consider starting a blog in your subject area. As of August 6, 2010, BlogPulse had identified over 144 million blogs. Fifty-two thousand new blogs started in the last 24 hours and almost one million people wrote a post in the last 24 hours.[9]

Yet, if you target a very specific niche, you may find little competition. If you're passionate about a niche subject and want to dedicate years to learning about it and blogging about it, you just might create a following. If blogging appeals to you and you have other purposes in blogging besides selling books (e.g., to help people, to establish yourself as a thought leader in a field, to sell your consulting and other products, etc.), then go for it!

My Counsel for Authors who Aspire to Blog

- **It's helpful for authors to have a central location to interact with their readers.** A blog is perfect for this. In this case, your goal probably isn't to become a leading blogger on your topic. For this purpose, you don't feel compelled to blog every day, or even every week. You still have time to write books and promote your books.

- **If your main concern is to market your books, concentrate on "going where people already gather" by getting reviewed and noticed on other people's popular blogs.** Why spend years trying to gather 100,000 followers, when you could get 10 established bloggers, who each already have 100,000 followers (1 million total), blogging about your book? Get further attention by commenting on their blogs and guest posting.

- **If you fall in love with blogging and decide to concentrate on building a massive following and potentially make your living at it, then you probably need to concentrate on blogging more than writing books.** You need to learn how to network, publicize your blog, and treat it like a business. To better understand what's involved, read the recommended sources at the end of this chapter, such as *ProBlogger*.

Observations, Reflections, and Principles

1. Your book doesn't have to be new for a blog campaign to work. My book had been published for over a year. No blogger asked me if it was new. These bloggers are more concerned about quality information and "of interest to my readers" than "hot off the press." In fact, if your book is so new that you don't have many reviews, I'd consider waiting until you have enough to impress these bloggers. They don't want to waste their time reading something without a proven track record.

2. Allow them time to read and review. While they often intend to read the book quickly, in my case they took, on average, a couple of months. Only at three months did I send a gentle reminder, in the form of an update rather than a reprimand.

3. Think creatively. When a small time blogger (ranked in the millions) with hardly any followers asked for a free review copy, I considered not wasting my time and money. But when I looked at her "Who We Are" page, I saw that she was a home schooler. I replied, "I'm trying to build a platform among home schoolers. If you like the book and see it as useful for other home schoolers, would you do a review that could attract other home schoolers?" She did, and I put the review on my press page, thus starting my platform in this niche.

4. Keep learning. Blogging and other forms of social networking are developing at breakneck speed. New techniques and applications will continue to help authors get the word out about their books.

5. Strategize for future years. How can you harness the relationships and platform you built during this campaign to do a more effective campaign next year or in five years? Each spring, I could offer posts on recommended summer reading or tips for new graduates on finances. To blogs that didn't respond to my first round of requests, I could offer free books for review and/or giveaway.

6. Remember that bloggers wield influence beyond their blogs. Since bloggers in your field share a passion for your topic, if they like your book, they're very likely to buy another copy as a gift and recommend it to others, *even if nobody bought a copy as a direct result of their blog review*. In addition to blogging, they may participate in influential associations, speak on the topic, comment on other blogs, host a radio show, write a newspaper column, etc.

7. How much time will this take? Once I've got my list to work from and my e-mail draft to copy and paste from (which I typically personalize a bit), I can look over the target blog and e-mail a request for review every seven to ten minutes. (Yes, I repeatedly timed myself.) Of course, if they request a copy, it takes time to ship out the books and to follow up.

8. Don't lose your focus on helping people. I wrote the book to help people. Shouldn't this blog campaign be about helping people? When I contribute a comment to a blog post, I'm helping someone. When a blogger gives away a book to someone who expressed why she and her family desperately need financial help, that giveaway helped someone. Even if nobody buys a book as a result of a review, I've helped people with my information and my giveaway, which was my ultimate goal anyway.

9. Nothing of this campaign reeks of pushiness or shameless self-promotion. Nobody objected that they felt they were being used or pushed to do something they didn't want to do. When they responded, they were typically delighted. I'm welcomed as a fellow financial enthusiast who offered them a favor.

10. Don't avoid the most popular sites, assuming they're long shots and are much too busy. They may actually have more time than some less popular bloggers, since they may be doing this full-time and work with multiple partners.

Do Something!

To put this chapter into action, I will...

1 –

2 –

3 –

Keep Learning!

- **See my free updates** to each chapter at www.sellmorebooks.org.
- **If you aspire to build a blog following, read the book, *ProBlogger*, by Darren Rowse and Chris Garrett.** They offer realistic advice without the sensationalism that often accompanies this field.

Chapter 15

Seek Reviews and Endorsements from Other Publications

Odds are, your efforts at courting the top early reviewers (chapter 13) left you standing in the rain for months, wilted flowers in hand. But don't let that stop you from courting. Rejection from the most desired Hollywood stars doesn't mean you're undesirable. And to be honest, stars and starlets are often quirky and opinionated, and have been known to humiliate their suitors in public.

Fortunately, *Kirkus* and the *New York Times* aren't the only fish in the sea. There are thousands. Here's why and how you should court them.

According to book marketing guru John Kremer, "Don't be stingy about sending out review copies."[1] Great reviews by respected reviewers can result in hundreds of sales and jumpstart an unstoppable word of mouth movement.

How Many Review Copies Should Authors/Publishers Send?

It depends upon your genre and your topic. If you write in a very niche field and very few blogs and magazines cover your topic, you may need to send only a few. If you write college textbooks, target the decision-makers and the publications they trust. Thus, one author may send twenty copies for review, and another thousands. But I agree with Kremer's rule of thumb – "Don't be stingy." Your book is your greatest marketing piece. Get it out there!

If reviews are one of your most powerful tools for book publicity, then your book is your most important marketing piece. Thus, contacting influential people and offering them free copies has a proven track record for selling books. That's why Doubleday printed 10,000 advance-reading copies of *The DaVinci Code* and put them freely into the hands of booksellers, reviewers, and other influential people in the book trade.[2] If you've got a great book, get it into the hands of influencers.

Where to Send Review Copies

1. Major Newspaper Columnists who write on your topic.

These columnists are not primarily book reviewers. Thus, publishers aren't routinely sending them the 600 to 700 books per week that the *LA Times* receives.

For a book on child rearing, find columnists who write about family issues. For a book on gardening, find papers that run – perhaps seasonally – articles on yard care, home improvement, vegetable gardens, etc. Since my last book was on money management, I targeted the major newspapers that offered personal finance column.

What to Expect out of Major Newspapers

Although we're past the big-time review columnists, we're still talking about major players here, so don't get your hopes up too high. Unless you've got a very attractive angle or they happen to be interested in your topic at the moment, you're still battling tough odds. But to me, the potential payoff is worth the effort, especially since some of these columns are syndicated to other papers as well.

Here's how I did it:

a. I searched Google for a list of "major newspapers," with links to each paper. I found one here:

http://www.newslink.org/metnews.html

See also this list of the top 100 U.S. newspapers, listed from largest circulation to the smallest.

http://www.infoplease.com/ipea/A0004420.html#axzz0x9LqH937

b. I visited each newspaper site, searching for financial columnists and their contact information.

c. I recorded the contact information in my marketing notebook, noting who I contacted and when, so that I could follow up or contact them later with other ideas.

d. I e-mailed first to see if they wanted a copy. Tell them in a paragraph or two why you think they'd like your book or how it would be useful to them, linking them to your press page and Amazon page. They will tend to check these pages to see what others say about your book. If you got early blurbs, as I detailed in chapter 7, your press page and Amazon page should present a convincing case that your book is worth reviewing.

Who Might *Not* Profit from Reviews?

If reviewers consistently slam your book, either because of poor writing (reread chapter 3), a niche style that many don't appreciate, or you've taken an unpopular stand on a controversial issue, choose publicity that doesn't involve getting reviews, like doing radio shows.

Read the e-mail I used in the below text box, which was adapted for each columnist. Note that the title isn't "Financial Book for Review," since they probably get many such requests and already have a pile of books for review by their beds. Instead, the title seeks to intrigue them with a column idea for an upcoming, timely event: graduation.

I say up front how writing about this book could help him to write something of benefit to his readers. To a columnist, it's all about his readers. With graduation season coming up, he could give financial advice to grads and recommend it as a graduation gift.

My E-mail to Major Columnists

Title: Financially Illiterate Graduates

Dear (name of columnist),

Thanks for your columns and for all you do to help us with our financial decisions. I'm also a fan of your financial book (name the book) and recommend it from my site.

With graduation season just around the corner, I know that many of your readers might want advice for graduating high school and college seniors, who, as we are well aware, are typically clueless concerning personal finance. Also, your readers might want recommendations for graduation gifts (why not the gift of financial wisdom?)

My book, targeting young people (ages 16-30), just came off the press. I'd love to send you a free copy for review. I think you'll find it well researched and documented, but written in story form to make it a quick, fun read. It covers getting and thriving in jobs, as well as saving and investing money. It's called: *Enjoy Your Money! How to Make It, Save It, Invest It and Give It.*

You can find out more about it, including reviews and an author interview here:

http://wisdomcreekpress.com/press_kits.html

Hopefully, during these difficult economic times, the book can help young people catch a vision for managing their money before they get into serious financial trouble.

If you're interested in a free copy, let me know an address and I'll send it on.

Thanks again for your columns!

Sincerely,

J. Steve Miller

(my e-mail address here)

e. I mailed each requestor a signed book, along with a brochure, a copy of the e-mail exchange, and a press release. This gave them plenty of information to write the article, including my press page, Amazon page and a phone number in case they needed to contact me. **The point is to make it easy on them!** I wrote "requested material" on each package to distinguish it from unsolicited mail.

> **Helpful Free Tool**
>
> Although it's in beta as I write, Media Sync looks like a promising tool for finding and contacting journalists, bloggers, and other movers and shakers in your field of interest. Check it out at:
>
> http://www.mediasynconline.com.

The results: Perusing about 50 newspapers, I found and e-mailed 30 financial writers. Eight requested a book. One reviewed it – a personal finance columnist for the *Oakland* (California) *Tribune*. He wrote a very nice review, dedicating his entire column to my book. I noted an immediate spike in sales the day the column appeared, which tapered off slowly over the next few days.

But even if no copies had sold immediately, I'd acquired a valuable link to my book information from a well-traveled site, which searchers can find even after the article's been archived. Further, the review serves as an endorsement from a reputable source – raising my platform to a new level.

From now on, as I contact other media, they can check out my press page to see that I've been reviewed by a major financial writer, giving me a stamp of approval from a significant peer.

2. Other Book Review Organizations

You'll encounter much less traffic among reviewers once you're past the big-time early reviewers like *Library Journal* and *Kirkus*.

Why send books out to these smaller reviewers?

a. You can use each review in your online press kit and various other places.

b. Some reviewers submit their reviews to other review organizations, giving you links and recommendations from many other sites. (Example: *Dead Trees Review* sends the review to 17 review sites, including Amazon.com.)

c. Some reviewers are top Amazon reviewers. Since readers check boxes to indicate that their reviews are helpful, their reviews wield more influence.

Where to Find Reviewers

Each of these web pages provide links to many review organizations:

- http://www.midwestbookreview.com/links/othr_rev.htm – This list, by Midwest Book Review, lists 140 review organizations.
- http://www.aldaily.com/#bookreviews – Links to big-time reviewers, including the *Washington Post* and *Wall Street Journal*.
- http://www.newpages.com/NPGuides/reviews.htm – Another list.
- http://www.dirk-wyle.com/newsl.htm – Short list of one reviewer's favorite review sites.
- http://en.wikipedia.org/wiki/Category:Book_review_magazines – A Wikipedia list of book review magazines.

Narrow Down Your List

I clicked through to each book review site listed on Midwest Book Review, culling it down to 25 reviewers who seemed appropriate for my book. Another list of 32 reviewers yielded me only two potential reviewers.

For my book, I could eliminate reviewers who:

- reviewed only fiction
- charged money for reviews
- reviewed only books by major publishers

How They Work

Typically, a review company will put your book on a private web page so that their reviewers can choose which books they wish to review. If a reviewer chooses yours, she'll contact you requesting the book.

What to Expect

The top companies still receive a lot of requests for reviews. In 2009, *Midwest Book Review* was receiving 2,300 books per month. If *MBR* reviews your book (they reviewed mine) they'll place the review in:

1) their online review magazine, *Small Press Bookwatch*

2) *Cengage Learning*

3) *Gale interactive CD-ROM series Book Review Index* (published four times yearly for academic, corporate, and public library systems).

4) the review databases of *LexisNexis and Goliath*

5) the archives of the *Midwest Book Review* site

Each company tells where they will place your reviews. Often, Amazon.com is included.

Niche Book Reviewers

If your book falls into a category that attracts its own specialty reviewers, search for them on Google. Example: If your book is distinctively Jewish, search "Jewish Book Reviews" in Google to find many reviewers of specifically Jewish books. Similarly, some sites/publications may review only financial or scientific books. For those niche reviewers, search "financial book reviews" or "scientific book reviews."

I submitted my financial book to *The Voice of Youth Advocates* at http://www.voya.com, which reviews books for those who manage the youth collections of libraries. This review in all likelihood helped me to obtain a distributor to libraries.

On Building Your Platform for More Reviews

One reviewer said that she chose my book because of the existing good reviews.

* * *

Tip: reviewers are checking your previous Amazon reviews to decide if your book is worth their time to review.

* * *

Thus, jump-start your Amazon page with early reviews from those who gave you input before publication, as I recommended in chapter 3. Early reviews build a platform to attract later reviewers. Great reviews beget more great reviews.

> **When to Hire a Publicist**
>
> It takes time to find contact information for magazines and newsletters that target your niche. For those who don't have the time or patience, consider paying a publicist who may have already prepared the list for another client. Moreover, she may have relationships with some of the editors you want to target.
>
> Even if you outsource this task, it's good to know the process to see exactly what you're paying for.

Magazines, Newsletters, and Smaller Newspapers

The web-obsessed marketer may object, "Won't printed newsletters and magazines soon be relics that we read about in Social Studies? How 1980s!"

Think again.

While some web enthusiasts envision all knowledge moving from paid sources to free sources, you wouldn't know it by watching print magazine subscriptions. If the magazine industry were ailing, you'd expect to find the periodicals that target web-savvy professionals on life support, since their clientele can get plenty of free information from the Web.

Yet, the print version of *Wired Magazine* – the magazine that coined phrases like "the long tail of the web" and "crowdsourcing" – had 700,000 subscribers in 2009, *increasing by 50,000 subscribers* to 750,000 in 2010. And their subscribers average 35 years of age – hardly old geezers who resist iPods and Kindles.[3]

If you're writing about cutting edge trends and the latest groundbreaking technology, cultivate a relationship with *Wired* and similar magazines. Three quarters of a million paid readers represents quite an audience for your book. And don't forget the thousands of people who read free issues in libraries and share copies around the office.

**

In 2009, the number of paid subscriptions to magazines in the USA was larger than the entire U.S. Population!

**

Although single copy magazine sales through newsstands and bookstores has dropped, the total number of paid subscriptions in 2009 (310,433,396) is a bit higher than paid subscriptions in 1999 (310,074,081). And this increase was during a grueling recession! **Since 1975, magazine subscriptions have almost doubled.**[4]

Don't Forget Smaller Publications

If someone offered you the opportunity to speak to a group of 1,000 people about your book, would you consider it a great opportunity? Of course! Then why do we often overlook smaller publications that influence thousands of people? And the competition for space in these publications is often minimal.

Here's the perspective of web-marketing guru David Meerman Scott and marketing professional Jeffrey Eisenberg:

> "...you will be much more successful if you forget about trying to get the huge article. Big yields come from cultivating many small relationships rather than focus on trying to get that one mega-success." – Scott
>
> "The big hits come by getting to the little guy." – Eisenberg[5]

You can always return to the big publications with new pitches after you get written up by the smaller publications. By then, your platform will be larger and stronger. In Eisenberg's case, the *Wall Street Journal* covered his book without his ever pitching it to them. The buzz created by smaller publications was picked up by the larger.

Success Story

Barry Golson wrote a book about retiring abroad entitled *Retirement Without Borders*. Lynda O'Connor found all the retirement magazines and sent them a press release, author photo, bio, and book cover. Fourteen responded and wrote articles! They even got a write-up in the retirement section of the *Wall Street Journal*.

Whenever I check out the book on Amazon, it's selling very well. Their secret? "The very best way to get readers…is to go directly to the editors of the magazines that target your audience. You want to be in the publications that your audience reads"[6]

To Succeed Like Warren Buffett:

Celebrate the Tedious Stuff

The prospect of searching for niche newsletters and magazines by flipping through giant reference books for hours on end sounds as exciting as spending a lovely afternoon watching paint dry. But Warren Buffett seems to relish the tedious stuff. It's an essential part of what made him a billionaire investor. Much like we need to understand the media that can publicize our books, Buffett needs to understand the financial details of businesses, so that he can decide which ones to invest in.

In a TV interview, someone asked Buffett what advice he'd give to a young person who wanted to learn to invest like him. He replied,

> "I'd tell him to do exactly what I did 40-odd years ago, which is to learn about every company in the United States that has publicly traded securities."

The moderator responded in disbelief: "But there's 27,000 public companies!" To which Buffett replied, "Well, start with the A's." And he has continued this intense study of companies throughout his life.

At age 75, he couldn't find enough undervalued U.S. companies, so he began exploring internationally. First, he narrowed down the countries, then acquired a book the size of a large telephone book that listed the financial details of South Korean businesses. After mastering the terms and symbols used in Korean reports, he bulldozed through the tome to distill a list of attractive Korean companies that could fit on one legal sized sheet of paper.

No wonder he's so successful! Who's as thorough as Buffett? In the end, his sifting of pan after pan of dirt yields gold and precious stones.

Your patient sifting of niche publications will likely yield similar nuggets, putting you in touch with writers who share a passion for your subject matter. *Your* passion resulted in a book. *Their* passion resulted in editing a newsletter or magazine or blog. You're not bothering them. They live for new information. Many would love to have a free copy of your book, an opportunity to review it, and to take future pitches from you concerning topics related to your book. And some of these editors recommend books to schools, serve on influential committees, and speak at important conferences. You just never know when the editor of a small newsletter will end up providing a vein of gold so rich that it makes all your efforts seem insignificant in comparison.

Once you realize you're sifting for gold, research becomes less tedious.

How to Find Newspapers, Periodicals and Newsletters

Here are some of the most useful resources:

- **Ulrich's Periodicals Directory –** http://www.ulrichsweb.com/ulrichsweb – This multi-volume resource lists almost a quarter of a million resources, categorized by subject so that you can find everything from an e-letter specializing in fish bait to a newsletter targeting people in wheelchairs.

- **Standard Rate and Data Services (SRDS) –** http://www.srds.com/portal/main?action=LinkHit&frameset=yes&link=ips – Marilyn and Tom Ross, founders of the *The Small Publishers Association of North America* (SPAN) prefer this resource. Note especially the volumes *Business Publications* and *Consumer Magazines*. If you want to concentrate on publications with the largest circulations, this is a great reference tool.

- **Writers Market** - http://www.writersmarket.com – lists only 2,000 magazines, but gives detailed information about contacts, what type of articles they write, what they pay, etc.

- **Chase's Calendar of Events –** http://mhprofessional.com/?page=/mhp/categories/chases/content/about_chases.html – So you wrote a novel about a girl and her horse. Wouldn't it be great to know if there's a horse-related holiday or event on the horizon, so that your pitch could be time sensitive ("With the Kentucky Derby coming up next month, perhaps you'd like to review....")? Chase lists thousands of events, 45 of which relate to horses.

- **Gale Directory of Publications and Broadcast Media –** http://www.gale.cengage.com/servlet/BrowseSeriesServlet?region=9&imprint=000&titleCode=DOP – Covers about 54,000 newspapers, magazines, journals, radio stations, and television stations.

- **Bacon's Media Directories** – http://us.cision.com/products_services/bacons_media_directories_2010.asp - Their Newspaper/Magazine Directory contains 24,000 trade and consumer magazines, newsletters and journals.

- **Standard Periodical Directory** - http://www.oxbridge.com/SPDCluster/theSPD.asp – "The largest directory of U.S. and Canadian periodicals" (magazines, newspapers, journals, newsletters, directories).

- **The All In One Media Directory** – http://www.gebbieinc.com/aio.htm - more than 24,000 media listings (newspapers, radio, TV, etc.).

- **Encyclopedia of Associations** – http://www.gale.cengage.com/servlet/ItemDetailServlet?region=9&imprint=000&titleCode=EA1G&cf=n&type=3&id=241774 - lists local, regional, state, national, and international associations. Associations often list recommended resources, send out newsletters to their members, post articles on their sites, etc.

- **The National Directory of Magazines** – http://www.oxbridge.com/NDMCluster/theNDM.asp – over 20,000 publications in 260 categories.

How to Use Ulrich

I'll give you an example of how I use one of the resources: Ulrich. You can probably search it digitally, free of charge, through your local public library or university. But from my experience (perhaps I was searching ineffectively) I feel that these searches tend to miss certain resources. Thus, I prefer the print version in four volumes, which weighs enough to put a bar through and do a decent set of bench presses.

To use Ulrich, imagine that you've written the book, *Teaching Literature to Boys Who Prefer Halo over Hemingway* (a fairly large portion of the young male population, I'd assume) and want to find compatible publications.

1. Open volume one and flip to the page "Subject Guide to Abstracting and Indexing" (in the Roman Numeral section before the 1, 2, 3 page numbering begins).

2. Find a category that relates to your topic. "Education" looks promising. Write down the category and the associated page number.

3. Find that same category in the following "Subjects" section. In this section, you'll find subheadings under your chosen category. "Teaching Methods and Curriculum" fits. Write it down.

4. Repeat #2 and #3 until you've found all your relevant categories and subheadings.

5. Look up each category on the page numbers indicated. You'll likely find hundreds of magazines, newsletters, etc.

6. Skim down the middle of the column to weed out resources from countries or languages of no interest to you. I decided to start with only the U.S. I might come back at another time and search other English-speaking countries where my book is available.

Getting Large Reference Tools for Almost Nothing

If Only Books had Antlers!

Cherie and I bagged these reference tools (Ulrich's, Gale's, Literary Marketplace, etc.) for $1 each at our local library sale. With home responsibilities, I find it easier to research at home. Although they're a year out of date, I typically check updated information on each periodical's website anyway.

7. Write down whatever information you need. Although Ulrich's provides contact names and phone numbers, I'll probably check these against each website, so that I'm primarily writing down the name of the publication and the web address. I also write down any pertinent information about the publication (e.g., who it's targeting, how many subscribe) to help me prioritize whom to seek out first.

8. Think beyond your topic. Perhaps parents, especially home schooling parents, would be interested in your book on teaching literature. So find parenting magazines (under the category "children and youth") that might mention your book as well.

9. To find newspapers, see Volume 4 to find daily and weekly papers listed by city and state.

How to Use These Contacts

Start with an e-mail, as I did with the large newspapers above, giving them a link to your press page for more information and offering a free copy for review. Try to personalize it to let them know why their readers might be interested in your book.

Send Follow-up E-mails

Some publicists say that follow up often makes the difference between a book that gets reviewed and one that gets thrown into the trash.

The Initial Follow-Up: "Did you receive it?"

It may get lost amid all the other incoming packages in a busy news center. Thus, send a short, polite e-mail a week or two later asking if they received it. It's also a good reminder.

The Second Follow-Up: "Here's some more pertinent information about my book."

If you don't hear something back in a month or two, consider following-up again. I know it's getting into the "bugging" category now; but after all, you did take the time and expense to send a free book that they requested for review. I resist doing this, so to make it less "bugging" and more "informing," I don't word this e-mail as a reminder. Instead, I give them more helpful information. I might say:

> "With graduation season almost upon us, your readers (it's all about "their readers," isn't it?) will be searching for graduation gifts and eager to hear advice for new grads. The book I sent you a couple of months ago, *Enjoy Your Money!*, just got a great review by a high school principal, which you can see here:

> http://wisdomcreekpress.com/press_kits.html
>
> If you've lost it or it never arrived, let me know and I'll send you another copy."

From a marketing perspective, a follow-up e-mail might fit under the much-heralded business concept: "It's easier to retain an old customer than to gain a new one." After all, these are people who showed enough initial interest to ask for the copy. I know they're interested in the topic and my book. Who knows, I may have missed seeing an article they wrote on my book. If I follow up, they can point me to it.

By disciplining myself to follow-up, I got an article in *Young Money's* popular website.

Another side benefit of following up: In cases where the editor who requested the book had been replaced, I received an automatic e-mail suggesting that I write the replacement editor at another e-mail address. It was like a referral! So when my initial contact at *Better Homes and Gardens* had been replaced, I followed up with the new editor, saying that the former editor had been working on this and would they like for me to send her replacement a copy as well. I suggested that I could also write an article based on the book if she preferred.

Ongoing Follow-up: "Here's another idea."

Publishing gurus Marilyn and Tom Ross suggest making a list of key media contacts that may run over 100 names.[107] After the initial contact, send an occasional postcard. Pitch ideas about your book that relate to current news. Successful freelance journalists repeatedly pitch story ideas to the same magazine editors, building relationships with them over time.

Follow the publications, getting a better understanding of what they like to publish. As you hatch ideas related to your book, update the editors (awards won, articles written, reviews received) and continue to propose articles.

Example Article

A year after my money book was published, I landed an article for *Young Money*, a magazine that targets the demographic of my book. Their site attracts about 150,000 unique visitors per month.

Note how I wrote an informative article, while mentioning my book and linking to it.

http://www.youngmoney.com/credit_debt/how-to-%E2%80%9Cenjoy-your-money%E2%80%9D

When Do I Stop?

Whenever it stops working.

Many of these editors don't care whether your book was published this month or ten years ago. They're all about helping their readers. If you're pitching quality information and the media keeps printing it and your books are selling as a result, why stop? In time, your press page will display link after link to your articles and reviews. When you pitch an article, editors will visit your press page and be assured that you're a professional and you can deliver. Each year you should become more effective as your platform for editors continues to grow.

Do Something!

To put this chapter into action, I will...

1 –

2 –

3 –

Keep Learning!

- **See my free updates** to each chapter at www.sellmorebooks.org.

Chapter 16

Attract Attention through Social Media

by J. Steve Miller and Cherie K. Miller

We're still in the process of picking ourselves up off the floor after witnessing firsthand the fact that a 16-year-old YouTuber can deliver us three times the traffic in a couple of days than some excellent traditional media coverage has in over five months.

- Michael Fox, founder of Shoes of Prey

The polling of Internet users shows that friends' recommendations are the most reliable driver behind purchasing decisions. Right now that market is largely untapped. Facebook and other social networks can allow that to happen.

- Yuri Milner, Russian social-media investor

Note: Among all the areas of publishing and marketing that are rapidly changing, social networking is the one that's careening the most wildly into the future. Although we've updated this chapter until the last minute before publication, things will have changed by the time you read this – perhaps significantly. We'll try to cover this topic much more fully and keep you up with the latest changes through a white paper, e-book, or just by regular chapter updates at www.sellmorebooks.org.

The Need for a Balanced View

> **Other Discussions of Social Networking in This Book**
>
> In case you're skipping around, we've already dealt with several aspects of Social Networking.
>
> - For using a blog and Facebook page in developing an online press page, see chapter 9.
> - For getting reviews from popular blogs, commenting on relevant blog posts, and starting your own blog, see chapter 14.

Social Networking has opened up new worlds for shy authors who'd prefer chasing a rabid weasel with a short broomstick over doing a book signing. Many authors delight in mingling online with endless people who share their passion for niche subjects and genres such as history, urban fiction, mysteries, fashion, business, or childrearing. In the process, they sell books.

On the other end of the spectrum are disillusioned authors who report that they're doing all the things their social media gurus confidently told them would result in a mega seller; yet, their books don't sell. They blog several times a week, tweet regularly, socialize on Facebook, dispense free advice on relevant forums, comment on popular bloggers' posts, and post videos on YouTube. Yet for all their massive input of time, their books aren't selling.

Why the polarized experiences?

Our personal results with social networking have been mixed. Some efforts have paid off in sales. Others have been a waste of time. To get a broader perspective, we compared our experiences with those of many other authors, read scads of articles on social networking for authors, read more broadly (outside book marketing circles) on marketing and social media, and attended a handful of social media conferences. We also asked the critical questions that we all need to be getting straightforward answers to, such as:

- **Question for authors:** "When you said 'Facebook is working great for me!' do you mean that you've got 1,000 'friends' and that some of them are now frequenting your blog, or do you mean that you're actually selling a lot of books as a result? If you mean the latter, how many are you selling from this effort and how much time did you invest?"
- **Question for publicists:** "If I have one hour per day to devote to book marketing, would it be better spent developing relationships in social media or using other methods such as getting reviews from high profile thought leaders in my field?"
- **Questions for social media experts:** "How likely is it that a low profile author can start a blog and become a recognized thought leader in his field? Are some fields easier to crack than others? Will it likely work for writers of novels? Even if an author builds a popular blog, will this guarantee a constant stream of book sales?"

Although we're not satisfied with the answers we're getting (case studies are emerging, but are still scarce), we do find authors selling books on social media platforms and enjoying themselves in the process. And we believe that the near future will unveil many more effective tools for authors.

Again, what works for one author may not work for another due to differences in personalities, interests, and topics/genres. So as you read, think through which methods and platforms may work best for *you* and *your* books.

Is Social Media the Ultimate Way to Market Books?

In our humble opinion, social media is just one more tool that can be used to market books. If other methods (radio, handing out business cards, doing seminars, etc.) are working great for you and pursuing social media would detract from your passions, don't be bullied into it by enthusiasts who claim that other methods are now passé. They aren't.

The Power of Social Media

For authors, the *purpose* of engaging social media isn't revolutionary. It's simply another way for authors to connect with influencers and directly expose potential buyers to their books, hopefully generating a word-of-mouth movement that results in large sales.

But certain aspects of social media make it especially attractive to authors:

- You can do it from home.
- You can connect with influential people in new ways.
- You can find niche audiences that once had few opportunities to gather and interact.
- A successful campaign can spread much more quickly than before.

The last point is why some say that social media puts word-of-mouth on steroids. It's no longer just one reader telling another reader who tells another reader. Today, with a couple of sentences and a couple of clicks of her mouse, an enthused reader can easily tell her 100 Facebook friends, five of which tell their 100 Facebook friends, some of which tell their 100 Facebook friends, etc. With this explosive, exponential sharing, tens of thousands of people – even millions – can quickly hear about your book. Alas, it doesn't always work that way, but the possibilities are indeed fascinating.

How Authors are Selling Books on Social Media Platforms

1. Establish a hub to make your social media efforts more effective. The "hub" is the place you'll consistently send people for interaction and to find in depth information about your books. We covered this in depth in chapter 9. For many authors, this hub will be their blog, which should include a press page (with author information, reviews, an interview, free chapters, links to radio and TV, etc.) and links to their other social media presences (outposts). For others, it will be a traditional website.

Michael Hyatt is CEO of Thomas Nelson, the seventh largest publishing company in the United States. He effectively uses his blog as the hub of his social media efforts, while other platforms function as his outposts. Note how the bottom of his home page (http://michaelhyatt.com) connects readers to:

- information about his public speaking
- his Facebook fan page
- his Twitter presence
- and his LinkedIn page.

Thus, when someone asks Hyatt, "How can I connect with you?" he doesn't have to hand them a list of all his social platforms. He can just direct them to his blog – the hub that directs them to all his online presences.

Here's how an effective hub helps authors sell books.

Someone searches "teaching your dyslexic child to read" in Google and finds your video on YouTube (an outpost). Impressed, she clicks on your YouTube profile to find out more about you. There she finds a link to your blog (your hub) and clicks through. On your blog, she clicks on a link to receive your new posts via e-mail and clicks on another link to find out more about your book on dyslexia. There she sees your impressive press page, which convinces her to order your book by clicking on a link to Amazon.com.

By guiding a visitor from an outpost to your hub, you both sold a book and added a follower.

So whether you're setting up your profile in LinkedIn or posting a response to a question in a forum, link people back to your hub so that they can get more information. Besides bringing in direct traffic, the incoming links will improve your search engine position and increase your Alexa ranking, helping others to find you in a search for your topic or genre.

Don't Make this Fatal Mistake!

The Priority of a Compelling Press Page and Amazon Page

I'm amazed at how many authors fail at this point. They spend loads of time interacting on social media platforms, but complain that it isn't helping their book sales. Yet, when I look at the pages they're pointing people to, I find no compelling reason to buy their books. The absence of reviews and blurbs tells me that the book is likely second rate.

It's so tempting to dive right into social networking to tell people about your book and start interacting over issues you're passionate about before getting good reviews and blurbs and putting them on your press pages. Potential buyers who read your comment on Facebook won't immediately drive to the nearest bookstore to find your book. Instead, they'll follow your link to either your press page or your Amazon page to find out more about the book and to see what people are saying about it.

People don't trust what we say about our own books. And they shouldn't. We're not objective about our own products. They trust what *other* people say about our books. Wow people with your press page and Amazon page. Entice them with great blurbs, reviews, and a helpful book description. Otherwise, your social media efforts may be "full of sound and fury, signifying nothing."

Again, I'm absolutely amazed at how many times I see this huge oversight. If your online press page isn't compelling, return to chapter 9 (on building a press page) and chapters 7, 13, 14, and 15 (on gathering reviews). Social media works best as a part of a broader marketing strategy.

2. Interact on social media outposts (Facebook, LinkedIn, etc.) that make sense for you and your book.108 On these outposts (social media platforms), people connect around their shared interests. Those who are fascinated with your topic or genre are the people who are most likely to buy your books. The wonder of social networking is that your best prospects are gathering in groups that you can easily connect with.

Before the Web, people who had very niche interests (they adored owls or were fascinated with sociological studies of European Gypsies) could connect with like-minded people at annual conventions, through snail-mail, or at a pub within walking distance of Cambridge University. Today, they can find thousands of global enthusiasts who share their passions on blogs, forums, Facebook, etc. Authors who write about owls and Gypsies would do well to find where those who share their passions gather.

To keep yourself from losing focus as you explore social media, keep in mind the three types of people we're trying to connect with:

1) Recognized thought leaders and key media contacts. These might be editors for relevant magazines, popular bloggers, textbook buyers for universities, or anyone else who has the potential to write an influential review, include you in an article, or purchase your book in bulk. Some authors use social media primarily to find these people and offer them free books for review.

2) Social media mavens. If you interact on a forum or listserv, you'll soon find that one or more members have established themselves as the most respected and passionate contributors. They may also wield influence outside of the platform – blogging, contributing to other discussions, or presiding over a trade association. By identifying these mavens and offering them free copies, authors get free and effective publicity whenever the mavens recommend their books.

**

> "Once you can understand where the conversation is, who leads, the type of voices and the best place for you to add your voice, you can then start becoming a more active participant." (Mitch Joel, President of Twist Image)

**

3) People who are interested in your topic. Since these aren't key media contacts or known influencers, authors don't offer them free books for review. Yet, this is the audience you wrote your book for. Let them know about it and they're likely to purchase it.

> **Note:** The platforms I mention below are not ordered by priority. Different platforms will work better for different authors.

Facebook

Facebook 101: Connect with Your Friends and Family and Tell Them about Your Book

Facebook has over 500 million active users (far more than the United States population), making it by far the largest social networking site on the web. Fifty percent of the active users log in on any given day. The average user has 130 friends, so that the potential for spreading information is truly astounding.[1]

If you're not already on Facebook, go to www.facebook.com, sign in, and start connecting with your friends and family. It's free and you may find it to be a wonderful way to keep up with people you care about.

It's also a wonderful way to get the word out about your books, so let's start with your friends and family. After *Enjoy Your Money* came off the press, we immediately announced it to both of our groups of Facebook friends. A few of them bought books immediately.

Between us, Cherie and I have about 1,000 Facebook friends. If half of those read their postings, that's 500 people who know about our books and just might purchase at a later time or recommend our books to use in classrooms or to give through their company as Christmas gifts.

"But I think it's inappropriate to market to my family and friends," someone may object. I agree. Since our Facebook accounts are primarily places to keep up with friends and family, we don't allow people to join unless we know them. Once they join, we don't market to them. Neither do we major on our books and our businesses.

Yet, we still occasionally talk about our books. The key is, we mention them only inasmuch as our friends would be interested in the book part of our lives. Some of them would likely be hurt if we'd published a book and never mentioned it to them. And if we win an award or get to speak somewhere about our books, we also mention it to our Facebook friends. They'd want to know.

I have a friend who's a musician. I want him to tell me when he has a gig coming up. I don't consider it marketing. I care about him and like to hear him play.

But we draw a firm line between "letting friends know about what's happening in our book lives" and "trying to sell books to our friends." For us, the latter is off limits in the "Wall" and "News" sections of our personal Facebook accounts. Since we've already let them know about our books, we don't advertise to them, press them to buy our books, or post frequently about our books. If our friends try repeatedly to sell us stuff on Facebook, we click "unfriend" by their names, so that we no longer see their posts. (Facebook doesn't alert them that we're no longer following them, so we don't risk a relationship.)

Facebook Profiles

When friends first connect with you, they'll often check your profile to find where you live, if you're married, where you work, etc. Include in your profile that you're "...the author of..." and include a link to your press page. That's not bragging. That's letting people who care know something interesting about you. Who knows, they may be searching for a book like yours and would be delighted to find it.

Also check your friends' profiles. If someone works for a company that could sell or give away your books, contact them personally and ask if it's a possibility.

Facebook 201: Contact Key Influencers and Niche Enthusiasts

Typically, although some of your friends and family will buy your book, they aren't the niche you're writing for. In my case, perhaps a handful of my Facebook friends would be interested in a book on book publishing. So let's move beyond our friends and family to connect with our niche audiences and the people who influence them.

Karen O'Toole wrote *Orphans of Katrina: Inside the World's Biggest Animal Rescue: What Really Happened on the Gulf and How You Can Help Save America's Pets Today*. Here's how she used Facebook to reach key media contacts in her niche:[2]

> "I got in a lot of national magazines easily, thanks to Facebook. I went to the bookstore, picked
>
> out the top dog and cat magazines, looked inside for the editor's name, and wrote to the editor directly, on Facebook. (Not on their wall, but where it says 'send a message to....')
>
> I did a brief intro, something like:
>
>> 'Hi, I have a new book out about animals. I'd love to send it for possible review in (name of their magazine). It's called *ORPHANS OF KATRINA: Inside the World's Biggest Animal Rescue*. Please let me know if you'd be interested. Thank you.'
>
> They all responded. They all wanted my book. I ended up in five well-known, respected magazines. I am out in *Bark* next for their big holiday special (they have almost 300,000 subscribers.)"

But couldn't Karen have accomplished the same thing by going directly to the magazine websites, finding the editors, and e-mailing them there? Perhaps, but often popular editors get so much e-mail that they scan it and miss a lot of detail. Some editors who love Facebook may pay more attention to someone introducing herself on Facebook.

Here's how Karen got the word out to general animal lovers:

> "I got 3,000 friends by putting in the search words DOG, CAT, ANIMAL, PAWS, KITTY, FUR, FIDO, PETS – every term related to animals – and asked those people to be my friend. Having that many contacts in your area of expertise, who are interested in your book's subject, and being able to reach high powered people directly, with no assistants involved – hey, you can see why I love Facebook!"

I think a large part of Karen's success is that she understood pet lovers and their relationship to Facebook. Here's how she describes it:

"I was looking for people who were dedicated to animals; not really to 'sell' them anything, but to stick my paw into the Facebook world of animal lovers. The animal world is very 'in the moment' where problems must be solved right away. (Blind cocker dies tomorrow in Robeson pound. URGENT. Anyone know a blind rescue or cocker group?) These emergency posts flow all day. Animal people NEED and WANT as many friends as they can get to spread the word and possibly save lives. The more eyes looking, the better chance they have to save that dog, horse, or wolf.

They were also the exact audience I needed to spread the word about my book. When someone adds me as a friend, or accepts my request to add them, I always send a link to my book's website. I never talk about it. I don't write: 'Thanks for adding me and please buy my book.' I say nothing. I just attach it so they can see it and decide for themselves. They 'get' it. I don't put them on the spot. But now my book link is on their walls, and all of their friends will see it too. If a bunch of their friends click 'like' on my comment, that helps to spread the word as well. I have over 1,000 'likes' on my Facebook page for my book and about 1,300 for my website"

When Your Facebook "Friends" Aren't Really Friends

Separating Business from Personal in Facebook

I asked Karen how this influx of animal enthusiasts into her general Facebook presence impacts her personal friends and family. She says that she never communicated with her friends and family on Facebook. They chat by phone and e-mail. Thus, for Karen, Facebook is a place to connect about animals and other topics of interest.

This brings up a vital point: Each person's Facebook presence develops its own following with its own distinct rules and expectations. If your Facebook "friends" are primarily business contacts that you've cultivated through the years, then it's appropriate for you to "talk business" on Facebook. Let's say you teach business seminars and most of your Facebook connections are people who have been involved with your seminars. You often discuss business issues and opportunities. They would likely want to know in more detail why they should be interested in your newest book.

Facebook "News" sections develop their own culture, with their own unstated rules and social faux pas. Some are all about family, baby pictures, and outings. Others have ongoing debates about political and social issues. Just do what's appropriate for the culture.

Tip: if your Facebook presence is more about your true friends and family, but you want to start interacting with a niche audience about your topic or book, consider opening up a second Facebook account, distinguishing your name (add an initial or use your full name) and using a separate e-mail address.

Set up a Facebook Page (formerly a Fan Page)

Karen mentioned using her Facebook page. This is separate from the place where you and your friends are primarily interacting. Authors set up pages for individual books or their topics. By having a page dedicated to her book, Karen could link people there to find out more about her book.

"But I've already got a press page on my Website that I link people to," you might object. "Why would I want to additionally have a Facebook page that duplicates a lot of the same information?" Two reasons:

1) Social media gurus tell me that **typically, more presences are better.**[3] Different people prefer interacting in different places and in different ways. If you have only a blog, you'll miss people who prefer interacting on Facebook.

2) **Facebook gives you the ability to send messages to everyone who has joined your page.** Don't overdo it, but when you have something of real value to share, you've got the opportunity to get the word out.

3) **People can discover your book in a Facebook search.** When I search "Orphans of Katrina" with Google, Karen's *author site* ranks high. When I search "Orphans of Katrina" on Facebook, her *Facebook page* comes up first. Since a Facebook search searches only Facebook, people would never find her author site in a Facebook search. If I'm interested in rescuing animals and do a subject search for "Animal Rescue" on *Google*, I don't find Karen's author site on the first page. But if I search "Animal Rescue" on Facebook, her Facebook page comes up first. That's valuable exposure.

Think of Facebook as a web unto itself, where millions of people hang out and search for information, seldom venturing out beyond Facebook. If you want people to find your book there, set up a page. It's not very difficult, and it's free. There's no need for me to go into detail here about how to set up a Facebook page, since details change and you can easily find tutorials on the web. But here are the basics:

- Log into Facebook, click "Account"/"Help"/"Pages for Businesses" to learn how to set it up and optimize it.
- Search "Author" and "Book" on Facebook to observe how other authors are using their pages.
- You can customize your page, adding additional pages much like a Website, and allowing people to interact.
- After it's set up, you can send a note to all your "friends" to alert them, link them to your page, and jumpstart the interaction.

Facebook tells options and best practices for their pages here:

http://www.facebook.com/FacebookPages

Answer Questions

As I write, a "Questions" feature is due to go live on Facebook this month. People will pose questions on Facebook and you can give answers. I assume that if you consistently give the most helpful answers in your field, you will be highlighted in some way that enables people to recognize you as an expert in your field (see this feature below on LinkedIn, which I assume Facebook is replicating), which could lead to book sales.

New Stuff on Facebook

Facebook is ever adding new features, some of which will surely be useful to authors. To keep up with new developments, see my resources at the end of the chapter.

Similar to Facebook

Before Facebook took the world by storm a couple of years ago, Myspace dominated the social media landscape. Many people still gather there, particularly those involved with the music and entertainment industry. As I write, Myspace is announcing a total revamping. Only time will tell if it can remain a viable social media presence.[4]

Forums and Listservs

These are some of the oldest social media applications of the Internet, originally allowing academics to crowd source by discussing topics of interest. Today they continue to assist people needing information on virtually any topic imaginable, from alternative cancer treatments to movies to technology. Whatever your topic, people are discussing it on forums and listservs.

Definitions

Forums and message boards allow members to ask questions, answer questions, and post helpful information on a specific topic. Although you may be alerted by e-mail when someone posts a response to your question, the conversation takes place on the site and remains there for others to learn from. Typically, posts can be found by anyone looking for information on a search engine.

Example forum: I frequent John Kremer's *Book Marketing Network*, where authors interact about book marketing.

http://thebookmarketingnetwork.com

Listservs allow members to ask and answer questions via e-mail. Ask a question or share a resource and it's e-mailed to all the members. Responses are also e-mailed to all members, unless someone decides to respond privately.

Example listserv: I participate regularly in the Self-Publishing listserv at Yahoo, where newbies and seasoned experts interact concerning all aspects of book publishing and marketing.

http://finance.groups.yahoo.com/group/Self-Publishing

Find the Best Groups for Your Niche

1. Search Google or Yahoo for your subject or genre. If you wrote a book about birds, search "bird forums." You can also use Google Groups (http://groups.google.com) to do a specialty search for forums, listservs, etc. (search "all groups" instead of limiting yourself to "Google groups.") To search groups in Yahoo, use http://groups.yahoo.com.

2. Peruse the forums that interest you, judging whether they're worth your time to participate.

- Does their Alexa Rank show that they're popular?
- Are participants looking for the information that your book provides?
- Are people regularly posting questions and answers?

> **Using the Alexa Toolbar**
>
> To see how popular a forum is, download the free Alexa Tool here:
>
> http://www.alexa.com/toolbar
>
> Whenever you visit a site, you can look at the toolbar to see how popular the site is. The lower the ranking, the more popular the site.

Find Relevant Discussions, Wherever They're Taking Place

Imagine that you're standing in a checkout line at Wal-Mart and you overhear a woman saying to her husband, "I'd give anything to have a book describing the best places to vacation with our kids in the Southeast." You can hardly believe your ears as you respond, "I've written a book on that very subject and have a box of them in my trunk. Would you like to see a copy?" After they purchase the entire box for their friends and family, you sit in your car, look at your GPS navigator and think, "If only they made a GPS to take me to wherever people are having this conversation."

But you're making this way too difficult.

While the odds of that conversation taking place in your checkout line are remote, the odds of that conversation taking place *somewhere* in the world this week, perhaps many different places, is very likely. If the conversation is taking place in a forum, you may be able to find it and respond. Here's how:

1. Search for conversations. Go to Google Groups at http://groups.google.com. Type "southeast United States vacations" into the box. Click "Advanced Search." Beside "Need more tools?" sort by date, so that the most recent conversations are displayed first. Beside "message dates," choose a time frame, such as the past 30 days. Click "Advanced Search" at the bottom to start the search.

2. Set up forum alerts. Rather than searching for existing conversations about your topic, why not get alerted by e-mail when conversations start? Try out BoardTracker free for a month (www.boardtracker.com), to see if it works for you. Here's how it works:

> **Free Google Alerts**
>
> You can also use Google Alerts (http://www.google.com/alerts) for this purpose. While Google Alerts searches news, blogs, etc., you have the option to set your alert to receive only "discussions."
>
> (Other such tools may have developed since I wrote this. Search "how to track forum conversations" and related phrases in Google.)

To recommend my money book, I'd like to know when a teacher is looking for a personal finance text so that I can recommend my book. To be alerted to these conversations, I give BoardTracker the phrase "personal finance text," so that whenever someone uses this phrase in a forum, I receive an e-mail about it, which allows me to respond. This could result in multiple sales, not only from the person asking the question, but from any others who follow the forum or find the conversation in a Google search.

Tips for Interacting on Forums and Listservs

- **If you join a very active listserv** (members of the Self-Publishing listserv send around 25 e-mails a day), set up a special folder to receive these e-mails rather than have them overwhelm your inbox. In this way, you can check them at certain times of the day or week and search them more easily for topics of interest.
- **Before posing questions and answers, lurk in the background for a while.** Each group develops its own culture, which you should learn. Some are very strident and opinionated, others are very open-minded and laid-back. Some are dominated by a few experts, others by the general population.
- **Be aware that some are slanted to particular viewpoints.** If you're interested in comparing publishing options on a forum, find out if the forum is hosted by a publishing company. If it is, the advice you receive on certain topics may be less than objective and candid.
- **Share about your books in a way that's appropriate for each culture.** Some groups may appreciate authors dropping by to mention their books. Other groups ignore or even ridicule authors who write a post about their book and leave. They deride them as "drive by's". It's typically fine to answer someone's question and include in your signature the name of your book and a link to your press page. If you interact regularly on the forum, offering valuable advice, you're more likely to gain respect and attract interest in your books.

YouTube

If a picture is worth a thousand words, isn't a video worth a thousand pictures? Yet, since authors love to read, it's easy to exalt the printed page and overlook the power of video. YouTube's explosive growth over the past six years (since 2005) demonstrates the world's appetite for brief videos. It's the largest online video community (over 300 million users), streaming over two billion videos each day.[5]

Advantages of online video for authors include:

- Videos rank high on searches, helping people to find you and your books.
- Flip cameras are cheap (under $200).
- Putting videos on YouTube is free, and not that difficult.
- The social networking components of YouTube enable viewers to comment on your videos and recommend them to others, giving them the potential to go viral.
- YouTube is only one of scores of video streaming sites.

Using YouTube to Sell Books

Marguerita McManus wrote a quilting book – *Crazy Shortcut Quilts*. Two years ago she put her first video on YouTube. Today she has over 34 short videos, averaging four to five minutes each. So far, people have viewed (uploaded) her videos over 350,000 times! Over 700 people have subscribed to her "channel" – the account where her videos reside. Especially if you've written a how-to book, study what Marguerita has done with video (http://www.youtube.com/user/CrazyShortcutQuilts).

Tips from Marguerita for using video to sell books

- **"Don't try to duplicate your book on video.** Instead, reinforce some of the techniques that you describe in your book. Or, give viewers additional information related to your book's theme."
- **"Don't sweat the equipment and technical issues.** Viewers want you to be real and understandable. Think functional. I do all my videos myself using an inexpensive camera, a second hand tripod and work lights. Now that YouTube lets you edit videos using their website, you don't even need editing software."

What's a Widget?

Go to Marguerita's website:

http://www.crazyshortcutquilts.com

On her right column, you'll see a box with the YouTube logo that allows people to subscribe to her YouTube channel *without ever leaving her site*. That's a free widget (a chunk of code) that Marguerita copied from YouTube and pasted into her site, no programming required.

- **"Make your book, your website/blog, and your e-mail address easily findable.** Provide a link to your book in your profile and the description of your video. Put your URL in any title credits you create for each video."
- **"Make it easy to subscribe.** Invite viewers to subscribe in each video and use the YouTube widgets to promote your videos on your website/blog. Once people subscribe, they are automatically alerted by e-mail each time I put up a new video. I can also contact my subscribers when I want to alert them about something new."
- **"Tag each video with popular search terms in your field.** This helps people to find your video in a search for your topic."[6]

Other Types of Videos Authors Can Create

- Put up a book trailer.
- Put up your TV interview.
- Put up parts of a seminar you taught.
- Do a short reading from your book.

Learning to Use Social Media Platforms

If we were to detail how to set up your accounts and begin using LinkedIn, Facebook, YouTube, etc., this chapter would be a book in itself and you'd likely be overwhelmed with the information, not to mention bored to tears.

Rather than check out a book from the library on "How to Use LinkedIn," **why not learn social media platforms as young folks do it: by visiting each site and fooling around.** Click on stuff. Poke around and see what happens. Don't worry about breaking something or looking dumb. When something doesn't work like you expect it to, rather than feeling stupid, blame the programmers for not making it more intuitive. To sharpen your skills, occasionally search the web for articles on "How to Use LinkedIn," etc.

Although YouTube is presently the most popular video streaming site, it's not the only game in town by far. Here's a list of the top video sites:

http://www.fridaytrafficreport.com/list-of-29-free-video-sharing-sites

LinkedIn

LinkedIn targets business professionals, helping them to connect with other professionals, display an up-to-date resume, recruit, ask questions, and get answers. It's the largest professional network, with 80 million members as we write. Here are some ways authors can use LinkedIn to sell books.

#1 – Set up your LinkedIn profile (www.linkedin.com). Link to your hub, Twitter account, press page, etc. People interested in your topic may view your profile, find your book enticing, and buy a copy.

#2 – Connect with people you know.

LinkedIn gives you ways to find and connect with your friends, associates, past colleagues, classmates, etc. (Click the Contacts/Add Connections tabs.)

As you post updates, your first level friends can see your speaking engagements, signings, awards, and other activities that involve your book. Again, this makes people aware of your books. You're not perceived as bragging. Since your books are a part of your professional life, people expect to see them mentioned on LinkedIn.

#3 – Browse your friends' profiles. Some may work for companies that could buy your books in bulk. Others may be members of local groups like Kiwanis or Chambers of Commerce, which might allow you to speak. Over and over, we hear from successful people that "it's all about who you know." LinkedIn connects you with people and gives you effective ways to leverage these relationships to sell your books. You can also contact first level friends through LinkedIn if you're speaking in their area.

#4 – Track down influencers.

I've been pretty passive in making connections and just have 54 people I'm connected to (first level connections). Yet, these 54 friends have over 10,000 friends (second level) that my first level connections can introduce me to. On the third level (friends of my second level) I have well over a million connections.

The beauty and genius of LinkedIn resides in these three levels of connections, each of which lists people's present and past industries, companies, interests, etc.

Once you start using LinkedIn, you can see why many journalists use it to track down people at companies and organizations that they want to interview. Similarly, authors can use it to connect with influencers in their fields. If you wrote a memoir about overcoming your high school addiction to meth, you could likely contact many influential people in rehab organizations, the juvenile justice system, and drug awareness groups who might be interested in your book, your speaking, and your expertise.

This is much like Karen O'Toole successfully contacted magazine editors through Facebook. While some people would be more accessible through an e-mail address on their company website, others would be more open to a contact through Facebook and still others through LinkedIn.

Here's how it works.

Under the "People" search box, click "Advanced." Let's say I wrote a historical novel concerning the Civil War and want to connect with Civil War enthusiasts. So I type "Civil War," into the "keywords" box. (There are many options here for narrowing down my search.)

LinkedIn searches my three degrees of friends, resulting in about 10,000 people who mention "Civil War" in their profiles. I also know what connection, if any, I have with them. If they are one of my first connections, I can contact them directly. If they are friends of friends (second level connection), I can ask a friend for an introduction. If they are in a LinkedIn "Group" that I'm a part of, I can contact through that group.

> To contact second and third degree contacts without getting an introduction, you can pay LinkedIn for a Premium account that allows a limited amount of "InMail".
>
> http://help.linkedin.com/app/answers/detail/a_id/437

5. Join a "Group"

LinkedIn Groups are their forums. For the person with the historical novel, search "Civil War" in the Groups search box and you'll find 15 or so relevant Groups. Use them to gently sell books in the ways we mentioned above in our discussion of forums.

6. Answer Questions

Since LinkedIn is a gathering of professionals, it's a great place to ask and answer questions. LinkedIn provides a way to ask questions that all members (not just your friends) can see and answer. People vote on answers so that the best answers rise to the top. Here are two ways to use the "Answers" area to sell books.

- **Find people who are searching for books like yours.** Search for questions asked about your area of expertise. In the top menu of your LinkedIn account, click More/Answers. In the "Answers" search box, type in something regarding your subject. When I searched "personal finances" or "best personal money management books," I found people asking advice about what books to recommend on the subject, and many other questions where I could legitimately recommend my book. (The results come ordered by "degrees away from you." For our purposes, it's more helpful to select the options to order results by "relevance" or "date".)

- **Answer questions in your area of expertise and become recognized as an expert.** Since readers rank answers, you can become known as the "go-to" person (indicated by a star) for questions related to your book. Obviously, if you're recognized as an expert, members will more likely view your answers and consider the book you mention in the text or in your signature.

Please note: Your impact goes way beyond providing an answer to one person's question. Anybody searching LinkedIn's Answer section can see your answer for years to come.

LinkedIn's "Less Hassle than Many Social Media Platforms" Environment

Unlike some social networking platforms, LinkedIn doesn't require regular interaction. I don't have people spamming me with random information (think: Myspace). I don't have to interact constantly with people and ward off countless invitations to participate in Farmville or Mafia Wars (think: Facebook). Relatives don't send me cute photos that I feel obligated to view. I can log in, use it for something practical, then return six months later and nobody seems to care that I've been gone.

Social Network Sites Where Book Lovers Interact

http://www.shelfari.com

- Find your book in Shelfari and edit its page so that visitors will understand what your book is about and why they should consider purchasing it.
- Find books similar to yours and edit their "more books like this" section to include your book.
- Find Shelfari's "groups" in your subject/genre. Add to discussions, mentioning your book when appropriate.[7]

http://www.goodreads.com

Use GoodReads in much the same way as you use Shelfari. Edit your book's page, find appropriate groups, and interact with them. A unique and useful feature of GoodReads is their "First Reads" program where authors allow people to sign up to win free copies of their books. Weston Locher, author of the humor book *Musings on Minutiae*, did two separate giveaways and had 1,800 people sign up. That's a lot of exposure! He also followed up on participants, reminding them that although they lost, they could purchase his book through Amazon.com. He provided a link and sold some books.[8]

Social Media Sites for Authors

http://www.writerscafe.org

Post your stories, poems, and sample chapters. Get advice and reviews. Enter contests. Talk books in the forum.

http://www.authorsden.com

"Where authors and readers come together." Create an author profile. Sell books in their "signed by author" bookstore. Network with fellow authors.

Twitter

What It Is

Twitter is a *microblog* in that you're limited to 140 characters per tweet (or message). Initially, 140 characters sounds like a terrible limitation. What can you possibly say of worth in 140 characters? Yet, brevity is Twitter's genius.

> **Why the 140 Character Limit?**
>
> Cell phones often limit texting to 160 characters. Twitter limits you to 140 characters so that up to 20 characters are reserved for your username.

If you concur with Strunk and White's (*Elements of Style*) observation that "vigorous writing is concise," then Twitter provides a marvelous mechanism to discipline the verbose writer. Type 141 characters and Twitter refuses to publish. It's that simple.

As a result, the writer who'd love to wax eloquent about "O recent New York Times article, how do I love thee? Let me count the ways..." must fortunately limit herself to:

> "Great NYT article every writer should read: www.nyt.com/coolarticle."

And people love it. As of September 2010, Twitter has 160 million registered users, tweeting 90 million tweets per day.[9]

How People Use It

Steve's first exposure to Twitter convinced him that it was the ideal time waster for egomaniacs who thought people actually wanted to know what they ate for breakfast. But when journalists began using real time pictures and cell phone tweets from the midst of political uprisings and earthquakes, he began to see the potential. Today, many consider it a primary way to communicate, network, and keep abreast of the latest developments in their fields. Businesses such as Best Buy, Whole Foods, Dell, and Pepsi use Twitter extensively for customer service, to get immediate and candid input on products, to offer coupons, and to announce new products.[10]

Using Twitter to Sell Books

John Kremer increased the traffic to his website – the hub where he sells his services and products – significantly using Twitter. By spending about 30 minutes a day on Twitter, he cut his Alexa ranking in half (smaller is better) over a four-month period. As a result, hundreds of new visitors come to his site each day from Twitter. This is a very significant change for an older, already-successful site.

Here are some tips from John Kremer and other successful Twitter users:

1. Set up an interesting, informative profile. People may look at it to decide whether or not to follow you. Let them know your professional and personal interests, your areas of expertise, the name of your book, your blog or press page, etc. Some may look at your profile, click on a link to your book, and decide to purchase it.

2. Tweet regularly. John Kremer posts about 10 per day. He posts quotes, ideas, questions, notices of updated website material, links to cool stuff, retweets, etc. The vast majority of your posts should be stuff that's useful, inspirational, or funny. A tiny minority should be about you and your products, unless you're a celebrity and fans are following you to discover what you eat for lunch and where your next concert will be.

3. "Follow" people who might buy or comment on your book. Follow not only people in your book's target audience, but also bloggers, journalists, and mavens in your field. Find these people by searching key words in Twitter's search – http://search.twitter.com. An "advanced" search (http://search.twitter.com/advanced) allows you to search an exact phrase and gives other helpful options. If you wrote a book on health foods, search key words/phrases such as health, healing, vitamins, healthy, nutrition, etc. Look at people's profiles and follow the ones that look the most interesting and relevant to what you'd like to communicate about. One author connected with someone who wrote about her book in the *Christian Science Monitor*.

4. When people ask to follow you, accept them only if you want to follow them. If you follow them for awhile and find them obnoxious, boring, or constantly trying to sell you stuff you don't want, unfollow them.

5. Make it conversational. Share ideas. Respond. Ask for assistance. Thank people for their help. Retweet thought-provoking or helpful tweets. If you major on conversation and developing relationships, an occasional mention of your book or services will be received far better.

6. Answer questions. John Kremer recommends using half of your tweets to answer people's questions. This moment, someone may be Tweeting a question that your book or special expertise can answer. Answer the question, then point them to your book for further information, when appropriate. It's obvious how this can lead people to visit your site or purchase your book.

Sometimes these questions show up randomly in your stream of Tweets. You may also search for questions that contain key phrases in Twitter's Advanced Search (http://search.twitter.com/advanced). So I might search the phrase "book marketing" and check the blank indicating that I want Twitter to show me only Tweets about "book marketing" that are written as questions.

If you prefer to be alerted by e-mail when someone tweets about a specific topic, sign up for alerts with an application like http://tweetbeep.com or http://twitter.com/TWEETLATER.

Is Twitter Worth Your Time for Marketing Your Books?

Granted, authors have used Twitter to successfully sell books, land publicity, build their site traffic, and do scores of other cool things. But the larger question remains: Is Twitter the best use of an author's time? After all, each minute spent tweeting takes a minute from other book-selling activities.

While we can't give the definitive answer for every author, perhaps the following considerations can help. Adapt them to evaluate other social media platforms as well.

a) Do buyers/influencers in your niche tend to use Twitter to find books like yours? Imagine that you publish textbooks and market them primarily by developing relationships with the decision makers at each university and sending them advance reader copies for review. It works wonderfully, but to do it right requires all your marketing time. Should you take 30 minutes each day from a proven method to use one that's yet unproven with textbooks? Probably not. Even if you hired a volunteer intern to work with Twitter, could she be effective if she weren't an expert on textbooks? Could she really answer academic questions in a way that would gather a following and point people to your site?

Idea: If the publisher in this case markets to the university decision-makers, perhaps the textbook authors could Tweet about their topics and develop a following, if it doesn't conflict with other successful initiatives in which they are already involved.

b) Could Twitter serve other purposes in addition to selling books? Perhaps you don't think Tweeting would likely pay off in enough sales to warrant a 30-minute per day commitment. Yet, Twitter might also help you to make contacts that lead to paid consultations, discover speaking opportunities, land writing assignments, and publicize your blog posts.

c) Are you attracting one-time buyers or lifelong customers? It makes sense for Dell and Whole Foods to pay people to attract customers and interact with them over Twitter. After all, attracting one customer may bring thousands of dollars per year. Similarly, a publisher with many books or an author with a long line of books might get more benefit per minute spent than a person who's trying to market one book.

d) Does your topic lend itself to a social media crowd? People passionately discuss and debate health foods, alternative medicines, movies, celebrities, and a host of niche topics. But if you're writing about a topic that has primarily a regional interest, like a history of Jekyll Island, Georgia, people may not discuss it as widely and fervently on Twitter.

Idea: You could still set up alerts to notify you when people are discussing Jekyll Island or asking questions about it. This passive strategy would take very little time, but could pay off in some useful contacts.

e) Do you enjoy it? Much of successful book marketing comes down to finding a method that not only works, but that you truly enjoy. When we read John Kremer on Twitter, we can tell that he truly loves it. He seems to enjoy answering people's questions, meeting interesting people, passing on useful information, and learning new things that may have nothing to do with marketing his books. We doubt the author who dreads his "Twitter Time" but guts out his 30 minutes per day would have the same success as a passionate John Kremer.

f) Are you a fast reader? If you're following thousands of people, it helps to be able to speed read your posts. Cherie reads significantly faster than Steve, making Twitter more manageable for her.

g) Are there other marketing methods that are likely to work better for your book and your personality/strengths? Although we keep saying this, it's worth re-emphasizing. There are hundreds of ways to market your books, of which Twitter and other social networking methods are just one subset. We find many successful authors who use one or a handful of methods that work wonderfully to sell their books. One method tends to work best for one author, another method for another author. You can't do everything. Do what works best for you.

Learning More about Twitter

On Getting Started: http://business.twitter.com/twitter101/starting

Best Practices: http://business.twitter.com/twitter101/best_practices

Case Studies of Businesses Using Twitter: http://business.twitter.com/twitter101/case_bestbuy

The Future: Where's it all Heading?

Social media platforms appear and morph at a dizzying rate. Twitter, Inc., was founded only four years ago in 2007.[11] YouTube started six years ago,[12] Facebook, seven years ago.[12] By the time you read this, new platforms may have made these obsolete.

What does the future hold for authors and social media? Here are our guesses:

Prediction #1 – **While today's social media tools are helpful to some, tomorrow's tools may be essential for all.** Scads of helpful applications for authors will continue to emerge.

Prediction #2 – **More people will congregate in smaller niches.** Authors who write about Leopard Geckos or Spiritual Urban Fiction set in Seattle will be able to quickly and easily find and communicate with their audiences.

Prediction #3 – **The most helpful, innovative, and interesting books will find themselves rising quickly to prominence through the social media actions of their readers: their conversations, their voting, their reviews, and their initiative in forwarding book recommendations to friends and networks.** Increasingly, although authors with big money and creative advertisements may still have the edge in initial exposure, the candor and passion of actual readers will have the final say in which books thrive and which ones die. May God hasten that day.

Do Something!

To put this chapter into action, I will...

1 –

2 –

3 –

Keep Learning!

- **See our free updates** and other resources on this subject at www.sellmorebooks.org.
- **For a good introduction to social networking, read Dan Zarrella's *The Social Media Marketing Book.***
- **Shiv Singh's *Social Media Marketing for Dummies* is sensible and considers recent studies.**
- **For using Twitter to sell books and bring traffic to your site, see John Kremer's Twitter resources (http://www.bookmarket.com/twitter.htm) and read his *Twitter Mania Manual.***
- **To build a following around your blog, read Darren Rowse and Chris Garrett, *ProBlogger.***
- **To find the latest articles and case studies on social networking, rated as to importance by readers, see http://sphinn.com.** Click Hot News/Social Media.

Chapter 17

Optimize Digital Sales

E-Books, White Papers, Members' Collections, and More

E-Books and Beyond

As I write, e-books and e-book readers (Kindles, Nooks, Google's Web Readers, etc.) are all the rage.

- E-book sales jumped 150 percent in July, 2010.[1]
- Over 250,000 e-books were downloaded from Apple's iBookstore on its first day of operation, with millions downloaded since.[2]
- Amazon's e-book sales tripled in the first half of 2010. Amazon reports selling more e-books than hardcover books. In June, 2010, they sold 180 digital books for every 100 hardcover books.[3]
- If these trends continue, e-books can only increase in their importance to authors. And no wonder they're popular. The many advantages of e-books include:

Are Paper Books Dying?

My take: if so, they're not disappearing any time soon. In fact, they're looking pretty healthy. So don't stop publishing your paper editions!

Some people graph the rise in digital sales over the past year and conclude that paper books will soon disappear entirely. But geeks with calculators can fail to take into account significant data, such as:

- **Adult paperback sales have *increased* by 15.7 percent for the year 2010 (through May).**

- **Portability** – you can travel with hundreds of books in your pocket.
- **Immediacy/Convenience** – you don't have to visit your bookstore or wait on shipping. They're immediately downloadable.
- **Global Access** – order wherever you can access the web.
- **Affordability** – e-books are typically cheaper than paper books.
- **Large Author Royalties** – self-published authors are currently receiving up to 70 percent of the list price from e-book publishers such as Amazon or Apple's iBookstore.

- **Although Amazon sells more e-books than hard-cover books, this doesn't seem to negatively impact the sale of hard-cover books.** Hardcover sales have *increased* so far in 2010.
- **Trade e-book sales still comprise less than nine percent of book sales.**

Perhaps the proliferation of e-books is encouraging reading in general, which leads to better sales of paper books. For whatever reason, the paper book looks pretty secure for the near future.

The Marketing Benefits of E-books

Obviously, if my book isn't available in the formats that large groups of people read, I'm bypassing a huge market. But beyond publishing, digital formats allow me to *market* my books in new ways. For example:

- I can give away digital chapters as samples at no cost to myself.
- I can give away (or significantly slash the selling price of) an e-book for a limited time to get the word out, jump-start reviews, and shoot for exposure through the top-selling categories of Barnes & Noble and Amazon.com.
- I can hook readers on a series by offering the first novel of the series free of charge.
- I can take advantage of the unique marketing tools each digital platform offers (discount coupons, networking with readers, etc.)
- Easy global access. Anyone with a computer and web access – on a ship, on a scientific outpost in Antarctica, in a remote village – can download a free version of Kindle and order digital books with a credit card.

This is all great news for authors!

So let's start this chapter by discussing e-books before considering other digital options for writers.

How to Publish an E-Book

> **Tip:** The options for e-publishing are changing rapidly, with important news breaking every few months. So get the latest scoop by consulting publishing forums and searching Google for the latest posts and articles on "how to publish an e-book."

First, consult with your publisher or printer. If you don't hold the rights to your book, get the necessary permissions (in writing) to pursue any new editions. Also, your publisher or print on demand service may have helpful suggestions or a valuable relationship with e-publishers.

Second, put your book in the most popular e-book formats and get it distributed on the most popular e-book sites. You can either submit your manuscript to each individual platform or simplify matters by submitting it to one place that will distribute it for you. Since people read e-books in many different ways, some readers will need your book formatted for Kindle, others for iPad, and still others for their computers.

One way to make your book available on multiple platforms is to put it in each of the major formats yourself. Example: To publish it for Amazon's Kindle, go to their Digital Text Platform (https://dtp.amazon.com/mn/signin), read the instructions and submit your manuscript. It's free to publish a Kindle version and the author receives 70 percent of the selling price. After your Kindle version is set up, work your way through each of the other platforms (Nook, iPad, Sony Reader, etc.) on their sites. By dealing with each platform separately, you have more control over the look of your book and will receive a higher percentage of each sale than going through someone else. Cherie recently uploaded one of her books to Kindle as a pdf and was amazed at how easy it was. In an hour or two, it was done.

Others report more frustration with formatting their documents for e-books.[4] Especially for those whose books were formatted in InDesign, trying to convert it to a simple Word document (for some e-book formats) can be frustrating and time consuming. That's when some resort to shortcuts like Smashwords.

Simplify through Smashwords

Rather than manually submitting their books to each platform, some authors prefer submitting their manuscripts to a service that does much of the formatting for them and distribute their manuscripts to the other main platforms.

The service most highly used and respected as I write is Smashwords (www.smashwords.com). Format your manuscript to their specifications in Microsoft Word, and then submit it to Smashwords. It's free. They will transform it into the most popular e-book formats and submit it to the most popular e-book retailers, such as Barnes & Noble, Sony, the Apple iPad iBookstore, Borders, Amazon, and all the major smart phone platforms. If you wish to publish some directly (like for Amazon's Kindle), you can specify to have Smashwords submit it to all the e-book sellers except for Amazon, thus securing your full 70% on each Amazon sale.

To ready your manuscript for Smashwords you don't have to know programming code – just Microsoft Word. How long should it take to format your text? Smashwords founder Mark Coker suggests that an experienced e-book formatter could do it in as little as one hour. But surely heavily formatted texts would take longer. One first-time user reported spending from 10-12 hours readying a heavily formatted text for Smashwords. **Option:** Pay an expert to do the formatting for you. Coker can recommend experts who charge $25 per hour and up.

> What if your book's only in hard copy? This service will scan your hard copy book into Word format for $25: http://www.blueleaf-book-scanning.com/book_scanning_service_order.html. Need to convert your pdf into Microsoft Word, free of charge? Try http://www.pdftoword.com.

When someone buys your e-book directly from the Smashwords site, authors receive 85 percent of the selling price. If one of Smashword's partners (such as Apple's iBookstore) sells your book, authors receive 85 percent of Smashword's *net* proceeds (net proceeds = the amount Smashwords receives from the selling retailer). In the latter case, authors typically receive between 42 percent and 60 percent of the selling price. Thus, for the sale of a $10 e-book, an author would receive $8.50 if it sold on the Smashwords site and between $4.20 and $6 if one of the partners sold it.[5]

How many e-books should authors expect to sell?

Coker candidly warns authors that some e-books don't sell at all. Like paper books, they must be well written and well marketed. Yet, he reports that one indie author, Brian S. Pratt, earned over $4,000 for his e-book sales (sci-fi/fantasy category) in a month through one retailer alone. The next month, he made even more. This author's strategy is to offer his e-books for under $6.00 and offer the first book in a series free of charge.[6]

The "Price Them Low" Strategy

And Pratt is far from alone. As I write (February 2011), I'm tracking low profile, self-published authors who are raking in thousands of dollars per month with strategies such as:

- **Offering the first e-book in a series very cheaply**, sometimes free, in order to hook readers into purchasing the rest of the series.
- **Offering a non-series e-book cheaply** – like 99 cents or $2.99 – but making tons of money as the Amazon/Borders rankings improve, thus giving improved visibility (more sales means more visibility), and making money through large volumes of sales.

The best blog I've found currently tracking these methods is by Joe Konrath:

http://jakonrath.blogspot.com/2011/02/guest-post-by-victorine-lieske.hml

He regularly analyzes his own e-book sales and those of other authors. Today I read a post of one author who was selling her single novel at 99 cents and increased her sales until she sold 21,000 e-books in January alone, netting her $7,300 for the month. (Admittedly, this was the January after everyone got an e-reader for Christmas and wanted to download their first books.)

Will this strategy stop working if everyone begins pricing their books this low? Probably. But for now, this looks like an excellent strategy.

Some Readers Prefer Short and Sweet

Could your book sell better in bite-sized chunks? Paulette Ensign sold over a million copies of her 16-page booklet, *110 Ideas for Organizing Your Business Life.* The same benefits that motivate readers to buy her paper booklets (short, cheap, to the point) can motivate readers to purchase e-booklets.

http://www.tipsbooklets.com/about.html

Digital White Papers and E-booklets

Imagine that you wrote a historical novel about Houdini, the great escape artist. Your readers often ask whether certain of the events in your book were fact or fiction. So to keep you from having to answer the same questions over and over again, and to add a potential stream of income, you write a 30-page paper in pdf format titled

"Houdini: Separating Fact from Fiction." Interested readers can click on a prominent link on the sidebar of your blog, taking them to a purchase page that explains: "This download is free, but if you'd like to give a donation for the time and effort involved in writing it, click here to make a donation."

Making Money from Ads

Some authors work with individual companies who put ads on their sites. Others use services such as Google AdSense, allowing Google ads on their sites. For the latter, you're paid by how many people click on the ads. From my experience, Google's ads are typically relevant to my site theme and unobjectionable. They're free to use, but the technically challenged (example: me) might need a programmer or friend to spend an hour pasting the programming code into your site or blog.

Some may call it a short e-book, but let's distinguish it as an **e-booklet**. Interestingly, many people prefer bite-sized bits over long books and will pay more per page for them than they'd pay for a 300-page book. Some authors charge readers for e-booklets; others give them away as an incentive to leave their contact information or to simply establish good will; still others request a donation. It's typically a good idea to charge for some information and give away other information. The latter builds traffic and promotes good will.

Sensing a market for works larger than an article but smaller than a book, Amazon launched ***Kindle Singles*** in October 2010. They specialize in e-books of 10,000 to 30,000 words (about 30 to 90 pages), offering them at a lower price. I plan to publish a few of these over the next year and will keep you up (on my blog) with the results.

Other authors write **white papers** – authoritative reports or guides that explain difficult issues or tell how to solve a problem. People charge wildly varying amounts for these papers, depending on the perceived importance of the subject matter.

Members-Only Collections

Rather than selling individual e-books, e-booklets, and white papers, it often makes sense to collect all your digital writing into one place and sell it as a collection. I do this with my character education resources at www.character-education.info. I write unique lesson plans, motivational people stories, and collect useful quotes and activities that teachers and parents use to teach character and life skills. For $14.75 per year, an individual teacher gets unlimited access to my extensive member resources. For $99.00, an entire school (teachers, administrators, students) can subscribe for a year. Educators from every state and over 30 countries have subscribed.

Benefits of a Useful Subject Site

Here are some reasons I love writing for members-only collections on my subject sites:

1. I have virtually unlimited space to publish my writing. One of my sites has over 1,000 pages of lesson plans, 150 articles, and a database of over 3,500 speakers' illustrations. Yet, it uses under five percent of my allotted server space, and costs me under $10 per month for hosting and a unique domain name (url).

2. I love to research and write. My sites provide my primary outlet. I read voraciously in nonfiction – particularly biographies – collecting interesting quotes and writing short, motivational people stories based upon my research. I thoroughly enjoy putting my writing to good use serving others!

3. It takes minimal upkeep, once I'm established. A traditional blog typically requires several quality posts per week to keep up its rankings. My subject sites require very little upkeep, after my initial years of writing to stock the sites with useful resources. Today I add resources only as I see the need, sometimes going months without adding anything to the sites. A couple of times per day, I may need to answer an e-mail from a customer who had trouble signing in, needs a scholarship, or needs me to fax an invoice to her school. Other than that, people access materials and pay by credit card without my assistance. Not having a physical storefront, I can maintain it from home, a coffee shop, while on vacation, or anywhere I can get web access.

Tips for Allowing Customers to Pay

On Your Site

You don't need to set up e-commerce (a way for people to pay with credit cards) to sell e-books through SmashWords or Amazon. Just link customers to those sites and they'll pay there. You *do* need to set up e-commerce if you sell e-books, white papers, or members resources *on your site.*

Suggestions:

- **Don't make a hasty decision.** Some people pay way more than they should. Search "e-commerce reviews" and such to learn all the options and narrow down the best companies for what you want to accomplish.
- **Get advice from acquaintances** who sell on their sites.
- **See if your site host recommends certain companies.**
- **Consider PayPal.** It's used widely. Since most customers have heard of it, they're likely to feel comfortable paying through PayPal. https://www.paypal.com

4. Allowing Google to put ads on my site gives me an added stream of income. To give you a ballpark for how many site visitors it takes to make some money from Google Ads, I'm typically making between $300 and $400 per month from Google Ads from a site that averages about 750 visits/sessions (12,000 hits) per day.

5. It provides me with a valuable e-mail list. When people sign in to use my resources, I request their e-mail address and they can check a box to receive my occasional e-letter. My 8,000 e-mail addresses give me the opportunity to provide recipients with valuable free resources and to announce new products.

6. Subscribers get a great value: lots of quality resources for their money. It's fun dealing with satisfied customers.

7. My expenses are low. I don't rent office space, pay a secretary, or pay a webmaster. I set up my sites and add materials to sites myself. I pay a programmer if I need special programming (like adding a database or setting up a members area) and pay a designer a couple of hundred dollars to go over my site and make it look better. Otherwise, I spend my time writing and publishing and marketing.

Example Authors Who Sell Their Writing in Digital Formats

If you think a subject site would work for you, study other subject sites to see how they do it – what they charge for, what they offer free of charge, how they present themselves, how they use blurbs, how they sell ads, etc.

Here are a couple of sites that sell memberships:

http://www.problogger.net – Darren Rowse sells membership and sells ads.

www.character-education.info – My character education and life skills site.

Here are a few sites that sell various products:

http://www.bookmarketingworks.com/index.php?cat=main&pg=home.htm – Brian Jud

http://www.bookmarket.com – John Kremer

http://www.parapublishing.com – Dan Poynter

Do Something!

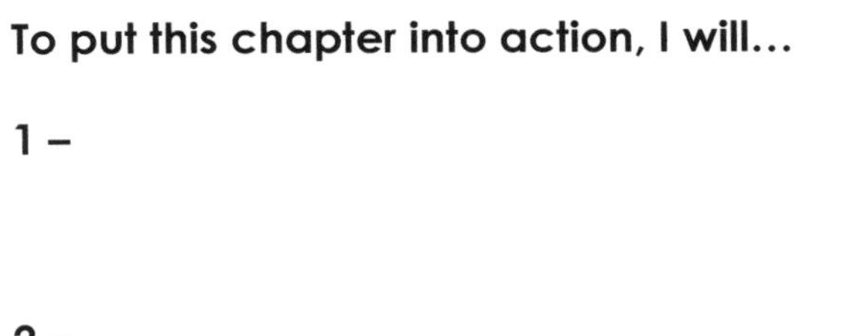

To put this chapter into action, I will...

1 –

2 –

3 –

Keep Learning!

- **See my free updates** to each chapter at www.sellmorebooks.org.
- **Publishers Weekly is a great place to keep up with the latest developments.**

Chapter 18

Sell Your Book in Brick and Mortar Stores (Not Just Bookstores!)

> *When A Time to Kill was published twenty years ago, I soon learned the painful lesson that selling books was far more difficult than writing them. I bought a thousand copies and had trouble giving them away. I hauled them in the trunk of my car and peddled them at libraries, garden clubs, grocery stores, coffee shops, and a handful of bookstores. Often, I was assisted by my dear friend Bobby Moak.*
>
> - bestselling author John Grisham, who's sold over 250 million books,
>
> from the dedication in his book, *Ford County*

David Cady sells hundreds of copies of his self-published first novel, *The Handler*, in places where other authors don't think of selling their books. It requires very little effort on his part – no daily blogging, writing articles, or competing for radio time. He simply drops by occasionally to ask the local restaurant manager if he's low on copies. The manager pays David his part of the profits, gladly taking another stack of books to sell at the cash register.

I believe that selling books through stores that don't primarily sell books is one of the most overlooked, underrated strategies. Yet, with the demise of large bookstores, smart publishers are rethinking their strategy. Some authors sell tens of thousands of books in places where there's hardly any competition at all. It may not work for every book, but I'm convinced that many authors could read this chapter, apply what it says, and sell thousands of copies of their books without doing any other form of marketing. Here's how:

1. Sell through Non-Bookstores.

To help break you out of the bookstore paradigm, let's look at book sales through the eyes of a book buyer I know rather intimately – my wife.

Cherie has a book addiction. To feed it, she acquires at least one new book a week – typically a novel, biography, or memoir. She reads a bit before bedtime each weeknight, but by Friday evening an uncontrollable urge drives her to binge read, often downing chapter after chapter until she finishes an entire novel before sunrise.

Feeding this addiction demands a constant inflow of books. Yet, she's not committed to any one supplier. Her fixes range from *Paperback Swap* to bookstores to resale stores to library sales to grocery stores. If she finds herself on a Friday without a fix, she's liable to purchase any bound pages in her path. If the cover looks interesting and the first page reads well, she's hooked.

I suppose Cherie's book-buying habits resemble those of many avid readers. Sometimes we diligently study reviews to find the most respected books in a field. But other times we purchase on impulse. Our impulse purchases put book-buying in a very different category from large purchases like automobiles, where we often must be exposed multiple times to a product, study *Consumer Reports*, and do extensive test drives. Thus, selling books by the cash register is less like a car purchase than a chewing gum purchase. A child spots gum at the checkout counter, tugs at mommy's pants and points to the rack. The only significant difference between the child's gum purchase and Cherie's book purchase is that Cherie's impulse isn't checked by an intermediary. She controls her own pocketbook.

And here's the big point that most authors don't seem to understand: **it doesn't really matter whether the cash register is in a bookstore, clothing store, or restaurant. In fact, being outside of a bookstore has a distinct advantage: there's less competition.**

So let's look at a few examples of people who successfully sell their books in non-bookstore venues.

David Cady

David is a former schoolteacher who's enjoying writing during his retirement. He sold about 200 copies of The Handler – a gripping novel about a detective trying to locate and rescue a lady from a snake-handling cult – in a single restaurant during the first six months of publication, and it's still selling there. He sells many copies through other locations as well, but let's focus on the restaurant. Here are some observations:

1) The restaurant is locally owned and operated. Not being a chain, the owner can make a quick decision without getting permission from the corporate office.

2) He designed his own cover, which by his own admission doesn't look professional. He wants to redo it, but in the meantime plenty of people keep buying.

3) He did some accompanying publicity. His local newspaper wrote an article about the book and he has had two signings at his local library. These probably enhanced local awareness about his book. I'd suspect that an article in a local paper about a local author in a small community (30,000 in the city, 80,000 in the county) could have more impact than a larger paper, since members of small communities tend to read their papers religiously to keep up with local events, deaths, etc.

4) He offers the book on consignment. The manager pays him for the books only if they sell – so that there's no risk on the manager's part and low risk on the author's part. Compare this to a large bookstore chain ordering 4,000 copies of your book. If they don't sell, you or your publisher are stuck with 4,000 returned copies, some of which are damaged.

5) They sell at the cash register. This sets up a unique selling opportunity. As people wait in line to pay, they nervously fidget with nothing to do. Someone picks up the book and starts leafing through. Someone behind her says, "I've read that book. It's great!" She purchases it.

6) His book is the only book for sale. David isn't competing with Sue Grafton on one side and John Grisham on the other. If a book addict finds herself in line and suddenly realizes to her horror that she needs her Friday fix, she finds one book sitting in front of her.

7) This would seem to be the ideal situation for an impulse purchase. Her credit card is out and she has only enough time to browse the cover and first page before making a decision. Otherwise she holds up the line.

8) This will probably work better from some genres than others. I think a novel of local interest would be ideal. Niche books like *Theoretical Physics for Fifth Graders* or *The Care and Feeding of Domesticated Weasels* wouldn't have a broad enough appeal for the restaurant crowd. Consider niche stores for niche books.

If it Works, Take it to a Larger Scale

David later offered free copies to gift stores near Chattanooga, Tennessee, in a touristy area (Rock City, Ruby Falls, etc.), close to his novel's Tennessee River setting. He told them about the book's success in his hometown restaurant and suggested a sales pitch they could use. "Keep all your profit from this first batch," David told them. "If you sell them all, I'll replenish your supply and we can split the profit from the next batches." Again, copies began selling. After all, tourists like to read books about the local area that they may not be able to get elsewhere.[1]

Here's how I advised David to take his sales to the next level:

> *Map out each nearby town along the Tennessee River. During the week, call the local Chamber of Commerce for each town to find out which locally owned restaurants and shops attract the greatest crowds. Convince your dear wife how much fun it would be to eat at a different, highly recommended restaurant each Saturday for lunch, followed by a leisurely, romantic stroll through a quaint community, browsing in interesting shops as you go. Give the restaurant manager your sales pitch about how much money your local restaurant made off the sale of your book. Drop off copies and offer your display, if they need it.*
>
> *If 30 restaurants and gift stores could sell 300 copies a year, you'd be selling 9,000 per year. Get 100 stores on board and you might sell 30,000 per year.*

But alas, David is more interested in hanging out with his grandkids and writing new books for the series than carrying the sales of his first book to a new level. Besides, he made a great contact with a Hollywood film company that has committed to produce a movie based on his book. They plan to begin filming on location this year.

Dr. Robert McGinnis

Dr. McGinnis self-published his non-fiction book, *In Search of Paradise*, as well as a series of *Paradise* novels for young people. When I told him the David Cady story, he responded,

> "I too have used the book sales next to the cash register idea and it worked well for me. I even purchased a rack for the books, which allows me to display more. I average about $100 per month from sales from a small deli. Not only were we both happy, but I didn't complain about the occasional free meals that were given to me as a bonus. I was given a special outside table, where on good days I could sit with customers and talk about my books. Another restaurant has placed a large picture of one of my better covers on their wall behind the cash register."

Besides restaurants, Dr. McGinnis has copies in his dentist's office, a used car lot, and a clothing store.[2]

To Learn More about This

Dr. McGinnis and I often exchange ideas with other authors at the John Kremer's *Book Marketing Network* at http://thebookmarketingnetwork.com. Find us in the forum area, where we often contribute to the popular discussions:

- "What's your biggest challenge with your book?"
- "What's working for you?"

Shops beyond Restaurants

For a general interest book, brainstorm places where a variety of people congregate. As we've said, "Go where people are already gathered." Some authors sell copies at grocery stores, gas stations, and beauty shops – anywhere lots of people go and either linger in a waiting area or pay at a cash register.

I noticed a local Soho Hero (offers services to small businesses such as printing, Fed Ex mailing, etc.) selling a local author's children's books on a low shelf. The manager told me that they sell quite well. A parent makes copies or mails a package while her bored child spots a colorful book and begins reading. By the time mom's ready to leave, the child is only halfway through, dying to know how the story ends. What parent can resist buying a book for her child?

After seeing the Soho Hero success, I theorized that my money book might sell well in stores that sell new and used video games. My reasoning? "Soho Hero is a place where children have to wait on their parents. I need to find a place where parents have to wait on their teens. Young people drag their parents into video game stores, browsing through the games and even trying a few out while their parents fidget like the children at Soho Hero. It worked. A locally owned video game exchange store sold it from the counter. According to the manager, "You have to hand sell it. I tell the customers how much I respect what you're doing with your kids and they get interested." Thus, coach the sales people a bit and encourage them to read the book so that they become fans.

For niche books, think of niche shops – a local health club for your weight loss book, the unemployment office for your career book, the school supply store for your home school book.

Overcoming the Shyness Factor

At first, I was reluctant to ask managers if they'd like to carry my book. Sometimes I'd circle the block before working up the guts to walk into the store. To my delight, I found owners looking for alternative streams of income. Offering my book on a consignment basis gave them a no-risk opportunity to try out a new product. I wasn't bugging them; I was doing them a favor.

I typically offer them a free copy to look over, asking them to feel no pressure to take it. I want them to sell it only if they're sold on it. If it doesn't sell well in their store, I ask them for their evaluation as to why it didn't sell and thank them for trying. This is a no pressure selling technique that I'm very comfortable with.

You'll find a number of authors in the e-book *John Kremer's Self Publishing Hall of Fame* who've had great success selling locally, including a job hunting and career writer who sells his books in dry cleaners – where job hunters get their suits pressed for interviews.[3] Others sell their books in beauty parlors, barber shops, and hotels. Christopher Wright and his wife sold 5,000 copies of his children's books in the first month and a half through gas stations, restaurants, gift shops, and hotels. They would go on to sell over one million copies of their *Michigan Chillers* and *American Chillers* series. (He writes under two pseudonyms: Johnathan Rand and Christopher Knight.)[4]

Inexpensive, Attractive Book Displays

If stores need something to display your book on their counter, consider the white cardboard counter displays (mine was 8 5/8" wide to fit my book) from http://www.meridiandisplay.com at $4.34 each for a box of 25 or $3.65 each for 50.

The Vast, Untapped Potential of Local Sales

- 18,000 people live in my town of Acworth.
- 700,000 live in my county (Cobb), which is a part of metro Atlanta.
- 5.5 million live in metro Atlanta.

How many thousands of restaurants, beauty salons, and hotels operate within an hour of my house? Even if I just targeted my county, since my current caretaking responsibilities restrict my traveling, keep in mind that local folks are wired to the world. Remember the Christopher Paolini story? After he spoke in a school about his novel, *Eragon*, someone recommended him as a speaker on a teachers' forum, resulting in scads of invitations to speak. Now he's selling millions of books.

With all the hype about "the long tail of the Web" and connecting with our niche markets globally, it's easy to conclude that the key to marketing is to focus on those global niches that gather online. Yet, we forget that local folks in our neighborhoods and cities are wired to these global niches. Let's call this phenomenon "the long arms of net-savvy neighbors." The local high school student who hears me speak, buys my book, and talks it up on *World of Warcraft* or a readers' forum could easily take my message global. An article about me in the local paper will be published on their website, with the potential of being picked up by larger papers or key influencers scouring the Web for information on their favorite topis.

Why Some Authors and Small Publishers Don't Target Bookstores

1. You risk losing money on returns. So you convince *Books a Million* to order 2,000 copies for their stores. They sell 50 copies over three months and ship the remaining 1,950 copies to you. Some of them are damaged. Now you're out the cost of the printing and must store or sell all those books.

2. You may lose money on other sales. If you publish through Lightning Source, you'd need to set your discount at 55 percent to make it attractive to bookstores. But this would make your profit per book on Amazon sales far less than if you had chosen the 20 percent discount.

3. It's typically difficult and discouraging for small-time authors to get their books into bookstores and keep them there.

4. There are plenty of great places to sell books besides bookstores.

You can see why self publishing guru Dan Poynter has famously stated, "Bookstores are lousy places to sell books."

Expectations for Local Sales

Your book may or may not sell well in any given store. It really depends on the type of book, how the store displays it, and how the sales people push it.[5] You may have to get it into scores of stores before you find which ones work for you. If it doesn't sell at all after a few months in one store, thank the store owner profusely for trying and take it to another store. But remember, just by having your book on display, you got free advertising that increased local awareness. Some customers may have seen your book in a store, thought about it later, and ordered from Amazon. Others didn't have an immediate need, but later wanted a book on your subject and picked it up at a local bookstore.

Approaching Non-Bookstore Chains

It typically makes sense to start with locally owned stores and get a good track record with sales before pitching your book to a larger chain. Although you might have to go through more hoops with big chain stores, many of them will consider your offer. Even Wal-Mart has a way for local managers to purchase local products they wish to sell in their stores: their "Local Purchase Program."

Kathleen Antrim self published her first book, a political thriller entitled *Capital Offense*. She sent a copy to the book buyer at Costco who loved it and put in a large order. Kathleen in turn did a book tour of 15 northern California Costco stores. It was eventually picked up by a traditional publisher and became a best-seller.[6]

2. Sell through Bookstores

I've already discussed the slim odds of both getting your book into bookstores and keeping it there long-term. The only guaranteed winners are books by established, best-selling authors.

- Their books will almost certainly land some big-time early reviews.
- Their publishers will pay for priority placement in bookstores.
- Their publishers will pay big marketing bucks to drive customers into the stores to make purchases.

But some small-time authors beat the odds. Here are some tips:

a. Consider writing books that have backlist potential.

Contrary to popular belief, bookstores don't make the bulk of their profits off their new books by top-selling authors. Rather, they profit from their backlist – books published years ago that keep on selling year after year.

Marc McCutcheon subscribes to *Publishers Weekly* to discover what types of books are selling well and what holes exist that need to be filled. He studies reference books like *The Encyclopedia of Associations* to find out how many people belong to environmental associations, boating associations, gaming associations, etc. These people buy books about their passion. In his book, *Damn! Why Didn't I Write That?* he shares a strategy that allows him to make a good living writing nonfiction full-time – getting accepted by publishers, getting his books into bookstores, and keeping them in bookstores long term.

b. Publish your book for optimum bookstore receptivity. Major publishers are often better received than small, independent publishers. Self-publishers should set up their own publishing company to appear more professional. Subsidy publishers should avoid having the subsidy publisher's name on the book. It should appear professionally designed, professionally edited, professionally laid out. It should contain all the proper numbers (ISBN, etc.) and sell at a competitive price.

c. Make it available through the distributors/wholesalers that bookstores order from. Mainstream bookstores tend to order from one or both of the major wholesalers: Baker & Taylor and/or Ingram. Christian bookstores typically order from wholesalers like Spring Arbor. Bookstore managers don't have time to order through each publisher or author.

d. Offer it to bookstores at an attractive discount. If you publish through Lightning Source, you can choose your discount. Bookstores prefer to order through wholesalers at the standard 55 percent discount.

e. Make it available with a return policy. If you publish through CreateSpace, you can pay to have your book available through Baker & Taylor with a return policy. This is the way bookstores do business. If they stock a book that doesn't sell, they can return it to the publisher for a refund. If you encourage bookstores to order your book, but they look it up to discover that it doesn't have a return policy, why would they stock it when they have plenty of great books they can order that do have return policies?

f. Drive people into bookstores with your publicity. When Robert Kiyosaki published *Rich Dad, Poor Dad*, it wasn't available in bookstores. To get it there, he did extensive radio reviews and told people to buy it in their local bookstores. When enough people showed up asking for it, bookstores started ordering. Kiyosaki would eventually sell millions of copies.

g. When you set up publicity, let the local bookstores know. If you're speaking to a writers' group or at a conference, let local media know about it. Then, let the bookstores know so that they can order copies. Offer to sign the copies so that they're more sellable and less likely to be returned.

h. Remind bookstores to reorder. Typically, only best-selling authors are on automatic re-order. Local author Ray Atkins has sold hundreds of books through his local mega-bookstore, but he still has to remind them to reorder every time they run out of copies.

i. Target independent bookstores. Managers in chain bookstores tend to have little say-so concerning what titles they keep in stock. It's all done through the corporate office. Independent bookstores can do whatever they dang well please. Talk to managers, giving your elevator speech about not only how good a book it is, but why you believe it will sell. If they don't take your bait on the first cast, offer them copies on consignment. After all, that's the way bookstores do business.

j. If your book does well in one or more stores, get testimonies from the owners and use them to get your book into more stores. Think like a bookstore owner. If the owner of the bookstore in the next town is getting rich off your book, wouldn't you want in on the action?

Do Something!

To put this chapter into action, I will...

1 –

2 –

3 –

Keep Learning!

- **See my free updates** to each chapter at www.sellmorebooks.org.
- **Read *John Kremer's Self Publishing Hall of Fame*,** the longer e-book version on his website.
- **Read *How to Make Real Money Selling Books,* by Brian Jud.**
- **Read this helpful blog post on local sales:** http://www.selfpublishingreview.com/blog/2010/04/16/10-ways-to-promote-your-book-in-your-own-backyard.

Chapter 19

Help Reporters and Journalists with their Articles

Last month, a major hailstorm hit our neighborhood. Within a few days, a roofer appeared at my door, asking if he could do a free inspection for hail damage. Since he's not local, I assume he watches the weather to discover where storms hit – the most likely locations for people to need his services.

That's a great strategy for roofers. It's also a great strategy for book marketers.

- What if we could know where news is breaking about our subject matter, giving us the opportunity to offer our expertise to local reporters? Today, we can find breaking news on our niche topics by setting up Google Alerts.
- What if, rather than pitching our ideas to editors who may or may not be currently interested in our subject, journalists could let us know when they need our expertise for writing an article? Today, journalists ask for expert contributions to their articles through several services.

Here are two easy, no-cost strategies that low profile authors can use to get publicity.

Strategy #1: Set up appropriate Google Alerts.

Rather than try to create news, find out where your topic is already newsy and offer your services. With Google Alerts, you can catch news as it's breaking, giving you many varied opportunities to publicize your book.

How Can Authors Use Google Alerts to Sell Books?

- **Contact media in the location of the event to offer your expertise.** You wrote a hiking book that has a chapter on protecting yourself from wild animal attacks. So you set up Google Alerts for "Animal attack," "Bear Attack," "Grizzly Attack," etc. When the *Atlanta Journal* reports a black bear roaming in a Cobb County neighborhood (yes, it occasionally happens), you contact area newspapers and radio stations to offer your expertise on protecting yourself from black bears, referring to yourself as "author of…."

- **Send out a news release,** connecting news to your book. If I get an alert that a newly released study finds teens financially illiterate, I can send out a press release noting the study and showing how my book promotes financial literacy.

- **Discover a person or an agency that could use your book.** You wrote a book to help teens resist drugs. You receive an alert of a new state anti-drug task force, so you e-mail the leaders, offering your book as a useful resource.

- **Post a response to a relevant blog post,** with your signature – including your book title and a link to your Amazon page or press kit.

- **Discover where grants are starting new initiatives.** You set up an alert to receive news about obesity. You receive an alert that San Diego State University received a $400,000 grant to study and combat childhood obesity. Since you wrote a memoir on your struggle to overcome childhood obesity, you offer to speak to area groups and send a free copy for review. They may wish to purchase and distribute $20,000 worth of your books.

How to Set Up Google Alerts

1. Brainstorm a list of terms you'd like to be alerted for. Put several phrases into Google's Keywords Tool (search the phrase: "Google keywords tool") to find more key words and phrases. A travel writer could start with terms such as "travel" or "tourism."

2. Start your Google Alerts on the set-up page: http://www.google.com/alerts.

- **Type in a search term.**

- **Choose a type** (news, blogs, discussions, video, everything). I choose "everything."

- Alerts will come via e-mail. **Choose how often you want the alerts to come** (as it happens, once a day, once a week). I like them to come "as it happens," since an early alert might give me the opportunity to have the first response after an important blog post.

- **Choose e-mail length** (up to 20 results, up to 50 results). I allow up to 50.
- **Type in your e-mail address.**

If you prefer, you can have alerts delivered to your RSS (really simple syndication) feed:

http://www.google.com/support/alerts/bin/static.py?page=guide.cs&guide=28413&topic=28417

Strategy #2: Receive Requests from Reporters Wanting Help with Their Articles

A freelance writer in New York City was writing an article on teens and money for the popular Microsoft Network (MSN). She needed some real life stories, so I told her about how one of our boys was handling his career and finances in a unique way. She called for more information and wrote the article, including a link to my character education site.

A few months later, I started receiving more than my normal e-mail concerning my character site. I checked my analytics to discover that the number of unique daily visitors had increased from less than 1,000 to about 10,000! The article had just appeared on MSN, sending a swarm of visitors to my site. As Murphy's Law would have it, *Enjoy Your Money* had not yet come off the press, but it served as early publicity and the article stayed up with the link to my site.

How did that writer find me? She posted a request on ProfNet, which e-mails a list of reporters' needs several times a day. Blythe Daniel, my literary agent and Colorado publicist, saw her request and forwarded it to me for a response. It's really that simple.

You may not think of yourself as an expert, but having written a book on a subject, many will look at you as an expert. And often, reporters are looking more for real life stories that all of us have – like a story about someone who trained their dog to gnaw on raw hide bones rather than antique furniture. As HARO's (Help a Reporter Out) logo states: "Everyone's An Expert at Something."

Choose One or More Services

Here are the three services I'm aware of:

HARO – http://www.helpareporter.com. This is a free service that Cherie and I often use.

Bill and Steve Harrison's Reporter Connection – http://www.reporterconnection.com – A newer free service, much like HARO. I'm using this as well.

Profnet – https://profnet.prnewswire.com – Profnet was established long before HARO or the Reporter Connection. Although it's a paid service, your publisher or publicist may have an account so that they can send you requests as they come.

Tips on Responding to Reporters

- Don't just volunteer to help and leave an e-mail address. **Actually tell them, briefly, a well-worded answer to their question and offer to give them more detail if needed.** Provide a phone number as well as an e-mail address.
- **Provide a brief bio, mentioning that you are "author of...," linking to your press page.**
- **Set up a Google Alert for your name and the name of your book, so that if a reporter uses your input but forgets to let you know about it, you may be alerted to it.** When the article goes live, always link to it from your press page to continue building your platform. If your book gets a mention in the *Wall Street Journal*, you can forever pitch your book "as mentioned in the *Wall Street Journal*."

What to Expect

Cherie responds more than I do, estimating that she finds a request that matches her about once a week. A reporter actually uses her information about one time out of ten. So don't despair if you respond over and over and get no response. Remember, many people are responding and the reporter can't use everyone's input.

We're encouraged by our results and plan to keep responding to these requests. Besides the MSN interview, over the past year Cherie's been covered by an Associated Press writer, the *Wall Street Journal*, the *Baltimore Sun*, the *Atlanta Journal/Constitution*, *CBS*, the *Chicago Tribune*, the *Fayetteville* (North Carolina) *Observer*, *MSNBC*, *Redbook Magazine*, *St. Louis Today*, etc. *The Today Show* even asked if they could send a camera crew to interview our children. (Our children weren't interested.)

Just remember, publicity often acts more like serendipitous magic than a predictable machine. You might respond for a year or two and get mediocre results; but then, when you least expect it, you make that special contact that can result in a media frenzy and thousands of sales. Many of Cherie's media opportunities came from one response that was picked up by other media sources.

Obviously, some topics come up more regularly than others. Whereas journalists regularly request input on personal relationships, business, and personal finance, they need information on very niche topics (e.g., restoring antique cars) less often.

Benefits to this Approach to Marketing Books

- **It's not very time consuming.** Contrast it with some publicists' recommendation to start your own column in a local paper, so that it might one day be syndicated and give you lots of exposure for your books. Although this may work for some, the odds of succeeding are slim and it's very time consuming. Responding to journalists is pretty quick and easy. Just scan the topics at the beginning of each e-mail to see if anything's relevant and e-mail a few choice ideas.

- **It results in experts mentioning your book.** If you write your own articles, you're pitching your own book. People tend to be more persuaded by others mentioning your book.

- **You know precisely what they're looking for,** as opposed to pitching ideas that you hope editors might be interested in.

- **You don't have to be pushy or obnoxious.** You're *helping* reporters, not badgering them. We're not poor authors scrounging around for a benevolent reporter who might do us a favor by including our books in her articles. Instead, we're the benevolent experts who go out of our way to help reporters with their articles. Sure, we need them, and they know that. But also they need us. Otherwise, they wouldn't have signed up for the service.

- **We're going to where people already gather, rather than trying to gather people around us.**

Do Something!

To put this chapter into action, I will...

1 –

2 –

3 –

Keep Learning!

- **See my free updates** to each chapter at www.sellmorebooks.org.

Chapter 20

Consider Radio (Even if You're Shy!)

So what's a chapter on radio doing in a book for shy, low profile authors?

1) Shyness in personal relationships doesn't necessarily translate into ineptness and fear in the media. Johnny Carson successfully hosted "The Tonight Show" for 30 years, earning him the title, "The King of Late Night." Incredibly, for every one of those 30 years, he led the ratings for his spot – nobody could compete with him. Among his many accomplishments were six Emmy Awards, a Peabody Award, and an induction into the Television Academy Hall of Fame.

He appeared so comfortable on camera that you'd assume he'd be comfortable in any social situation – the life of every party. Yet, Donald Trump described Carson as so socially shy that it was painful to watch him try to deal with his adoring fans.[1] Talk show host Dick Cavett, a contemporary of Carson, said, "I felt sorry for Johnny in that he was so socially uncomfortable. I've hardly ever met anybody who has as hard a time as he did."[2]

So if you're incredibly shy and socially uncomfortable, consider applying for a late night TV spot!

2) Many authors credit radio with large numbers of sales. Many best-selling authors, from Jack Canfield and Mark Victor Hansen (*Chicken Soup for the Soul*), to Scott Peck (*The Road Less Traveled*), to Robert Kiyosaki (*Rich Dad Poor Dad*) all credit radio with much of their success.[3]

Radio is a proven medium that's certainly worth a try, even if your first inclination is to run screaming in the opposite direction.

3) Radio personalities interview low profile authors all the time. Sure, they'd love to interview the President of the United States. But their main concerns are that you can help their listening audiences and handle yourself on radio, which is easy to prove to them by getting some small-time radio interviews (where hardly anyone is listening) under your belt, getting testimonies from the interviewers, and linking to the interviews from your press pae.

Why Aren't I Pushing Television?

Many authors seem to think that if they can only get on Oprah, their marketing concerns will all be behind them. Yet, I know of authors who've been on Oprah and seen no sales at all. After all, you might be only one of many guests in the episode who get their two minutes of fame. Don't get me wrong; I'm not against TV. I've done TV and will continue to do TV to get the word out about my book. But it's not a high priority for me. Here are my reasons:

1) It's pretty intimidating. You may be the next Johnny Carson, but to most of us, it's more unnerving than radio. Besides thinking about what to say, I'm thinking of where I'm looking (camera or interviewer?), whether or not I'm slouching in my chair, appropriate body language, etc. With radio, I can be in my pajamas, displaying hair art from a fitful night's sleep, with notes scattered in front of me to help me out with difficult questions.

2) I have to be on location. I can do a California radio interview from my home phone in Georgia. To be on California TV, I typically need to fly out there. That's a lot of time and money.

3) It's very competitive to get on the big shows. Same with radio, but it's still a factor.

4) I'm typically seeing meager results from many authors. I don't have a large enough sampling to make a strong point here, but many authors are telling me that their sales from TV spots are surprisingly disappointing. Sure, some authors get on national TV and sell tons of books as a result, but I think they're the exceptions. I was on two of the largest Atlanta stations during graduation season (*Enjoy Your Money* makes a nice graduation gift). Both interviews went great. The hosts pushed my book and held it up for the audiences to see. But as far as I could tell (it was only available through Amazon at the time and I could track daily sales), nobody (zip, zero, zilch) bought a book as a result.

Perhaps avid TV viewers aren't avid readers. As some say, "Viewers view; readers read." Yet voracious readers are still likely to listen to the radio on the way to work. But here's another explanation. Perhaps there's not actually much difference in response between TV and radio interviews; but radio can be used on a much larger scale. It's not practical to do a TV show every week or every day (travel, expense, bookings, etc.). But many successful authors have done radio on such a scale. While many of their radio interviews may result in no sales, if they do 200 of them, the magic kicks in, word of mouth takes over, and voila! Books start selling by the truckloads.

So I still do TV interviews. They build awareness. They also leave me with professional videos I can put up on YouTube. I can link to the interviews from my media kit, showing other media that I can come across well. The shows link to me from their popular sites, helping my site in search-engine rankings. If I do enough small shows, I may land a big-time show and get national exposure, which is much more likely to sell books. But for the above reasons, I don't pursue TV as the ultimate publicity.

Is Radio for You?

Admittedly, radio's not for everyone and it certainly works better for some books than others. It may not work for you if:

- **You've written a geographically niche book.** If you wrote "Where to Catch Fish in Panama City," try for some local stations near Panama City, but don't pitch Chicago radio.
- **You've tried small local stations, but froze up every time,** like Richard Dreyfuss in "What About Bob?" (Tip: Don't watch this painful scene before you go on the air.)

Some shy folks can shine on radio, perhaps because they're not visible to the audience. Maybe it's akin to the phenomenon of people who are extremely comfortable instant messaging, texting their friends, and communicating on Facebook, but freeze up face-to-face.

Rather than provide a course on radio interviews, let's learn from a low profile author who started from scratch and is succeeding with radio. At the end, I'll give a few tips and recommend further resources.

Danny Kofke Pursues Radio and Sells Lots of Books

Danny doesn't have a big platform, nor does he have a lot of time. He teaches full time in a public elementary school (special education) and is raising two young children. Yet he's selling far more books than your typical author, largely through his own publicity efforts. I mentioned his simple, yet functional blog/press page/author page in chapter 9. Examine it (http://dannykofke.blogspot.com) and you'll find links to interview after interview. And it's not a brand new book. It's been out over two years and his media exposure keeps growing. The book's called How to Survive (And Perhaps Thrive) on a Teacher's Salary.

How did a low profile author from Hoschton, Georgia (population 1,070), land over 150 radio interviews (and counting)? Here are the tips I gleaned from several interviews with him. (Note: he started with radio but now gets TV and print coverage as well.)

JSM: Danny, I'm so impressed with your passion for marketing. Can you give other low profile authors some tips?

DK: Sure! **First of all, I'm having a blast marketing my book.** It's not a chore; it's fun! I've been at it for over two years and I still get a charge out of doing radio, TV, and other media. I still fondly recall the excitement of doing my first radio interview.

Second, authors need to face a sober fact: It takes time and effort to sell books. They don't sell themselves.

JSM: Do you avoid the smaller stations?

DK: No. You never know what might pay off. I did an interview with *Bank Rate* that got picked up by the FOX site. Another interview went secondarily to AOL's home page. My point? Just get out there and do something, even if it's small. Do something enough and cool things start to happen.

JSM: So give us your process. How do you find all these stations?

DK: In brief, I research viable media and send e-mails (pitches) to them.

- **I start with a Google search** for such topics as "radio stations about teachers," "financial radio shows," etc. Then, I find them on the web and study each show. If a show's all about, for example, recommending stocks to buy, I don't pursue it.
- **Next, I find the contact person on the site and e-mail a pitch.** It must be powerful. Remember, it's not about your book; it's about their audience. With the first paragraph, share a startling statistic or something to grab them, demonstrating that their audience would love to hear what you have to say. If you've gotten publicity before, link them to your media page so that they can read or (better) hear past interviews.

JSM: Do you follow-up when they don't respond, or just leave it in their hands?

DK: I've found follow-up to be very important. I'll pitch anyone and everyone; then I write on the calendar to e-mail back in a month or so if they haven't responded. If they don't respond to that, I may e-mail again several months later, saying something like, "Hey, I just spoke on this station and was mentioned in this article. If you'd like to interview me...." And I keep following up unless someone says they don't want to hear from me anymore. Getting back doesn't seem to annoy them. I suppose they're used to getting multiple pitches from the same people.

JSM: With as many contacts as you're making, I suppose you have to keep good records.

DK: Good record keeping is vital. I calendar items that I need to do at a later time. I keep records in a notebook of whom I've e-mailed, how they responded, and when I should touch base. If someone declines and wants no further pitches, I note that as well.

Example: I contacted the TV show "The 700 Club" early in my marketing. They declined to interview me. But recently I e-mailed again, telling them what other events I've done and linking them to my author site so that they can see my other interviews. This time, they booked me!

JSM: Does it get easier over time?

DK: For me, it's been a snowball effect. Once I get that first show, it's easier to get the next. And the media isn't interested exclusively in new books. Once you get one interview and put it on your media site, it's easier to leverage more reviews. Now the media has something to judge whether or not you're a fit for their program. The more interviews you get, the more impressive you look. It's called building a platform from scratch. You leverage one opportunity to land more and bigger opportunities.

I sent ten e-mails over time to CBS about getting on their early show, but to no avail. But I finally got on CNN. So I wrote CBS and said, "Hey, I was just on CNN." This time, they replied and asked to see the CNN interview. That's the way this industry works. If you've been on a station that they think is cool, they want you on *their* program.

A Typical Pitch E-mail from Danny

Hi,

I hope this note finds you well. According to a recent 2010 report by PayScale.com, elementary education is listed as the second worst paying college degree. I would like to know if I could be a guest on your program to show others that people can do well financially even if they don't make a large salary.

My name is Danny Kofke and I am currently a special education teacher in Georgia. I am an elementary education major and taught kindergarten and first grade before moving into special education. I have done something to show others how they can do well despite earning a modest income.

I have written the book "How To Survive (and perhaps thrive) On A Teacher's Salary." I've been a teacher for ten years and am proud to say that passion for the craft keeps me in the classroom but smart savings and a basic understanding of financial principles have kept my wife (willingly!) at home with our children. Many find it hard to believe that one teacher can support a family of four, but "How to Survive" explains the steps necessary for others to follow suit and save for life's journeys.

In my book I show others how to:

- Retire with a sizable nest egg
- Teach in a foreign country
- Own all of their possessions - including their cars and houses
- Invest in Roth IRAs and 403bs
- Establish a weekly budget
- Live a financially secure life on a modest salary!

I have been featured in a number of publications including USA Weekend, Bankrate.com, PARADE, Instructor Magazine, CBS MoneyWatch.com, FoxBusiness.com, AOL.com, The Atlanta Journal Constitution, Woman's Day, The Wall Street Journal, ABCNews.com, Yahoo Finance, Consumer's Digest, Bottom Line Personal, Your Family Today and The Huffington Post. I have also been interviewed on over 150 radio shows and on numerous television shows including The 700 Club, ABC News Now, FOX Business Channel's Varney & Company, HLN's The Clark Howard Show, Fox & Friends, CNN's Newsroom and MSNBC Live.

A lot of people think that figuring out financial matters and investing are difficult and are intimidated by it. I want to show others that if this 34 year-old schoolteacher can figure it out then they can too.

Once again, I would like to know if I can be a guest on your show.

> Please let me know what you think and if you need more information from me.
>
> Thank you in advance for your consideration.
>
> Sincerely,
>
> Danny Kofke
>
> How To Survive (and perhaps thrive) On A Teacher's Salary
>
> HYPERLINK "http://www.dannykofke.blogspot.com" www.danny-kofke.blogspot.com
>
> (Personal e-mail here)
>
> (Personal phone number here)
>
> HYPERLINK "http://www.tatepublishing.com/bookstore/search.php?search=kofke"http://www.tatepublishing.com/bookstore/search.php?search=kofke

JSM: Off topic, but I noticed you got a mention in the *Wall Street Journal*. How'd you wing that one?

DK: I responded to a HARO (Help a Reporter Out – see chapter 19) request.

JSM: Your media page seems central to your strategy. Tell us about it.

DK: It's not fancy but it gives the media exactly what they need, all there on one page where potential interviewers don't have to waste time searching for information. They can click sample interviews and see that I can handle myself well on interviews. It's also free and takes minimal time to maintain. It's consistent with what I teach in my book: Don't pay for things you don't need. It's also easily up-datable. You don't have to use complicated web design programs like DreamWeaver or ExpressionWeb. You don't have to hire a web-master. Blogspot gives you all the basic tools you need.

JSM: Is this the bulk of what you're doing to promote your book? What about all the other thousands of promotional things you could be doing?

DK: With a full time job and a family, I don't have time to do everything. I'm certainly open to other opportunities. I'm exploring doing presentations to school faculty, but so far this works for me. I enjoy it and it's getting results. Why replace something that's working so well with posting daily blogs?

JSM: Many authors probably contact a few stations, get no reply, and give up. What kind or response should we expect? Out of the 20 first contacts that you made, how many ended up actually booking you?

DK: I'd guess that four or five replied and maybe two booked me.

JSM: How many respond now that you've been in major media?

DK: Producers want to see how you can fit into their show and help their listeners/viewers out. It is not about you or your book most of the time – it is about your message. Since I have been on numerous TV and radio shows, producers can take a look at these samples and judge whether I would be a good fit for them. They no longer have to guess what I would sound/look like since they can see first-hand. **I would say I now get about eight responses out of 20 pitches.**

JSM – Do you spend 90 percent of your marketing time pursuing radio?

DK: No, I would say about 60 percent radio, 30 percent television, and the rest various print outlets. At first, before I had any television exposure, I mainly pursued radio. But now, since I have had exposure in all three areas, I pitch appropriate people in all of these areas.

JSM: How many pitches (new and follow-up) do you average each week?

DK: I would estimate 100 or so. Some weeks more, some weeks less.

JSM: How much time do you think you average marketing your book each week?

DK: It is an endless job since there are so many ways to market. I have to balance being a good husband, father, teacher, and marketer. I have to limit myself since I could probably work on marketing ten hours a day! I **would say I spend an average of 15 to 20 hours a week working on book stuff.**

JSM: Many of us aren't very sure of ourselves. Tell us about your feelings on your first interview and how you'd advise authors to deal with the nervousness factor.

DK: I still remember it like yesterday. **I was very nervous and was afraid that I would sound nervous and not be able to get my points across in a way that would help the listeners. But I knew my subject matter, which gave me some confidence. At the same time, I was really excited.** I'd never been interviewed on radio before. It was so cool to think that someone wanted me on his show!

JSM: I personally cringe at the sound of my voice on radio. Did you initially like hearing your voice?

DK: No! Even now, I still don't like how I sound on radio. I guess I will always be my harshest critic.

JSM: Anything else that might encourage shy authors who think they could never do radio?

DK: Radio is a great way to get your point across in a non-threatening way. You can do interviews in the comfort of your own home and go into the room where you feel most at ease. Another thing to think about to ease your discomfort is to think about your message and how important you feel it is. I think that I have some powerful advice I can provide to others and, if I get nervous and am not able to get this advice out, I feel I am actually being selfish and preventing people from bettering themselves.

In addition, radio is great practice for larger platforms. After doing radio interviews for a couple of years I have now been on national television a number of times. Since I had time to practice delivering my knowledge on radio many times I did not feel nervous when I was delivering it to a much larger audience.

JSM: Thanks, Danny, for being so generous with us! That's great information!

More Tips for Radio Interviews

Preparation

1. Have suggested questions, with your answers, available from your online press page. This makes it easier on interviewers and helps them know what you're comfortable talking about.

2. Over-prepare ahead of time, then just enjoy the interview. This was suggested to me by the award-winning, long-time radio personality Rhubarb Jones, who now teaches mass media at Kennesaw State University. I'm self-conscious about my memory, which can fail me at the most inopportune moments. So I needed someone to tell me, "Stop rehearsing things in your mind and just go with the flow of the interview."

3. Write down questions you think you might be asked and practice answering them.

4. Have a friend ask the questions and practice answering. (That's harder for me than actual radio! Maybe it's the face-to-face thing.)

5. Record yourself answering questions and listen to them, critiquing them. (Warning: This can be painful as Danny and I both hate our own recorded voices!) If you notice a lot of annoying filler words like "uh," eliminate them.

6. Practice speaking in sound bites. Write down pithy (condensed, interesting, forceful) sentences, interesting quotes, and short people stories that you could use in answering interviewers' questions. Ideally, try to answer in a few sentences, typically under 30 seconds. This keeps the interview conversational. Of course, stories and analogies may take longer. Condense stories down to their essence.

7. Prepare a summary response, in case the interviewer asks, "Is there anything else you'd like to say?" or "What's the most important thing you'd like us to remember?"

8. Use counter-intuitives. You're not interesting if you just repeat what everybody already knows.

9. Be energetic, but in a genuine way. Don't try to imitate big-time radio personalities. Be yourself.

During the Interview

1. Talk standing up. You'll tend to sound more lively and engaged.

2. Imagine that you're speaking to one person. While 5,000 people may be listening, they're not gathered in a stadium. They're typically listening by themselves in their kitchens and cars.

3. Have notes you may need in front of you (some use notecards), but try not to depend on them. People can typically tell when you're reading a response. Write the details of helpful statistics and studies to add authority to your opinions.

4. Have water handy in case your throat gets dry.

5. If the interviewer fails to mention your book, mention the title yourself, letting the audience know where they can purchase it.

After the Interview

1. E-mail the host, thanking him for the interview.

2. Tell him that you'd love to return some day. Suggest other topics you could discuss.

3. Ask if he'd mind writing a sentence or two that would help you land more interviews.

4. Post the blurb on your press page and link to the interview.

Confronting a Major Concern

"What if they ask a question that I don't know the answer to?"

Don't let the thought petrify you! You can offset some such questions by letting the interviewer know up front what you're most comfortable discussing. Here are a couple of responses if this happens:

"The Deflection Maneuver" – Do like politicians and change the subject back to something you're comfortable with. "You know, John, that's an interesting question, but I think the bigger issue your listeners need to consider is…."

"The Honest Abe Answer" – "You know, I could tell you what I think about that, but that's not really in my area of expertise." Some, like me, would respect you even more when you gave that response. A college philosophy professor once told us in class, "The older I get, the more comfortable I get with that little phrase, 'I don't know.'" I'm getting more comfortable with it as well. It's much better than giving a B.S. response that everyone recognizes as B.S.

Just do it!

Let's face it; we'll never be perfect at anything. So don't let your imperfections immobilize you. Start somewhere. Do something. Be daring. Be dangerous. Then learn as you go. Do you really want to one day admit to your grandkids, "After I wrote that book, I could have been on the radio, but I wimped out."?

Do Something!

To put this chapter into action, I will…

1 –

2 –

3 –

Keep Learning!

To Learn More about Radio Interviews

Highly recommended: Google "Tips for Radio Interviews" and similar search terms to find scores of tips. People are giving great, practical advice on the web concerning radio interviews. Learn all you can and consider making your own checklist. But don't get overwhelmed with all the advice!

To Find Radio Programs: (Since the following reference books are expensive, look first in your local library. Ask a good research librarian which resources she likes best.)

- **All In One Media Directory** – http://www.gebbieinc.com/aio.htm - more than 24,000 media listings.

- **Gale Directory of Publications and Broadcast Media –** http://www.gale.cengage.com/servlet/BrowseSeriesServlet?region=9&imprint=000&titleCode=DOP – Covers about 54,000 newspapers, magazines, journals, radio stations, television stations.

- **Bacon's Media Directories –** http://us.cision.com/products_services/bacons_media_directories_2010.asp – To find radio information – "Bacon's Radio/TV/Cable Directory contains detailed contact information on **every U.S. and Canadian broadcast outlet** – from all national and regional networks, to all broadcast and cable stations, network news bureaus, program syndicators, and news, talk, entertainment, and topical programs."

To Help Radio Programs Find You: Consider The RTIR Report (http://www.rtir.com/index.html)

After you've done a few small-time interviews, consider taking out an ad in the *Radio/Television Interview Report,* "a trade publication that goes to over 4,000 radio/TV producers across the United States and Canada." Your name will be listed with 100-150 other authors and spokespeople who are making themselves available to do free interviews. Best-selling author Robert Kiyosaki credits this publication with his initial success in promoting his book, *Rich Dad Poor Dad*.

Chapter 21

Consider Speaking (Even if You're Shy!)

The Power of Personal Presentations

Speakers have changed my life.

My sophomore year in high school I attended a ski retreat, primarily because a girl I liked was going. It wasn't a large group – perhaps 30 wiggly teens that also came to ski and socialize. But an evening devotional session changed the course of my life.

The guest speaker wasn't world-class. He didn't wow us with a multi-media presentation. He was decent at singing and playing acoustic guitar, but he was no Led Zeppelin. I suppose what most attracted me was that he was real. You could tell that he believed his message had changed his life and that if we took it to heart, our lives could change as well.

The impact of that message knocked me off the path of doing what everybody else was doing and going where everybody else was going. It landed me on the road less travelled. I no longer had to party and show off and live to please everyone else. I had a purpose in life that helped me to make wiser decisions and resist the lifestyle choices that many of my friends would regret and struggle with for decades.

The memory of that high school retreat, for me, still encapsulates the power of personal presentations. Such presentations continue to impact my life to this day.

With this background, you can see why I don't view speaking as a necessary evil – a bothersome necessity to sell my books. Rather, it's another way to share messages I'm passionate about, messages that could change the lives of others in the same ways that speakers have changed my life over the years.

The Media Revolutions Aren't Replacing Public Speaking

Even with all the revolutions in communication with e-books and blogs and YouTube, I don't see people's fascination with personal presentations diminishing. Next month I'll attend yet another social media conference to hear top thought leaders share their wisdom. These events are typically sold out every year. Isn't it thought-provoking that an event like this would attract anyone at all, since it targets technologically savvy people who could probably get the same information, free of charge, by reading the presenters' books and blog posts, and watching their latest presentations on YouTube?

Perhaps seminars save us time by distilling the essence of their wisdom into 45-minute talks. Perhaps it's the lure of meeting these people personally. Perhaps it's the opportunity to talk to participants about their experiences applying social media to their businesses and associations.

Whatever the practical benefits, there's simply something special about hearing someone in person. Maybe it's the difference between hearing a band on an iPod and hearing them live. There's a "live, in person" dynamic that's lost when spoken words sift through a medium.

That's why colleges will keep hiring professors, high schools will keep bringing in guest presenters, churches will keep hiring preachers, and hundreds of thousands of organizations will keep booking an endless array of guest speakers for their conferences and seminars.

As an author, you're perceived as an expert that event organizers love to book. If you're passionate about your message, why not share that passion in person?

The Shyness Factor

Echoing my chapter on radio, I justify including a chapter on public speaking in a book for shy authors on two grounds. First, some people who are shy and awkward in personal relationships are remarkably effective speaking in public. Second, many authors credit public speaking with strong book sales and high levels of fulfillment. I've already described how young Christopher Paolini used hundreds of school presentations to sell his first novel, *Eragon*. His success is just one example of many authors who successfully speak at seminars and sell their books at a table afterwards. It's a tried and true method that we simply can't ignore.

For many authors, speaking ends up taking precedence over writing, so that they find themselves not so much speaking to sell their books, as writing books to get more speaking engagements. Many authors certainly make more money with their speaking than their book sales. A plus for me is that it has led to interesting opportunities to speak in such fascinating locations as Slovakia, Austria, Holland, and Russia.

That's all to say, even if public speaking doesn't initially appeal to you, consider giving it a chance to grow on you. You just might fall in love with it.

Overcoming Hurdles

What keeps you from booking speaking events? Is it a legitimate roadblock, or just a typical hurdle that successful speakers overcome? Here are several obstacles to consider:

- **"Public speaking feels awkward and unnatural to me."**

One of my favorite communicators is Bruce Wilkinson, a world-class speaker and best-selling author. I attended his series of seminars on becoming an effective speaker and asked him between seminars, "Did public speaking come naturally to you or did it start off feeling awkward?" He replied, "Do you play guitar?" I told him that I did. He said, "Did it feel natural at first?" I told him that it felt terrible. It hurt my fingers and I couldn't imagine how guitarists could coax their fingers to push strings to a guitar neck in such insane positions. Wilkinson replied, "Well, I wasn't a natural at speaking. Much like learning a guitar, I had to practice until it began to feel natural."

- **"I'm so aware of my goof-ups and flaws."**

Remember, Danny Kofke and I both hate the sound of our recorded voices. Jack Welch, one of the greatest managers of the last century, is much in demand as a speaker, but struggles with a stutter. I think it's safe to say that if you're doing "how to" seminars, people want solutions to their problems. Give them those solutions in a sincere way and they'll overlook your stutters, accents, and awkward body language.

But concern about your shortcomings can be positive. Isn't that what motivates us to become more effective? Those who are unaware of their flaws or show no concern about them may be no better as a speaker after 100 presentations than they were with the first.

- **"I'm nothing like the great communicators I've heard."**

We don't have to be like them. People want sincere, real speakers with useful information. If you're passionate about your subject and come prepared, you'll probably do fine. The main thing is to keep learning and getting input on how you can improve.

- **"But it takes so much time to prepare to speak."**

True, but if you speak on the same or similar topics over and over, the preparation time drops dramatically.

Tips for Making the Most of Your Speaking

I could mention hundreds of tips. But listing them all would simply overwhelm most authors. Here are a few key suggestions for first-time speakers. At the end of the chapter, I'll mention further resources to keep you moving forward.

Constantly Improve Your Presentation

1. Ask the event organizer exactly what she wants you to accomplish and how former speakers have best met those goals. If you're speaking at a library, ask the librarian about characteristics of the best and worst library speakers she's heard. Each venue tends to develop its own culture, with some audiences wanting primarily question and answer, others wanting to leave with more content, still others wanting a formal presentation with PowerPoint.

2. Audiotape or videotape yourself speaking and make a list of things you could do to improve. In a graduate school public speaking course, the professor recorded my speech. I was amazed to see myself rocking back and forth from heel to toe. I would have never picked this up from a book on public speaking, but seeing myself in action, I easily saw an irritating quirk I needed to correct.

3. Read a couple of good books on public speaking. Start where you are, but don't stay where you are. Keep learning. The following are short, sweet, and powerful. (What's the deal about sevens?)

> Dr. Howard Hendricks, *Teaching to Change Lives: Seven Proven Ways to Make Your Teaching Come Alive.*
>
> Milton Gregory, *The Seven Laws of Teaching.* A classic that Bruce Wilkinson re-reads every year.
>
> Bruce Wilkinson, *The Seven Laws of the Learner: How to Teach Almost Anything to Practically Anyone.*

4. Talk to early arrivals and ask what they'd like to get out of the seminar. Some people attend to get very specific information that you may or may not cover. Once you know what they want, you can either address it in your session or tell them that they can contact you later to get the answers they need.

5. If appropriate, allow for questions and interaction. I spoke recently to a book club. Since they'd already read my book, I saw no need to repeat that content. Instead, I told them, "I'll give you a few interesting morsels about how and why I wrote the book and how it's been received by people; but since this is a discussion group, I don't want to hinder the discussion. Fire any questions at me that you'd like to ask and we'll have a fun discussion." They asked great questions the entire time and we had a splendid dialogue.

Conversely, if I do a 45-minute seminar on book marketing, participants generally want rapid-fire ideas for marketing their books. Extensive dialogue would take away from that. So let the nature of the meeting and subject guide you as to whether to major on discussion or lecture.

6. Always get feedback. The last page of my handout allows participants to write something they liked about the seminar, something I could do better next time, and another place they recommend I should speak. If my wife or kids are present, I always ask them for candid input.

Learn to Sell More Books During Speaking Engagements.

1. Make sure that your ultimate motive is to help the people in your seminar. Participants complain about seminar leaders who come across like they're primarily there to sell their books and take your money. Give them what they need. Give them more than they expected. If they like you and feel like you care about them, they're more likely to buy your books.

2. Give them something. When you give, people want to give back. It's a well-established part of human nature[4] as well as simply a nice thing to do.

Marguerita McManus, author of *Crazy, Shortcut Quilts*, has sold about 15,000 copies over the past couple of years. Many of them sold through quilting conferences, where she gives away small, quilted samples that she calls "QuiltyBits." According to Marguerita, "The gift absolutely astonishes the audience." The quilted samples aren't just for looks. They demonstrate unique design elements that she features in her book.

Marguerita says, "I made them for several reasons:

- I knew that the audience would not discard them (none of these women would EVER consider throwing away fabric) and even if they didn't like or want them, they were very likely to pass them on to someone else. This is very different from a brochure that gets tossed at the end of the conference.
- I really wanted that 'WOW' factor when the audience received them. The 'QuiltyBits' were way over the top of what's typically handed out in these presentations.
- The 'QuiltyBits' show the important techniques of our book much better than any speech could and it was important to us that the audience "gets it" with regard to how different our technique is.

- The shop owners could place their 'QuiltyBits' on their shop counters. As customers pick it up and ask about it, the owner can recommend the book that explains the technique. It works! It's the perfect opening to sell our book to the class and it works like a charm! We were able to give the audience, right then and there, with no work on their part, the tool to promote a sell-out class and sell the book."

(By the way, Marguerita says that both she and her daughter – her daughter is the primary presenter – are shy. But that doesn't seem to hinder their effectiveness.)

I've given away bookmarks with my book cover on the front and book information on the back. Cherie punches a hole through a top corner and attaches a bit of colored yarn that makes it look special. It's no "QuiltyBit" – more of a "YarnBit" on a bookmark, but it's something unique and free that shows we care.

What affordable giveaway could be useful to your audience and show that you care?

3. Ask if the conference sponsors will include the cost of a book for each participant in the registration fee.

4. Put a book into their hands to leaf through during the seminar. Explain that they can purchase it afterwards. If it's appropriate, refer to a couple of sections as you talk.

5. Sign your books beforehand so that you can spend more time talking.

6. Offer them at a discount so that people will feel better about you and be more likely to buy now. *Enjoy Your Money* sells for $15.99 on Amazon, plus shipping. I sell them for $10 each when I speak, approximately half of the total price of the Amazon purchase with shipping. You don't have to discount it that steeply. Experiment with what works for you.

7. Do your part to make sure the event is well publicized. For smaller events, organizers may not follow through with their good intentions. You may have to put up posters, talk to the local papers, try to get on local radio, etc.

8. If you're building a contact/e-mail list (many authors say this is invaluable for building their followings), allow participants to sign up so that you can keep up with them and let them know of your future events and publications. If you have a Facebook page or a blog, encourage them to visit and sign in.

9. If you're selling a book to be used as a text or instructional book, tell them exactly how to use it and give them a handout (or a link to free web-based

resources) to walk them through the process. Marguerita has mastered this to the point that her publisher adopted her approach and uses it to train other authors. She separates herself out from other authors by teaching groups of quilters from her book (with her daughter as the main presenter) before she ever goes to the conference. This enables her to say to shop owners, "When you do a class in your shop, these are the questions they'll ask and here are the supplies they'll likely want (think: profits for their stores) to buy." She outlines for the quilt shop owners exactly how to advertise (verbiage and blurbs for newsletters and websites) and structure the quilting class. It's all there in her handouts for them to copy and use.

* * *

> "The key was for me to think like a shop owner (buyer) rather than an author (seller)."

* * *

This separates her from authors who are so enamored with their books that they assume teachers and shop owners will figure out for themselves how to use their books to teach a class. Anyone trying to sell their book to teachers can see the wisdom of this approach. According to Marguerita, shop owners are looking for a book that's "easy to follow, popular, already being used successfully in a class, and easy to train their staff to use." By giving them exactly what they're looking for, she sells thousands of books.

10. Network with authors of your genre who speak and sell their books. Share with each other what's working and what's not. Christopher Paolini dressed up in medieval armor to talk to school kids about his novel. Marguerita McManus has techniques that work extremely well for selling a "how-to" book that seminar attendees will be using as a text. Each type of book will sell differently, so that your most valuable advice will likely come from those selling similar books.

Set Up More Speaking Opportunities

1. Start small, free, and local. Then, build your platform. You've got to start somewhere. When you speak, get blurbs and recommendations that you can put on your press page or a specialized speaker page on your author site. Think from the event organizer's perspective. She needs hard evidence that if she books you, you'll do a good job. If she checks out your speaker's page and finds enthusiastic recommendation after recommendation from other event organizers, she'll likely book you. Also, link to samples of your speaking on YouTube.

2. Ask event organizers and participants to recommend other places you could speak. (Again, I ask this in my evaluation sheet.)

3. Network with other speakers. Serious speakers often join their local chapter of Toastmasters for sharpening their craft and learning the business side of speaking. Find more information and the nearest club at http://www.toastmasters.org.

Do Something!

To put this chapter into action, I will…

1 –

2 –

3 –

Keep Learning!

Read a book on public speaking. Here are the ones I recommended in the chapter:

- Dr. Howard Hendricks, *Teaching to Change Lives: Seven Proven Ways to Make Your Teaching Come Alive.*
- Milton Gregory, *The Seven Laws of Teaching.* A classic that Bruce Wilkinson re-reads every year.
- Bruce Wilkinson, *The Seven Laws of the Learner: How to Teach Almost Anything to Practically Anyone.*

Chapter 22

John Kremer's Twelve Tips for Low Profile Authors

Introduction by J. Steve Miller

It's such an honor to have John Kremer contributing to this book! He and Brian Jud (see next chapter) have mentored me from afar in my book marketing. John's *1001 Ways to Market Your Books* gave me the detailed specifics that I needed to chart my course in marketing my books. His *Self-Publishing Hall of Fame* e-book gave me hundreds of inspiring examples of how small time authors made it big. Find these and many other great resources at www.bookmarket.com. His resources show the depth of understanding and attention to detail that makes them invaluable for all types of authors. Every author and publisher needs the latest edition of his *1001 Ways* in his or her library, underlined and personally indexed for easy reference.

Introduction by John Kremer

Steve's excitement for book marketing is contagious and this book offers a unique and much-needed contribution to the field. While there will be some overlap with what Steve recommends elsewhere in this book, I'll highlight what I see working especially well for low platform authors. I should mention that very few of my *1001 Ways* target high platform authors. But since my *Self-Publishing Hall of Fame* book typically highlights low profile authors at the point where they're new to publishing, I'll often pull from their stories in this chapter. There's no theory in that book, just story after story of people who started small and made it big. Whether you're traditionally published or self-published, we can all learn a lot from their successes.

Recommended Strategies

Let's assume, as Steve detailed in chapter 3, that you've written a marketable book. Great books are so much easier to market than mediocre books!

Tip #1: Write down your marketing strategy for your book.[1]

Don't just take an idea here and an idea there and try each of them on a whim. Decide what has the most potential for your book and start by concentrating there. Some strategies, such as getting on radio, take some time to learn. Further, it takes time to build your reputation among radio stations. By narrowing down what you want to do first, second, and third, you can focus your efforts on one campaign at a time and give each the time to pay off.

Tip #2: Find the movers and shakers in your field who can get the word out

I recommend this to all authors, but as a low profile author, you especially need the endorsement and recommendation of high profile, influential people. So start by identifying those people. You're looking for influencers who are passionate about your topic: bloggers, radio personalities, magazine editors, and newspaper columnists – people who might review your book or at least recommend it to others. Your list should number easily in the hundreds, more probably in the thousands.

Tip #3: Contact those movers and shakers, offering them a free book for review.

Your book, in the hands of influential people, is your best bet for sparking and stoking a blaze of word of mouth publicity. As I said in *1001 Ways to Market Your Books*,

> "Send out review copies. Send out lots of them. Send out more than you think you should. Hit every major magazine that you think might be at all interested in the subject of your book. In most cases this means sending out somewhere between 200 and 500 review copies.[2]

To save money and to make it more effective, send e-mails first, asking if they want copies. That way, when your book arrives, it comes as solicited mail rather than unsolicited, giving it a better chance of being opened and read.

Sending out books takes some time. It takes some money. But if you've written a captivating book, you need to get it into enough influential hands to make word of mouth effective. If you send out copies over time, the resulting increase in sales one month may more than pay for sending out next month's books.

Tip #4: Sell through venues where your target audience gathers.

Notice that I didn't say exclusively "where they buy books." As I gather stories about self publishing successes, although some of them do tons of traditional book signings in bookstores, I find others selling in places that most people don't think of buying books.

- Aliske Webb sold her novel, *Twelve Golden Threads: Lessons for Successful Living from Grandma's Quilt* at **quilt shows**. After selling over 25,000 copies, HarperCollins won an auction between four major publishers to handle the book. Webb received a healthy sum of money for the deal.[3]

- John Erickson sold the first of his *Hank the Cowdog* children's books at **cattle auctions**, **rodeos**, **Rotary meetings**, and **schools**. So far, the series and accompanying audio tapes have sold over six million copies.[4]

- Dawn Hall sold 70,000 copies of her first cookbook through **grocery stores**, **gift shops** and **health clubs**. She also made **author appearances**, gave **cooking demos**, and **presented in classes**. As of today, she's sold over one million books.[5]

Tip #5: Make Things Happen Locally

If you study my collection of self-published successes, two things might surprise you: how many books the authors sold (typically hundreds of thousands or millions), and how many credited local or statewide initiatives with the bulk of their early sales. Many authors, wowed with all the fascinating opportunities on the web, may be overlooking local possibilities that seem rather rinky dink on a small scale, but can add up to very, very significant sales when taken seriously.

- *The South Beach Diet* started as a series of pamphlets that Arthur Agatston gave to his **patients**. They shared it with **local friends**. Then a **local TV program** interviewed him, showing a clip each night with a menu for the next day. Then **local supermarkets** began stocking the pamphlets. A literary agent got wind of these local happenings and sold the book idea to a publisher. It ended up selling over seven million copies and a spinoff cookbook sold over two million copies. But Agatston's success began locally.[6]

- Ken Blanchard and Spencer Johnson sold 20,000 copies of *The One Minute Manager* **in the San Diego area alone** before selling reprint rights to William Morrow.[7] It went on to sell over 12 million copies in 25 languages.

- Ken Harper sold 9,000 copies of his book, *Give Me My Father's Body: The Story of Minik, the New York Eskimo*, **primarily through his general store** on Baffin Island (which has a total population of 11,000!). Pocket Books bought paperback rights for six figures. The *Book of the Month Club* bought book club rights. Actor Kevin Spacey optioned movie rights.[8]

- *Publishers Weekly* called E. Lynn Harris "the patron saint of black self-publishing." He sold 10,000 copies of his novel, *Invisible Life*, through **beauty salons** (with a "please don't remove" note and instructions to

call him to buy a copy) and **black-owned bookstores** and **book parties** hosted by his friends. After selling his novels to Doubleday/Anchor, they have sold millions of copies, making the *New York Times* bestseller list six times.

Tip #6: Relish trying new methods and exploring new technologies.

You can't do every newfangled thing, but when you hear of something that makes sense for you and your book, give it a try. Great booksellers are willing to try new things.

When I first saw Twitter, I thought, "What a complete waste of time!" But when I took a closer look, I began to discover its marketing potential. My early attempts were largely trial and error, but you've got to start somewhere. Once I learned the more subtle techniques and began connecting with people, I doubled the number of visitors to my www.bookmarket.com site in a mere four months! If you think Twitter might work for you, I wrote *The Twitter Mania Manual* to take you step by step through how to use Twitter to sell more books:

http://www.bookmarket.com/twittermaniamanual.htm.

Tip #7: Be persistent with an initiative; but if it doesn't yield fruit, move on to the next tactic.

I often hear authors make statements like: "Book marketing just isn't working for me. I contacted fifteen radio stations and not one of them responded." If they're going about it the right way (often they aren't), I tell them:

> "Fifteen isn't nearly enough. Especially for first time authors who haven't established themselves on radio, you've got to make contact after contact until you find someone willing to take a chance on you. Once you narrow down talk shows that like your topic, contact one hundred of them, starting with small time stations. Once you've establish yourself on radio, with links from your press page to your interviews, it's easier to get more radio spots."
>
> If you don't get any response with your first fifty tries, then maybe radio's just not receptive to you and your topic. As W.C. Fields put it,
>
> > *"If at first you don't succeed, try, try again. Then quit. There's no point in being a damn fool about it."*
>
> But if you quit radio, don't quit book marketing altogether! Radio's not for everyone. Move on to another of the hundreds of ways to market books."

Tip #8: Don't dismiss opportunities that you think are reserved for only best selling authors.

Small time authors get published internationally. First time novelists get movie deals. Small time authors get on Oprah. Remember, high profile authors had to start somewhere. Also, remember that once your book starts selling and you're able to land some decent publicity, you no longer have a low profile.

I see low profile authors get big-time coverage all the time. The reason? The media needs interesting, entertaining information that appeals to their listeners or readers. Offer them what they need and they'll cover you. Publications are information-eating monsters that require constant feeding. After years of writing columns and interviewing guests, they've got to keep coming up with fresh material.

Sure, multitudes bombard them with story ideas. But they live for those ideas! One *New York Times* columnist has the byline: "I eat ideas for breakfast." The last thing he wants is for people to stop sending story ideas. Sure, it helps if you're a nationally known authority, but it's not critical.

I'll say it again: The media wants stories that are interesting and helpful to their audiences. Consistently offer them those kinds of stories on a large enough scale and you'll likely get some responding. And when they do, look out! You just got national exposure!

Here are a few keys to landing big-time media.

#1 - Pitch great ideas rather than your book. As a low profile author, the fact that you just published a book isn't news. Scads of new books come out every day. So pitch ideas that relate to your book, ideas that allow you to say, "As I discovered while researching my new book...."

#2 - Pitch ideas that relate to current, newsy events. So you've written a relationships book and a new study was just released about an increase in failed marriages. Pitch an article tying those statistics to your analysis of causes and cures in your relationships book. Is Valentine's Day coming up? The media has to come up with new angles every year. Meet their need and you just might get some press.

#3 Join groups like *HARO, Bill and Steve Harrison's Reporter Connection*, or *Profnet* and respond to reporters' requests.

Tip #9: Do five promotions a day.

I find that authors respond better to a specific goal rather than a general commitment like "I've got to do more publicity." It doesn't have to take a lot of time and money; just make five promotional contacts every day and things will begin to happen.

- Respond to someone's blog post.
- Tweet about something.
- Participate in a forum.
- Mail a letter or postcard.
- Call someone on the phone.
- Send a news release.

It might just take fifteen to twenty minutes a day, but five contacts a day add up to thirty-five contacts per week, 150 contacts per month, 1,800 contacts per year.

Tip #10: Find fun ways to market your book.

They will differ for every author. Some authors love author signings. Others dread them. Life's too short to spend it doing things you hate. Besides, I find that authors are more effective when they're doing something they love.

Tip #11: When you find something that you enjoy and that works for selling your book, perfect it and pursue it with a passion!

Sure, there's probably some new author out there who got published, immediately got featured in *The New York Times*, and didn't have to do any more publicity. But those people, if they exist, are very rare. Typically, low profile authors who sell a lot of books (and many, many of them do) are doing publicity on a much larger scale than authors whose books aren't selling.

You don't have to do all my *1001 Ways*! Instead, use the book to get an overview of the wealth of possibilities. The successful authors I've studied seem to do a few things well rather than 100 things haphazardly. And when they find something that works for them, they pursue it relentlessly.

- Dave Chilton did hundreds of interviews the first year after publishing *The Wealthy Barber*. Two years later, it made the Canadian best-seller list and was still there five years later. It went on to sell over three million copies. **Chilton believes that publishers' tendency to spend only six months or so publicizing a book doesn't allow enough time to establish word of mouth. Instead, according to Chilton, "Stay focused on the project for at least two to three years."**
- Larry James has sold 100,000 copies of his self-published books so far. His advice to authors?[9] **"Promote! Promote! Promote! Never stop promoting."**

Tip #12: Never stop learning!

My resources, Brian's resources and Steve's resources are great places to start, but please don't stop there! I don't mean that to sound discouraging. I'm just saying, fall in love with learning. If you do, you'll find great ideas everywhere. Someone in your local writer's group knows the best shop in town to sell your books. But if you've stopped learning, you won't think to ask your writer's group for their tips on book marketing. And you'll never learn about that one shop that might sell thousands of your books.

One of the most enjoyable ways to learn is to join the Book Marketing Network and hang out in the Forum, asking questions and making suggestions. Subscribe to *Publishers Weekly* and some book marketing newsletters (see "Recommended Resources" at the end of this chapter). How else will you know when Facebook comes out with a new killer application for authors or a new book award is announced that targets books like yours?

Conclusion

Writing a book is a huge accomplishment. But it's not very fulfilling if nobody reads it. I challenge you to find some ways to market your book that work for you. Pursue them. When you do, you just might be surprised to find that the joy of selling your books exceeds the joy of seeing your books published.

Do Something!

To put this chapter into action, I will...

1 –

2 –

3 –

Keep Learning!

Recommended Resources by John Kremer

John's site is huge, offering tons of free and low cost resources. Go to his site and browse for a couple of hours to see the vast resources he offers authors: **http://www.bookmarket.com.**

Here are a few of his many resources:

- **Books by John Kremer include:**

  1001 Ways to Market Your Books **–** Every author should have a copy of the latest edition. The 6th edition contains 700 pages (compare to 450 pages in the 3rd edition) of detailed information on every imaginable way to market your book. Write your own personal index in the back, noting the pages that are most likely to work for your book. You'll find yourself referring back to it over and over like a reference book.

  John Kremer's Self Publishing Hall of Fame – It's both motivational and instructive – motivational in that I discover hundreds (over 500 so far – he keeps adding) of low profile authors who are selling truckloads of books. Reading a few stories each evening motivates me to press forward with my book sales. It's instructive in that many of the stories tell how they marketed their books, helping me to see what actually works. Get the e-book, which has many more examples than the print version.

- **List of 36 recommended e-zines, highlighting those he subscribes to.**

- **Twenty free audio and video seminars.**

- **His own "Book Marketing Tip of the Week Newsletter." (I'm subscribed.)**

- **Links to Recommended Book Marketing Resources and Services.**

- **E-books by John Kremer include:**

  Book Marketing 101: How to Create a National Bestseller

  Book Marketing 104: 192 Marketing Ideas I've Learned from Other People

  Book Marketing 105: Choosing a Book Distribution System

- **His free Book Marketing Network gives authors and publishers a place to share their ideas, successes, frustrations, and dreams. Join it here: http://thebookmarketingnetwork.com.**

Chapter 23

Bulk Sales beyond the Bookstore
An Interview with Brian Jud

Introduction by J. Steve Miller

Brian Jud – best-selling, award-winning author and book marketer extraordinaire – started Book Marketing Works back in 1996 to help publishers market their books. No collection of book marketing volumes would be complete without his latest title: *How to Make Real Money Selling Books (Without Worrying About Returns): A Complete Guide to the Book Publisher's World of Special Sales.*

I've frequently participated in his free book publicity webinars and have always been inspired with his enthusiasm. I'm amazed at the amount of information he can pack into a talk.

Special sales have been important to the marketing of my books. That's how I sold 100 copies of *Enjoy Your Money* the day it came off the press. A CPA purchased them to give away to high school and college graduates. My music book sold to colleges and graduate schools. I continue to push for special sales today.

The Interview

J. Steve Miller: Brian, many authors struggle to get their books into bookstores. Do you find low profile authors making significant sales outside of bookstores?

Brian Jud: Yes, they can sell in large, non-returnable quantities in non-bookstore markets. Here, buyers are looking at the content of the book, not necessarily a "name" author. They want well-written material that can be used as a premium or ad specialty to help the corporate marketing people sell more of their products, or human resource managers to train, reward or motivate employees.

J. Steve Miller: What are some markets outside of bookstores that low profile authors should consider?

Brian Jud: The market differs from book to book.

- Rick Warren pushed his devotional book, *The Purpose-Driven Life,* with pastors, who bought it in bulk for their congregations. It became the largest selling hardcover book in history (besides the Bible). By 2007, over 30 million copies had sold.[1]
- Richard Bolles printed and sold the first 2,000 copies of *What Color is Your Parachute? A Practical Manual for Job-Hunters and Career-Changers* to campus ministers, who used them to help students. Today eight million copies are in print.[2]

Once you start looking beyond the bookstore, you'll find thousands of places to sell books. A large portion of our population never shops in bookstores. But many of these buy books at seminars, hospital gift shops, grocery stores, and health food stores. They also read books at well-stocked corporate libraries, military bases, prison libraries, and university libraries.

J. Steve Miller: So how can an author discover the best places to sell her books?

Brian Jud: First, define the target readers and find out where they congregate or buy products. Then segment the potential market into sub-groups of people who buy for similar reasons. For example, an author of a children's book could sell it to daycare centers, children's museums, PTOs, home-schooling associations, the armed services, or toy stores. Publishers can get an overview of the myriads of possibilities. In *How to Make Real Money Selling Books*, I offer hundreds of pages of advice for locating sales channels and working them to your best advantage.

J. Steve Miller: I've read it, underlining the ideas that fit my books and making my own index in the back, referring me to the tips I need to implement. Great book! What are some of the biggest markets out there that we should consider?

Brian Jud: The United States federal government is the largest buyer of goods and services in the world.[3] Twenty-three percent of all its purchases must come from small businesses. If you've got a book about getting jobs in a poor economy, for example, it might be a great fit. Try selling to your local government before talking to state and regional agencies. Find your local city government site at www.officialcitysites.org. And be aware of "fiscal year frenzy" – when many agencies need to either spend their remaining budget dollars or lose them. For some branches, the fiscal year ends in September. Begin contacting them in July if you think your book might be useful to them.

Schools are in constant need of textbooks, supplemental resources, and age-appropriate library books. With 50 million K-12 students in public schools, and many others in private schools and home schools, authors have a huge opportunity for sales. Many authors have found success offering readings, question-and-answer sessions (English and Literature teachers love exposing students to authors), talks on specialty subjects, etc. Jason Spencer-Edwards self-published his young adult novel, *Jiggy*, and convinced the *New York City Department of Education* to approve it for school reading lists. Then, he went from school to school, dropping off sample books and offering to speak in classes. In two years alone, New York schools bought 50,000 copies.[4]

The Military offers vast opportunities for book sales. We are talking about over 1.4 million people in active duty. Add to that 700,000 civilians working for the Department of Defense and two million military retirees. They have their own libraries, stores, book clubs, and schools. You can target them through military exchange services, like the Army & Air Force Exchange Service (aafes.com), military newspapers (e.g., *Marine Corps Times*), and military magazines (e.g., *Salute Magazine*).

But it really doesn't matter which markets are the biggest. What really matters is finding the best markets for *your* book. Many health books sell well in nutrition stores. A novel with a local setting might sell well through local restaurants, gas stations, and stores in tourist destinations. If you've written a strategy book for poker players or a riveting novel that involves gambling, forget the government, schools, and military. Market it in Las Vegas, Macau, Atlantic City, or in any local club where people play poker.

J. Steve Miller: What are the benefits of special sales over traditional bookstore sales?

Brian Jud: Unlike bookstore sales, you don't risk losing money on returns. The buyer typically pays for shipping. You can sell large quantities of books at one time.

It's not unusual to see businesses purchasing 5,000 copies of a book to use as a giveaway to accompany a purchase. Another business may order 1,000 copies as a free gift to their top workers.

J. Steve Miller: Why aren't all authors doing this? There must be some drawbacks.

Brian Jud: Most authors can't think outside of the bookstore, which relegates them to a competitive arena where authors and publishers fight for extremely limited bookstore space. The main drawback to special sales is that making the big deals often takes time – sometimes months or even years – to cultivate relationships and give decision-makers the time they need.

J. Steve Miller: Going after the larger corporations sounds rather intimidating for low profile authors. Any advice here?

Brian Jud: First, write down any personal connections you have with companies that might buy your book to use as an incentive, gift, or promotion. I don't just mean executives. Your acquaintances that are secretaries and cashiers often have connections within companies and can give your book a personal recommendation to whoever makes these decisions.

After you've exhausted your personal contacts, visit local businesses. While everybody else is trying to court Coca Cola and Wal-Mart, you might be the only person courting a local company that employs thousands of people. And don't overlook the local mom-and-pop businesses. Here's how starting local could work if you've written a nutrition guide or a memoir of defeating an illness:

- **Visit your local, independent health food store and offer your book to the manager.** Independents are typically an easier sell than chains because they can make their own decisions on the spot without having to refer you to corporate.
- **Contact *Nutri-Books*, a wholesaler to the health-food market.**
- **If a locally owned health food store sells lots of your books, get a blurb from the store owner that you can use with other independent stores.**
- **Finally, offer it to the big chains with your record of success in independent stores.** Approach big decision-makers with more than "It's a great book...really!" Instead, show them all your glowing testimonies from other stores, with their track record for sales, and you've got an attractive proposal.

Do you see how the "start local" strategy can apply to other markets? You donate a copy of your novel to your local library, which displays it prominently for a month as a book by a local author. Many people check it out. You get a testimonial from the librarian and use it to sell books to other libraries.

J. Steve Miller: I suppose I should allow you to tell about your Premium Book Company, although I really hate to do this. It just encourages more competition to a book that I have with you guys.

Brian Jud: How selfless of you! *PBC* is helping a lot of authors with their special sales. Basically, you pay us an initial, one-time set-up fee to put your book in our special sales program for as long as it is in print. This includes a catalog, custom search engine, and exposure at over 60 trade shows annually. We work through a national network of more than 5,000 experienced, promotional-products sales representatives who sell books to known buyers in corporations, associations, schools, and government agencies. These representatives are paid on commission, so that they don't make money unless they sell products. Once orders are made, sales are not returnable. We pay shipping. It's a new venture, but we think it's a model that has a lot of potential.

J. Steve Miller: And even books by low profile authors have a chance at these large sales?

Brian Jud: Sometimes they have a *better* chance. If a business wants to buy a free gift, the last thing they want is the best-selling book that everybody already has. Sometimes it helps to be unique.

Do Something!

To put this chapter into action, I will...

1 –

2 –

3 –

Keep Learning!

Recommended Resources from Brian Jud

Start here to explore his many resources: http://www.bookmarketingworks.com.

Note especially:

- Brian's free *Book Marketing Matters* e-letter. I receive it. Sign up and see back issues at http://www.bookmarketingworks.com/mktgmattersnews/.
- *How to Make Real Money Selling Books (Without Worrying about Returns): A Complete Guide to the Book Publishers' World of Special Sales* – Brian's book, containing 375 pages of specific details on how to sell your books outside of the bookstore.

- http://www.premiumbookcompany.com – Join this program (I have) to get 5,000 representatives trying to sell your book in bulk to corporations, associations, schools, and government agencies.
- Sixteen free webinars on topics ranging from "Sell More Books in a Slow Economy" to "Media Training."
- Over 70 free articles on special sales, promotion, planning, pricing, distribution, and product development.
- Personal consulting for special sales. I've done one of these and received many helpful tips.
- Find printers, reviewers, editors, designers, publicists, and distributors – over 3,000 of them – all rated and reviewed by other users: **http://www.bookcentralstation.com.**
- Note his eight e-booklets with hundreds of marketing tips on topics ranging from getting on radio and TV to finding effective distribution.
- Consider his media training.

Chapter 24

Send Press (News) Releases

With news releases…you can talk to the world.

-Brian Hennigan, marketing communications manager for dbaDIRECT, a data infrastructure management company.[1]

Press Releases are nearly useless.

- Tom Foremski, *Silicon Valley Watcher*[2]

Do Press Releases Still Work?

Over the past few years, several thought leaders have been announcing the death of the press release. "It was once a useful tool," they say, "but today we can communicate freely with the press and the public through our blogs and web-based media rooms."

Yet, when Stephanie (my Atlanta publicist) and I paid Bostick Communications $175 to send a press release about my money book in 2009 (http://www.bostick-communications.com/gpage2.html), I received 26 responses requesting a copy for review and/or an author interview. Here's the breakdown:

- Six TV stations: Washington, DC, Atlanta, Cincinnatti, Baltimore, and Sacramento
- Three newspaper editors: Detroit, Knoxville, and Whiteville, NC.
- Fifteen bloggers/reviewers
- A university bookstore
- A radio station in Ocean City, Maryland. (I did this interview.)

Obviously, influential people are receiving and reading Bostick's releases. Bostick also tracked the results to show me where it was being read and reviewed.

Brian and Jeffery Eisenberg's book, *Waiting for your Cat to Bark?: Persuading Customers When They Ignore Marketing*, hit number one on the *Wall Street Journal* business bestseller list. How did these marketing experts market their book?

Games Press Release Companies Play

Is it just me, or is choosing a press release company feeling more and more like talking to used car salesmen? Here are some common practices and phrases that companies may excuse as "industry standard language," but mislead the newbie:

- *"We send your release to over 300,000 journalists."* (So did they buy that list, or cultivate it? Is it accurate? Is it kept current? How many journalists block their releases as spam? Does anybody actually read them?)
- *"We send your release to the major news wires, like AP and Reuters."* (Associated Press and Reuters aren't news wires that automatically deliver your releases to reporters. Anybody can find an e-mail address of someone at AP or Reuters, but that doesn't mean they'll read your e-mails. The best press release companies get read by virtue of their reputation and the trusting relationships they cultivate with the media.)

First, they targeted their existing customers their blog and newsletter. Second, they sent advance-reading copies to hundreds of bloggers and other influential people. Third, they sent out a press release every day through PR Web for several months so that the ideas from the book would get out in the marketplace and be picked up and discussed by bloggers and consumers.

How News Releases Can Bring Traffic to Your Site

High-traffic sites often post releases in their entirety or write articles based upon them. If they include a link to your site, not only will people likely follow that link to your site, but search engines will begin to rank you more highly so that more people can find you. One of the most important factors considered by search engines is the number and quality of incoming links.

The news releases worded the book's ideas in many different ways, titled with eye-catching headlines such as:

- *Is Google Responsible for Marketing Failures?*
- *Why Your Customers are More Like Cats than Dogs*

The result? "Some 300 bloggers wrote about the book, developed conversations around its ideas, and helped push it along to many thousands of consumers via word-of-blog."[3]

These successes indicate that press releases can still be effective if done in the right way.

What We'll Cover

I thought this would be an easy chapter to research and write. But alas, the digital revolutions have unleashed a veritable Pandora's Box of bewildering press release options.

Hopefully, this chapter will save you a lot of time, frustration, and money as I attempt to answer these questions:

- "Do media releases make sense for my book and my budget?"
- "Which companies would be most effective at distributing my media releases?" 150+ press release companies are in operation.[4] Some are reputable and straightforward. Others are as slick as a bucket of greased eels.
- "Who actually reads these releases?"
- "Do journalists read press releases from only select companies?"
- "Does Google News post releases from all press release companies?"

- "Prices range from free to $700+ dollars for one press release. Do I simply find the least expensive one?"
- "What are some tips to write more appealing press releases?"

How Can Press Releases Work for Authors?

There are several ways authors can use press releases.

First, you can cultivate your own list of media contacts and send newsworthy information directly to them. This still works. For example, find e-mail addresses and phone numbers of your local newspapers, radio and TV stations. Whenever you're speaking – doing a book signing, organizing a charity event, or coming out with a new book – send them a news release, giving them all the information (who, what, when, where, why) that they'd need to interview you or write an interesting article.

It's free, it's easy, and it can be effective.

In fact, a newsy item in a local paper can go national or even global. Example: Undercover agents bust a drug ring in a metro Atlanta high school, making major news because high-ranking school officials had known of the problem but refused to deal with it. Your memoir of overcoming a drug habit that started in a similar high school provides a personal side to the story – the potential long-term impact on the students. So you offer your perspective (via e-mailing a press release and following up with a phone call) to a local journalist, who mentions you in her article.

The journalist thinks the article may have national appeal, so she submits it to the Associated Press, allowing journalists nationwide to consider publishing the story as well.

Besides local media, you can also collect contact information on national media, cultivate relationships, and send appropriate stories directly to them

> **Tip:** When the press responds to your releases, keep their contact information and note their responses. Since they've shown interest in your topic, this could be the beginning of a fruitful relationship.

Second, you can pay a respected news release company to send your story to influential media contacts. This type of release can be costly (e.g., $175 to a targeted list or $400 to northeast states, per release) but it can work for authors who present news angles that appeal to journalists and radio personalities. If they're intrigued, they may mention you in an article, e-mail you to request a copy of the book, or try to set up an interview. **For this to work, you must send your release through the respected services that journalists actually read, not**

the ones that they block as spam. If nobody opens the e-mails, the size of the contact list doesn't matter. I'll show you how to find the most respected companies in a moment.

Third, you can send releases to internet news sources like Google News, Yahoo!, Lycos, etc. This method of getting news out, made possible by the digital revolutions, is recommended by marketing experts such as David Meerman Scott. You still have to send them through news release companies. But they charge less for this than other services. Some offer it free of charge, making it affordable for authors to send out multiple releases. **Tip:** If you send a regional release, like one targeting Los Angeles, the company will typically send it to Google News as well. Read the small print to make sure.

Who reads these releases on Google News?

People who search for your topic on the Internet and anyone who has set up a Google Alert or RSS Feed to receive news or articles posted on a certain subject.

Caution: Sending out a paid release through a respected company doesn't guarantee that Google News will automatically pick it up and disseminate it. We never saw our last two paid releases (through one of the top-rated companies) on Google News. And even if runs in Google news, it won't necessarily go out in a Google Alert. According to Google, "In order to be included in Google News Alerts, an article must be included in Google News and appear in the top ten results of Google News for specific search terms."

Scott is impressed with this method's ability to reach bloggers.[5] Although journalists can read them as well, they are no longer the gatekeepers. All interested parties can access news directly. This has led many to call them "news releases" instead of "press releases." News can go directly to the world instead of through intermediaries.[6] As a result, Scott calls news releases "one of the most important direct marketing tools at your disposal."[7]

Keeping Current: To find the latest on how Google receives and distributes news, see their informative articles here:

http://www.google.com/support/news

To find out specifically about how it handles press releases, search "press releases" in the box beside "Search Help."

* * *

"...you can reach hundreds of web sites with a single news release."[8]
– David Meerman Scott

* * *

What Can You Write Press Releases About?

Many things, as long as they're newsworthy. "New Novel Published this Month" isn't news. Thousands of new novels are released each month. The media might comment on a new novel by Stephen King, but why would they cover a relatively unknown author, unless you've got an intriguing angle?

"New Novel Explores the Roots of Corporate Corruption" might catch a business writer's eye, especially if lies and deceit led to the recent fall of a highly visible business.

But remember, we're not just targeting the traditional press, which must limit itself to topics of interest to the general public. Specialty bloggers and newsletter publishers feed off Google Alerts in their fields of interest.[9] Thus, release information when:

- you can offer interesting information from your book or on your topic.
- you have information that solves a problem.
- you know fresh research that dovetails with your book's thesis or story.
- you won an award.
- you wrote a helpful white paper.
- you're speaking at a conference.

What Should a News Release Look Like?

It depends upon whom you're targeting. Some people, like traditional journalists at

Is Google News Posting Releases From Your News Release Company?

Google News blocks certain press release companies. Yet, according to Scott, getting onto Google News should be one of your main considerations in choosing a news release service.

To find out if a company's being blocked, use this nifty Google hack: "site:".

Example: Let's see if Google News is accepting press releases from the press release company, PRWeb.

Go to http://news.google.com. In the Google News search box, type "site:prweb.com". Click "Search News." This hack limits the search to web pages in news.google.com. If Google News is posting their releases, you should see a list of posts from prweb.com. This technique is actually recommended by Google to check out your press release service.

big-time publications, may prefer press releases in precisely the traditional format. Many other busy writers would prefer a fleshed-out article that they can edit minimally and run as an article.

See my example press release, in a traditional format, at the end of this chapter.

Which are the Best News Release Companies?

This depends upon your budget and the ends you're trying to achieve.

1) If you're going after big-time media, use the press release companies that they actually read. To find the top performing companies, consider the top ten, as rated by independent rating service TOPSEOs:

http://www.topseos.com/rankings-of-best-press-release-distribution-companies

This service sizes up companies by surveying their clients to discover:

- how many of their press releases get read.
- their return on investment.
- their satisfaction with the experience.
- conversions (e.g., requesting more information or purchasing a product).
- effectiveness and reach.
- how long it took Google News and Yahoo News to pick up the releases.[10]

Helpful Templates for Social Media Friendly News Releases

The below releases contain all the bells and whistles that make them more easily passed on through social networks. Typically, companies charge more for their inclusion.

http://www.shiftcomm.com/downloads/smprtemplate.pdf

http://www.shiftcomm.com/downloads/smr_v1.5.pdf

2) If you're targeting a specialty list, find a service that offers the list you want. Example: If you're targeting librarians, consider Librarian's News Wire http://liswire.com/. If you wrote a book specifically for a Christian audience, seeking exposure in periodicals, television and radio that target Christians, try a service like *Bostick Communications* which offers, among its many targeted lists, one for Christian media: http://www.bostickcommunications.com.

3) If you're targeting people (such as bloggers) who read web-based news sources such as Google News, Yahoo! and Lycos, look for the best rated free or inexpensive services. See if TOPSEOs recommends a company that offers a free option. Further, Google "top press release sites," "best free press release sites," etc., to see which press release companies other people are using and achieving good results with.

Recommended Companies for Free Releases in 2010

Recommended by Stephanie Richards: www.i-newswire.com/submit.php, www.dbusinessnews.com, www.24-7pressrelease.com, http://www.newswiretoday.com/. As of August 2010, Google News is carrying press releases by each of these organizations.

From Subhub, Feb, 2010, (http://www.subhub.com/articles/the-best-free-and-paid-press-release-websites-and-when-to-use-them): www.prlog.org , www.pr.com and www.pressrelease365.com .

Rule of Thumb: An article on Subhub (http://www.subhub.com) suggests using top paid services for the most important releases, and free releases for all the rest.

How to Do a News Release

At the end of this chapter you'll find the press release that I mentioned at the beginning of this chapter. It's in a traditional press release format and doesn't include social networking elements. Each company that you use will specify how they want your release formatted and will typically give you some tips for getting the best results. Follow their step-by-step instructions for how to send out a press release from their sites.

Tips from the Trenches

1. Consider hiring a professional publicist who understands the book industry to assist you in sending your first release. I paid Stephanie Richards, President of The Write Way, LLC, to edit my first release and hold my hand through the process. After that, I felt I could do my own releases. You may want to use publicists to do all your press releases. Besides keeping up with the latest trends in press releases, they typically have their own cultivated list of contacts.

2. Make the title and content newsworthy. Journalists skim titles before deciding which releases to read. Make them count.

3. Appeal to bloggers and your potential buyers, not just the traditional press. Strike a balance between "useful for journalists" and "useful for the general public."

4. Optimize your release for search engines by including appropriate key words and phrases. Make it easy for those searching Google News and Yahoo! to find your release. Use Google's Keyword Tool (see chapter 4) to learn which phrases people use to search for the topics covered in your release. Searchers may never find you unless you include those phrases!

5. Content is king. Write terrific (useful, interesting, well-worded) content.

6. Link your news release to a press kit on your blog or site that compels the media to take you seriously (including blurbs and reviews). This page should give them plenty of information to easily write about you and your book. Provide example questions and answers for reviews. If you're shooting for radio or TV, demonstrates that you can handle yourself in those arenas by including podcasts or videos of you in action (see chapter 16). Here's my press kit for *Enjoy Your Money*:

http://wisdomcreekpress.com/press_kits.html

7. Many experts recommend sending releases frequently, not just when you have "big news."

8. Offer customers something that compels them to respond – a discounted review copy, free chapters for download, a free white paper, exclusive information, etc.

9. Realize that sending out review copies can be expensive. Some may respond to the release by requesting a review copy. Don't feel obligated to send it to everyone who asks. Some may request it from faraway lands, which can require $14 in postage. You could mail five copies nationally for that amount. Also, people with blogs that nobody ever reads will request a copy. Check out the requesting blogs or news sources. Are they truly influencers? Could they really get the word out, or are they just looking for free books?

10. If it's within your budget (adding these to a release often costs more), include social media tags for DIGG, del.icio.us, etc. so that readers can easily spread the word.

11. It's okay to send out the same free release through several companies. Since some members of the media read releases from one company and others from another, you may get a wider reading by using several companies. Also, Google News doesn't publish every press release. If other news in your subject area appeals to their editors more for that day, they won't publish it. Thus, search Google News for unlikely phrases (like your name) to see if your article gets posted. If it doesn't, send out the same release in coming days with several other companies.

12. Post the release on your website (e.g., in your "media room" or press section of your author or publisher site). Keep it there as long as it's still appropriate. Since online news sites may delete such news after a month, you'll still have a copy for searchers to find.

13. Monitor the effectiveness of your release. Can you know for sure that it was sent? Does the company let you know how many members of the press opened the release or responded (blogged about, forwarded, clicked through to your site) in some way?

14. Make the most of your results. As I mentioned earlier, I got a book request from a book review blogger who got very little traffic. Was it worth sending her a book? I looked at her profile to discover she was home schooling a child. I sent her a free copy, requesting that she review the book as a possible text for homeschoolers and received a valuable review. Give these opportunities some creative thought to get more benefits out of each reviewer.

15. Keep an annotated list of those who responded with interest. You may be able to pitch ideas to them in the future.

16. If your organization is a "not for profit," ask if they offer discounts. Example: PR Newswire waives its $190 yearly fee for nonprofits, so that they have to pay only the per release charge.

17. If you want to send out many paid releases over a year's time period, ask if there's a way to get a better price per release. These deals are often available and widely used, but not typically mentioned on their sites.

Example Traditional News Release

News Release
For Immediate Release

July 16, 2009

Contact: Stephanie Richards
info@wisdomcreekpress.com
www.wisdomcreekpress.com

Personal Finance Book Helps Generation Y Thrive Despite Current Economic Climate

Enjoy Your Money! How to Make It, Save It, Invest It and Give It, by J. Steve Miller, teaches Generation Y to go "counterculture" with their money.

ATLANTA — Wisdom Creek Press has released a personal finance book for Generation Y to help them thrive in the current economic climate and beyond. *Enjoy Your Money! How to Make It, Save It, Invest It and Give It,* by J. Steve Miller, follows the adventures of four diverse students who form "The Counterculture Club." The club is led by an eccentric, financially savvy teacher who agrees to mentor the students on how to earn money, control expenses, and find more happiness in the process. Miller, founder and president of Legacy Educational

Resources, wrote the book as a fictional story to appeal to teens and twenty-somethings that want a successful financial future.

"Although the book is well researched and documented, *Enjoy Your Money!* is more about people than numbers," said Miller. "One way to help Generation Y learn critical financial principles is to package the information in an engaging story about young people they can identify with. Also, rather than telling young people what to do with their money, the book shares stories of how successful people like Warren Buffett and Sam Walton succeeded. Then, readers can adopt whatever financial management plan works for them."

The characters in *Enjoy Your Money!* represent four different cultures and each character challenges traditional stereotypes. While the book targets ages 16 to 32, people of any age can benefit from the financial principles provided in the book, including how to:

- Get out of debt and accumulate wealth
- Get ahead, even when the work you love doesn't produce big bucks
- Find your strengths and passions and make a living with them
- Live a more fulfilled life

"I've read scores of books and periodicals on personal finance. It's rare and refreshing to find a book so enjoyable, so accurate and so life changing. I'm purchasing hundreds of copies to give away to graduating seniors," said Larry Winter of Winter & Scoggins CPAs, certified valuation analyst, certified fraud examiner, personal financial planning specialist.

According to Miller, "My original motivation for researching and writing this book was personal. My wife, Cherie, and I have seven boys, from 14-year-old twins to a 27-year-old. I don't want my children to live their lives experiencing the misery of financial bondage. This book sums up what we're trying to teach them about finding financial freedom, and my hope is that it will benefit others across the country as well."

For more information, including reviews, interviews, etc., visit www.wisdomcreek-press.com or see customer reviews on Amazon.com at http://www.amazon.com/Enjoy-Your-Money-Make-Invest/dp/098187567X/ref=sr_1_2?ie=UTF8&s=books&qid=1237211789&sr=8-2.

About the Author

J. Steve Miller is the founder and president of Legacy Educational Resources, a nonprofit organization that provides web-based character and life skills teaching tools for educators in every state and over 30 countries (www.character-education.info). Miller has published books, developed extensive curriculum, written numerous articles, and established an illustration database for speakers. Miller is a frequent speaker and has presented at conferences from Atlanta to Moscow. For more information about him, visit www.jstevemiller.com.

# # #

Do Something!

To put this chapter into action, I will...

1 –

2 –

3 –

Keep Learning!

- **See my free updates** to each chapter at www.sellmorebooks.org.
- **Read David Meerman Scott, *The New Rules of Marketing & PR.***
- **Peruse PR Newswire's knowledge center, with 28 case studies and 15 white papers.** http://www.prnewswire.com/knowledge-center/white-papers

Chapter 25

Sell Even *More* Books!
Taking Book Sales to the Next Level

What Jack Welch Can Teach Authors

Jack Welch was one of the most respected managers of the 20th century. As CEO of General Electric – one of the world's largest corporations – his success depended upon the success of hundreds of talented and motivated associates. He gives them credit for his success in the first page of his autobiography:

> "Please remember that every time you see the word *I* in these pages, it refers to all those colleagues and friends and some I might have missed."[1]

But in my mind, the credit goes back to Welch for hiring and/or retaining these successful people. What characteristics did Welch look for in people that he felt would make them successful at GE? Can small-time authors learn something from Welch that could turn us into successful writers? I think so, because while *writing* a book is an art, *publishing and selling* a book is a business. Welch knows a thing or two about what makes people successful in business.

In hiring, Welch looked for tried and true characteristics such as integrity, intelligence, maturity, positive energy, and the ability to energize others. (Remember, Welch was hiring managers).[2] But one Friday night, flying back to headquarters after a week of reviewing personnel, GE's head of human resources turned to Welch and said, "…we're missing something. We have all these great people, but some of their results stink." What they missed was a very distinct characteristic that some smart, honest, and energetic people lack: *the ability to execute*. As defined by Welch:

> "It means a person knows how to put decisions into action and push them forward to completion, through resistance, chaos, or unexpected obstacles. People who can execute know that winning is about results."[3]

So you've made it to the end of my book. Although not one of my chapters contained a thrilling murder mystery or a daring vampire romance, you hung in there through hundreds of pages of often-tedious material. Congratulations! That accomplishment shows both passion and intelligence. But those two characteristics wouldn't be enough to compel Jack Welch to hire you as a book publicist. He'd likely say, "That's cool, but can you execute?" If you put this book down and pick up the next without formulating a book-selling strategy and executing it, don't be surprised if you fail to sell more books.

Authors who sell lots of books give legs to their ideas. They make things happen. They execute.

Here are some tips to make it happen for you:

1. Execute by writing down (or revising) your marketing plan.

- **Type your "Do Something!" list from the end of each chapter into a Word Document.** Don't obsess over noting every detail of how to do a press release or a blog campaign. Just type, for example, "Idea #12: do some free press releases – see chapter 24 for details."
- **Prioritize what you will do first, second, etc.** Consider what needs to happen before the book's published, what works best when it's new, what may still work after it's been published for years.
- **Put dates by each of your marketing initiatives.** After all, a goal is simply a dream with a deadline attached.
- **Post a summary of your plan next to your calendar, on your mirror, in your Day timer, or wherever you're likely to see it regularly.** Write in your monthly calendar what you plan to do and when. Tell accountability partners (your writing group?) to ask regularly how it's going.

Now you've got a marketing plan. It's really that simple.

2. Execute by doing something instead of nothing.

If you're not highly motivated or don't have much time, try to do at least something every day. E-mail an influential blogger. Talk to a local restaurant about selling your book on consignment. Mail a copy to a reviewer. It's only one task per day, but it adds up to 365 initiatives every year. And when you start getting good reviews and seeing your book sell, you just might catch fire.

3. Execute with more impact by radically increasing your scale.

If you want to sell hundreds of thousands of books, you'll need to think on a different scale than those who sell tens of thousands.

John Kremer recommends that you do more than *something* every day. Make five contacts per day, suggests Kremer, resulting in over 1,800 contacts per year. To sell even more books, make ten contacts per day and you'll make over 3,600 contacts each year.

Once you find something that works for you and your book, marketing becomes a simple numbers game. Put in the numbers and you'll sell more books. If sending out 50 books for review produced 500 sales, could sending 500 result in 5,000 sales or sending 5,000 result in 50,000 sales?

- That scale of thinking caused the publishers of *The DaVinci Code* to send out 10,000 advance reading copies.[4]
- That scale of thinking caused Christopher Paolini, once he saw that school assemblies worked for him, to do 135 assemblies. No wonder *Eragon* became a best-seller.[5]
- That scale of thinking enabled Canfield and Hansen to turn a book that over 100 publishers rejected into a publishing phenomenon. Most authors do a few radio interviews and a few book signings and wonder why their books aren't selling. Canfield and Hansen thought on a wildly different scale. To sell their first *Chicken Soup for the Soul* book, they got a list of radio shows and started calling them. They did 600 shows that first year.[6]
- That scale of thinking allowed Scott Peck to push *The Road Less Travelled* to best-seller status. When Canfield and Hansen asked him for his secret, he said that he did three interviews a day. Ten years later he was still doing an interview every day.[7]

* * *

When successful authors find something that works, they take it to an extreme level.

* * *

4. Faithfully execute – although the results seem meager – then watch for the magic. As we said in chapter 11, so much of successful book publicity is just doing the mundane things day after day, seeing very little fruit from most of your efforts. But then, seemingly out of nowhere, magic happens.

The magic has struck local author Pamela Jackson twice so far. When her first novel, *On This Side of Heaven*, was still in manuscript form, she took her son to batting practice, which just happened to be scheduled at the same time as

Andy Stanley's son's practice. Stanley is a highly successful pastor, author, and motivational speaker. They had never met.

They talked a bit and Jackson mentioned her novel (instead of doing nothing that day, she chose to do something), which was about a pastor who fell into moral compromise. Stanley was intrigued and asked if he could see the manuscript. Later, they crossed paths again and Stanley said, "I just want you to know that your manuscript ruined my day of preparation for my Sunday sermon. I normally reserve Saturday nights for final preparation, but my wife caught me reading your manuscript at 10:00 PM, when she told me I needed to put it down." He completed it the next morning, back stage between sermons. He wrote her a glowing blurb that went on the front cover and resulted in a lot of sales.

Her second touch of magic (she considers these touches from God) came in the midst of doing the mundane things you do before publication to get the word out. She paid to do one of those magazine ads that reads like an article. At the same time, she worked on her website and decided to host a writing contest. Whoever wrote the best article could put it on her site. The number of entries was rather disappointing, but an 11th grader, who'd read her article and decided to check out her site, turned in a wonderful article and she declared him the winner. He was excited about the win and contacted her to share his appreciation. "Is there anything my father can do for you?" he asked. As fate would have it, his father was the Southeast director for Borders, the mega-bookstore chain. "I'd love to get my book into Borders," Jackson said. He helped her to schedule book signings, giving her an incredible opportunity to sell tons of books through effective book-signings during the November gift-buying season.[8]

Philip Nork mentioned in the *Book Marketing Network* forum that he'd sold 1,500 copies of his book (not traditionally published), *Sensitivity 101 for the Heterosexual Male,* in the first three months of publication. Another forum participant asked for details. He replied that 1,000 of them sold in one fell swoop. Flying from Las Vegas to New Mexico, he was reading his book and talking to the lady next to him about it. Another passenger overheard the conversation and approached Nork after the flight. He was a buyer for gift shops and subsequently placed an order for 1,000 copies.[9]

* * *

Magic strikes when we least expect it, as we plod along with our daily, mundane, marketing efforts.

* * *

Once we understand how the magic works, it's easier to endure those dry times when nothing seems to be working.

5. To execute more effectively, never stop learning.

Jack Welch didn't just look for people who could execute; he looked for intelligence – not necessarily brilliance, but people who possessed "a strong dose of intellectual curiosity, with a breadth of knowledge to work with or lead other smart people in today's complex world."[10]

Authors who execute without intelligence execute the wrong things. They spend their days hanging out on Facebook, imagining that they're harnessing the power of social networking, and then wonder why nobody's buying their books.

That's why I hope that this book doesn't conclude your study of book marketing. I hope it's only the beginning. I hope I've helped you to see that learning a few tactics and modifying a few attitudes can make the difference between a non-seller and a best seller. But I may have failed to cover the best tactics for selling *your* book. That most effective method – your key to becoming a best-selling author – may be described in another marketing book, or on a blog post, or in a book-marketing forum. The most revolutionary social networking application for selling books may be in development as you read this chapter, to be released in a few months. How will you hear about it if you've stopped learning?

Al Rogers' words deserve repeating:

> *"In times of profound change, the learners inherit the earth, while the learned find themselves beautifully equipped to deal with a world that no longer exists."*

So don't stop learning.

Keep up through my website (www.sellmorebooks.org) and the sites of John Kremer and Brian Jud and Dan Poynter. Follow my suggestions for further learning at the end of each chapter.

I suppose my biggest temptation to stop learning marketing is this thought: "I've already got more ideas than I could ever execute. Why get more ideas until I've implemented these?" My answer? "I'm not just adding to my list. New ideas help me to reorder my list and to make my initiatives more effective." An idea I heard from an author this past weekend will likely take my presentations to a new level. I can't afford to stop learning!

6. Execute with more power by viewing yourself as helping people.

I made this point in chapter 11, but I want to conclude with it. A few years ago I heard Jeff Haynie, CEO of Appcellerator speak at a technology conference. Having succeeded at a startup of his own, he spends many days in Silicon

Valley advising others concerning their startups. Haynie observed something simple, yet profound, that often differentiates the successful startups from the losers. The losers start their pitches with "here's an idea that's bound to make a lot of money." The winners start their pitches with "here's an idea that could help a lot of people."

Like startups, writing a book is an entrepreneurial exercise. Your gut motivations will have a lot to do with whether your startup fails or succeeds.

Canfield and Hansen got over the stigma of marketing by focusing on helping people. "I never wrote books to get rich," Canfield said in an interview. "I wrote books to make a difference." As a result, they sold millions of "Chicken Soup" books.[11]

Christopher Paolini didn't do school assemblies just to sell copies of *Eragon*. He saw himself as motivating students to read and write.[12]

History demonstrates the awesome power of great books to give hope to the hopeless, wisdom to the ignorant, and relief to the suffering. Great books can transform a shy teen into a confident, powerful force for good. Great books mold impressionable minds. Great books change the course of history.

But they can't change anything until we get them into people's hands. That's what motivates me to

SELL MORE BOOKS!

Appendix 1

Never Stop Learning

At the crossroads on the path that leads to the future,

tradition has placed against each of us ten thousand men to guard the past.

- Belgian philosopher Maurice Maeterlinck

To keep up with this ever-changing industry, we must continually challenge both "the way it's always been done" and "what makes sense to me." Those who keep learning will maintain a huge advantage over those who stop learning.

In this appendix, I'll limit myself to some general tips rather than trying to recommend hundreds of specific resources. The latter would likely take 40 extra pages and raise the cost of the book, not to mention that it would be quickly dated. So I'll try to keep an updated, free list of specific books, sites, e-zines, organizations, blogs, forums, etc. at www.sellmorebooks.com.

Here are some general tips to optimize your learning:

1. Don't overlook older books on book marketing. Don't expect a 1995 book to cover social media and Amazon.com, but it might have excellent tips on local selling and building relationships with key influencers and distributors. Often today's authors become so enamored with the latest social networking trends that they overlook tried and true methods that may work even better for their books.

2. Re-read your underlinings and notations. When I first read a book, I remember and apply a tiny percentage of the wisdom offered. But since I underline key, relevant points and make notations in the back, it takes very little time to review these relevant portions. I should probably re-read my underlinings in Kremer's ***1001 Ways to Market Your Books*** once a year or so and realign my marketing goals accordingly.

3. Follow a publishing forum or listserv. Find the best ones with hundreds of participants who keep up with the industry. The ability to crowd source this up-to-the-minute wisdom is invaluable.

4. Give back by sharing your experiences (good and bad) and wisdom. So much of book marketing advice consists of:

- Here's how to do a press release...
- Here's how to set up a YouTube video...
- Here's how to do an author signing...

And yes, that advice has value. But beyond that, we need authors and publishers and publicists telling us their actual experiences with various methods so that we can better assess a method's viability for our books. Here's the specific information authors crave, but typically lack:

- "I tried this press release with this press release company and got no results at all. I made these specific changes and got 20 interviews which resulted in 50 books sold within a week."
- "I've been answering people's questions on LinkedIn, allowing me to become a respected thought leader in my field. But this has taken me an average of ten hours per week and I'm not sure that it has resulted in enough specific sales to justify my involvement."

The platforms (forums, discussion groups, etc.) are available to collect and assess these informal case studies, but without authors sharing candidly and on a larger scale, many publicity campaigns will continue to be shots into the dark.

5. Join local writers' organizations and attend writers' conferences. Yes, there's still value in meeting people face to face. Find the ones attended and run by interesting, helpful, experienced authors, and you'll find yourself encouraged and enlightened.

Appendix 2

200+ Ways that Low Profile Authors Can Market their Books (A Helpful Way to Choose Your Initiatives)

Sometimes a big list helps. You can easily circle the ideas that appeal to you, cross out the ones you'd never do, and highlight the ones you'd like to accomplish in the next sixmonths.

A Huge List: Discouraging or Encouraging?

Don't get discouraged by this list, as if you should do all these things or even most of them. Most successful book sellers that I know tend to do a few things very well rather than flit here and there trying one tactic one day and another the next. So let this list encourage you by realizing that if one tactic isn't working, there are plenty of others to choose from.

From Subhub, Feb, 2010, (http://www.subhub.com/articles/the-best-free-and-paid-press-release-websites-and-when-to-use-them): www.prlog.org, www.pr.com and www.pressrelease365.com .

I compiled this list from the suggestions of scores of authors and book publicists who offered ideas in about 25 book marketing books, over 100 articles, as well as numerous seminars, webinars and forums. For detailed descriptions of how to implement these strategies, visit www.sellmorebooks.org, where I connect you with helpful resources.

Making Your Book More Marketable

1. Choose a **memorable title**. Choose a **subtitle that is descriptive and contains much-searched words/phrases**. 2. Include **settings that make it marketable** in those geographic areas. 3. Include **subject matter** (a cancer survivor, a disabled protagonist, a character who continually eats jelly beans) **that opens possibilities for sales** and recommendations through related organizations, companies, newsletters, and blogs. 4. **Do research that journalists/bloggers would be interested in quoting**. 5. **Include an index** to make it more attractive to librarians. 6. **Do serious research that would impress experts and cause them to write good reviews.** 7. **Co-author** with a recognized expert or allow her to write a chapter or an introduction. 8. Work hard to **get blurbs by recognized**

experts or celebrities to put on the cover. 9. It should **look professional** in every way: editing, cover art, interior design, etc.

Blurbs

10. **Get lots of blurbs from all kinds of people**. Since you're building multiple platforms, different types of blurbs and different blurbers appeal to different audiences. 11. **List authors of similar books, thought leaders, leaders of industries, high profile people that either you or your friends know. Don't forget low profile people who represent your book's market.** 12. **Use blurbs on the front cover, back cover, in press releases, and in e-letters seeking reviews**. 13. When people tell you how much they liked your book, ask for their permission to use their comments. **Help them to word their comments** to better express how they feel.

Book Awards

14. **Find all the relevant contests** in *Writer's Digest*, *Literary Marketplace*, through Google, etc. 15. **Target the ones that fit your budget, offer the best chance of winning, the most prestige,** etc.

Reviews

16. **Study the big, pre-publication reviewers** and send them galleys according to their specifications. 17. **Find newspapers** that review books (book review columns) of your type. 18. **Find newspaper columnists in your subject area** and e-mail them to ask if they'd like a free copy for review. 19. **Find people interested in your genre/subject matter and ask them if they'd like a copy to review on Amazon.** 20. **Have many read it in digital format before publication** to get their input. After it's published, offer them a free copy to review on Amazon.

Research Niche Media

(There's less competition in a narrow niche)

21. Use resources at your library like *Gale Directory of Publications* and *Broadcast Media* to **find hundreds of newsletters, periodicals, radio stations, and newspapers that cover your niche.** 22. **Follow up** later with other newsy angles. If they do respond, note their interest and contact them again in the future.

Non-Bookstores that Don't Normally Sell Books

(No Competition with Other Books)

23. **Home Office (mailing/copy/etc.) stores.** 24. **Restaurants, Doctor's offices.** 25. When it sells well in one place, **get testimonies from storeowners** to use in

selling it to other places. 26. **Hairdressers, nail salons, auto repair waiting rooms** – anywhere people have to wait in line or wait for services.

Non-Bookstores that also Sell Books

(Less Competition than Bookstores)

27. **Office supply stores** (Staples, Office Depot, etc.) 28. **Costco, Sam's Clubs** 29. **Airport stores** 30. **Gift stores** 31. **Specialty stores** (pet stores for dog books, home school stores for textbooks, etc.).

Publishing for Effective Marketing

32. **Choose publishers known for excellent products and diligent marketing**. 33. **Don't let it appear self-published or subsidy published.** If you're doing either, start your own publishing company and use your own ISBN. 34. **Make sure your contract allows you to purchase inexpensive author copies** to use for reviews and giveaways. A good book is its most effective marketing piece.

Bulk Sales

35. Brainstorm: **What people or organizations might buy your book in bulk** for Christmas or birthday gifts, to give out free to promote a product, for graduation gifts, as training/inspiration for their employees, or as rewards for outstanding employees? 36. **Contact these organizations through friends who have contacts**. (LinkedIn might help.) 37. **Visit local organizations first.** 38. **When one organization uses your book, get testimonies to use in attracting other organizations.** 39. **Join Brian Jud's Premium Book Company** to have salesmen try to sell your books in bulk to companies and specialty markets.

Your Author/Book/Subject Site

40. **Develop a central place where potential buyers/interviewers/readers can connect with you.** 41. **Consider using a blog** for this purpose, since search engines tend to rank blogs higher. 42. **One of your pages should be a "Press Page,"** giving information about your book, listing reviews, linking to interviews, offering useable author photos and cover art, providing sample chapters, etc. 43. **Study the web presences of other authors** to get ideas. Don't pay more than you have to! A basic WordPress Blog is free, and may be all you'll ever need. 44. **Save time and money by learning how to add pages and write content yourself.** If it doesn't look professional enough, **pay a designer to go over it and make it look good.** 45. **Buy a web address** (url) for your name, the name of your book, the name of your subject, or whatever you want to emphasize and brand. 46. **Use Google's Keyword Tool to find what phrases are most used to search for your information.** Use those phrases in your tags, titles, bold print, headings, early in your text, late in your text, links, etc., to attract searches. 47. **Link to your online presence in your signature** with every e-mail and online

comment you make. 48. **Link to your online presence through the personal profile sections of all your social media presences.**

Supporting Materials

49. **Make a brochure** with your book cover, book description, blurbs and reader benefits. 50. **Create bookmarks** with your cover art on the front and ordering information on the back. 51. **Make a professional display** for book signings. It could display your book cover, blurbs, and benefits to readers. 52. Design **posters** to advertise events. 53. **Find or develop inexpensive, useful giveaways.** For a financial book, a cardboard investment calculator could demonstrate how quickly money can multiply. Giving gifts makes people more open to giving back by buying your products. 54. **Print your book information on 4x6 cards** and have students tack them on dormitory bulletin boards and anywhere they're appropriate.

Online Stores

55. **Make your book available from all the online stores where people might find you**: Amazon, Barnes & Noble, Powell's, AbeBooks, Alibris, etc. 56. Optimize your presence by **encouraging people to put up reviews**. 57. **Use the book description section to detail benefits to readers and outline the contents.** 58. **Use whatever tools the stores offer**, such as "search inside the book" to draw searches and give browsers the opportunity to read book portions. Add tags to optimize searches. 59. **Prepare a "Listmania!" recommended book list** on Amazon that includes your book. 60. **Prepare a "So You'd Like To..." guide** on Amazon that includes your book.

Develop Affiliate Sales

61. **Encourage others to sell your books** (especially e-books) from their sites. They get a portion of the profit, making it a win/win.

Speaking

62. **Contact your local chamber of commerce** to see if they know of or run seminars appropriate for your subject matter. 63. Would your topic appeal to **churches?** 64. Consider school **classrooms**, school **clubs**, and **assemblies**. Think kindergartens through universities, public and private. 65. Represent **an existing organization**. 66. **Create a seminar**. 67. Offer to do **seminars at established conferences.** 68. Contact organizations with local chapters such as Kiwanis, AARP, Rotary Club, etc. 69. Explore opportunities in **libraries**. 70. Search www.meetup.com to **find reading groups** (search your geographical area and "reading") and meetings organized around your subject area. Contact them with your book information to see if they'd like to read your book and bring you in for the discussion. Also check for reading groups through your local library and search "reading groups (your city or state)" in Google.

Writing Articles

71. **Use *Writer's Market*** (online or print) to find magazines that publish articles on your subject. 72. **Study each publication** to see what they're looking for (their publishing calendar), their style, if they take outside writers and how they like writers to submit articles. 73. **Offer titles/themes that are controversial, counter-intuitive, intriguing.** 74. People love to read about people. **Use personal stories or stories of interesting people** that others would love to read about. 77. If a magazine has a web presence, **offer an article for posting on their site** (less competition than their print publication). 76. **Link back to your articles** from your press page.

Newsletters

77. **Start a newsletter** either on your subject or for your following. 78**. Offer it on your site**, with a freebie to entice people to join. 79**. Give them valuable, free information** with each newsletter.

Producing Videos

(Search Engines often rank videos high)

80. **If you do a TV spot that works**, get permission to **put it up on YouTube, YahooVideo and other free video sites** (there are over 300 video-sharing sites). 81. **Title it and describe it with much-searched key phrases.** Link back to your press page or site. 82. **Video your talks and put up relevant portions.** Link to them from your press page so that organizers seeking to book you can see you in action. 83. **Video informal how-to segments on your book's topic to fill gaps in current video offerings** and to help people.

Festivals

84. **Share a booth** with other authors for more fun, less work, and less cost. 80. Book festivals are only one type. Would your book sell at country fairs, Renaissance Festivals, Dragon Con, or other **niche festivals**? 85. **Talk to other booksellers** at festivals to ask them what works and what doesn't. 86. **Have something to give away.** People will want to reciprocate by buying something. 87. **Have a contest or a drawing** (not for your book, lest they forgo buying it to see if they win it). 88. **Be friendly** to everyone, whether they buy or not. They may buy later or recommend you to others.

Distribution

89. **Make sure your book is being distributed in a way that best suits your goals.** If you want to maximize your profit per book sale on Amazon, choose the lowest possible discount from Lightning Source. If you want it to sell in bookstores, choose a 55% discount and set up a return policy. 90. **Find distributors that actively sell to niches you want to target** (e.g., libraries, schools, etc.). In

researching distributors, make sure their discount works for your book. It's often 70%. John Kremer maintains a list of distributors at http://www.bookmarket.com/distributors.htm.

Book Clubs

91. **Find all appropriate book clubs** that might carry your book. (*Literary Marketplace* lists 69 book clubs.) 92. **Study each company** to understand their audience and their terms. 93. **Offer your book** to appropriate book clubs. 94. **Discover local book clubs and offer to speak.**

Translations and Foreign Rights

95. **If you think your book has international appeal, search "foreign rights literary agents" in Google** to find agents who specialize in securing foreign rights. 96. **Prepare an e-mail explaining why your book would appeal to publishers in other countries.** Contact many agents and/or foreign publishers directly who might be interested.

Learning (See also "Leverage the Expertise of Others")

97. **Keep up with the** industry through publications such as *Writers Weekly*. 98. **Subscribe to book marketing newsletters** from John Kremer, Brian Jud, Rick Frishman, etc. 99. **Follow listservs and forums** such as *Book Publishing Professionals* on LinkedIn or the *Book Marketing Network* on Ning. 100. **Talk regularly with other authors in your field to learn from each other. Attend writers' conferences.** 101. **Collect a library of book marketing books** so that you can reference relevant chapters when you start a new initiative. 102. **Follow and participate in top book marketing blogs.**

Uncategorized Stuff

103. Search Google with phrases such as "best books on (your subject)" or "recommended (your subject) books." If your book's not included in certain lists, **track down the creators of the lists and offer them a free book to consider adding to their lists.** 104. **Install the free Alexa Toolbar** in your browser so you can immediately know the popularity of any site or blog. This helps you prioritize which sites are worth writing for, sending books to for review, etc.

Bookstore Strategies

105. **Start with local, independent bookstores.** 106. **Drive people into the bookstores with local radio, Facebook, personal contacts, and newspapers.** 107. **Use your track record of sales in one store to encourage other stores to take your books.** 108. If they won't buy your books (typically at a 55% discount) **leave some on consignment.** 109. **Leave free bookmarks** (book cover on one side, book info on other side.) 110. **Do book signings.** Tip: It's often more comfortable

with other authors. Advertise through local publicity. 111. Beyond your hometown, **consider towns where relatives and friends live.** Do they have connections with their local bookstores?

School Strategies

112. **Offer readings in classes.** 113. **Speak on writing as a career.** 114. **Speak in classes in your subject area.** 115. **Do assemblies.** 116. **Offer your book as a fundraiser.** 117. **Create a special web page** on your blog/site describing what you do in schools. Include pictures of excited, involved students and testimonies of teachers, administrators, and students. When you contact other schools, link them to that page for more information.

Libraries

118. **Offer copies to local/regional committees** that review books for possible library use. 119. **Provide a brochure** that lists awards and reviews. 120. **Offer to speak.** 121. **Give away a stack of free bookmarks with your book information on them.** 122. **Submit your book for review to organizations that libraries look to for reviews.** Example: VOYA – *Voice of Youth Advocates* – targets librarians who cater to young people. 123. **Contact a distributor that targets libraries.** (See "distribution" section.) 124. **Change your thinking about libraries.** Don't fear that you'll lose sales because your book's available free of charge. Think of it as another way of spreading the word! 125. **Mail information to libraries**, explaining how your book fills a niche that their community needs. Give options for ordering the book. (Many order through wholesalers or distributors.) Leave a link to your media page for more information.

Giveaways

(Provides a "taste" and encourages reciprocal buying)

126. **Provide free digital chapters on your website/blog/press page** 127. **Print a sample chapter to place in waiting rooms** and other key places.

Newsletters/E-letters

128. **Find the most popular newsletters** in your subject area and offer the writers a free copy for review. 129. **Offer a free guest article** appropriate for the newsletter. 130. **Start your own newsletter**, offering a free gift (valuable white paper, chapter, etc.) if people sign up for it on your site.

Blogs (see also "Your Online Presence" and "Social Networking")

Participating in Other Blogs

131. **Find the most popular blogs in your subject area.** Use Tecnnorati's search engine (search "blogs" instead of "posts"). 132. **Comment on their posts** with relevant information. 133. **Put your book title and a link to your press page in your signature.** 134. **Contact the blogger to offer a book for review.** 135. **Offer your book for use as a giveaway.** 136. **Keep records of bloggers** who liked your book. Continue to comment on their blogs. 137. **Offer to write guest posts.** 138. **Follow up on bloggers who didn't respond to your initial requests.** A non-response isn't a rejection. Often it takes several tries. 139. **Link to blog posts that review your book from your press page.**

Your Own Blog

140. **Choose a niche theme** that separates you from other bloggers. 141. If you're trying to gather a blog following, **blog regularly** – several times per week. 142. **Develop popular posts as "pillars"** – solid, unique content on a subject that people need and search for. Example: A post where you keep current statistics in your field, or recommend the top books/resources in your field. 143. **Actively seek links from other prominent blogs** in your subject area. 144. **Join an association of bloggers** in your field that promote each other.

Record Keeping and Follow-Up

145. **Keep good records of whom you've contacted, whom you sent books to for review, which came through with reviews, etc.** 146. **Follow up** on those who said they'd do a review but never came through. 147. **Thank** those who do reviews, recommend your books, and do favors. 148. **Note which strategies worked best and allocate future marketing time accordingly.**

Target Special Seasons

149. **Consult this year's edition of *Chase's Calendar of Events*** in your library to find every event that connects with your book's subject matter. (Example: The media might be more receptive to interviewing a personal finance author during *National Financial Literacy Month*.) 150. **Consider each season.** If your book targets graduates, time articles to come out during graduation season.

Comment on Current News

151. **Set up Google Alerts** for key phrases in your subject area. 152. **When news about your subject breaks, comment on blog posts**. 153. **Offer your expertise** to local reporters on relevant events.

Help Reporters/Journalists/Bloggers

154. **Subscribe to services** such as HARO (free), Bill and Steve Harrison's *Reporter Connection* (free) or *ProfNet* (paid). 155. When reporters use your material,

keep the name and contact information for future reference. 156. **Thank them** for covering you.

Leveraging the Expertise of Others
(See also "Learning")

157. **Hire great publicists** when you need their contacts or expertise. 158. **Ask your writers group for input**. 159. **Join a local writers association** to meet writers, publicists, editors, literary agents, etc.

Press Releases

160. **Send one to announce your book**, tying it to a newsy topic. 161. **Write effective copy**. Emphasize, a) what reporters would like to write about, and b) what readers want to know about. 162. **Use multiple companies** to send free releases. 163. **Use key words and phrases** that are heavily searched. 164. **Find the most effective companies** at http://www.topseos.com/rankings-of-best-press-release-distribution-companies

165. **Consider companies that use updated lists of the people you want to target** (e.g., Christian media, librarians, etc.) 166. **Set up your book and your name to receive Google Alerts** so that you'll be alerted when your book gets mentioned. 167. **Send releases over time** on topics related to your book that journalists could easily write articles about. 168. **Consider sending press releases announcing your speaking event, your helpful white paper, a book award you received, an interesting/controversial (newsy) position you're espousing**.

Radio and Television

169. **Start local.** Once you get some smaller interviews under your belt and link to them from your press page, larger radio stations are more likely to interview you. 170. **Search Google for radio shows on your topic.** 171. **Consult the huge media directories** at your library to find more: *All in One Media Directory*, Gale *Directory of Publications and Broadcast Media*, *Bacon's Media Directories*, *U.S. and Canadian Broadcast Outlet*. 172. When you do a good interview, **get a quote from the interviewer** about how well you did. Put the blurb on your press page. 173. **Link to your interview** from your press page, so that potential interviewers can hear you in action. 174. **Over prepare, but relax** and enjoy the actual interview. 175. **Stand up** during the interview to come across more energetic. 176. Remember: it's all about the listening audience. **Pitch interviewers with how your interview can help their audiences.** 177. **Add humor and fun.** Entertain as you educate. 178. **Don't force your book** into the conversation. Typically, the interviewer will mention it and you won't have to. If you need to mention it, do it in unobjectionable ways, like "When researching my chapter on Canine Obesity for my book, *Enjoy Your Puppies*, I discovered...."179. Ask your publicist for advice on how to make the most out of an interview. 180. **Get media training** to make your interviews more effective. 181. While

you can always start your own program, it takes a lot of time and personal drive. Unless you always wanted to have your own show, **"go where people already gather" by getting on other people's shows.** 182. Although TV sounds more glamorous, **typically prioritize radio over TV**, unless you're talking about a huge national show like Oprah. Authors often report disappointing sales from TV appearances. 183. **Put an ad in the Radio-TV Interview Report, which radio shows use to find people to interview.** The ad will probably be more effective if you've already gotten some reviews under your belt and linked to them from your press page.

Planning Your Marketing

184. **Write a marketing plan.** 185. **Plan long-term** so that you can see how today's publicity can help you to be more effective in five years.

Social Networking

Facebook

186. If you're the last person on earth to get on Facebook, **sign up today.** 187. **Be friendly and conversational**. Encourage friends during good times, console them during hard times, and celebrate their birthdays. 188. Announce your book on Facebook when it first comes out. 189. **Let your friends know about book events** appropriate to share among friends. 190. **Start a Facebook page** (formerly "fan page"), as a place you can be more direct and specific about everything related to your book. 191. **Visit your friends' profiles** to see if they work for companies that might use your book as a giveaway, incentive, prize, or gift.

LinkedIn

192. **Start a LinkedIn page** for professional networking. 193. **Put book information in your profile.** 194. **Answer people's questions** (See LinkedIn's "Answer" section) concerning your book's topic, establishing yourself as a trusted resource and thought leader. 195. Ask questions and **use the answers in articles** you write that relate to your book. 196. **Find LinkedIn groups** that relate to your book and participate in them, putting your book title and a link to your media page in your signature. Some of these participants would love to give input on your manuscript and later write reviews on Amazon. 197. **Connect with influencers** in your book's subject area through your connections and by trolling the "Answers" section. Go to the "Advanced Search" feature in the "Answers" section. Search key words that relate to your subject area. Here you'll find key influencers who answer people's questions about your subject area. Contact them (did they list their email address or blog or place of employment in their profile?) and ask if they'd like to review your book.

Squidoo

198. **Search Squidoo to find the most popular "lenses" in your subject area.** Study each of these lenses to determine why they're so popular. What can you offer that's not already being offered (your niche)? 199. **Create and maintain one or more "lenses" to help people in your subject area.** (Could some of your "pillar" blog posts become Squidoo "lenses"?) 200. **Recommend your book**, listing reader benefits and linking to your site/blog/book page. 201. **Link to your lens** from your other web presences.

Forums, ListServs, and Message Boards

203. **Search Google to find the most active ones on your topic.** 204. **Participate in discussions**, including a link to your press page in your signature. 205. **If there are no good forums on your topic, start one.** 206. **Use them to connect with people about your topic while you're writing your book.** Ask for ideas, run ideas by people, and find early readers to give you input. Many of these will later give you Amazon reviews.

Index

End Notes

Chapter 1: Four Digital Revolutions that Can Make Nobodies Awesome

1 http://www.publishersweekly.com/pw/by-topic/industry-news/bookselling/article/42783-aap-book-sales-dipped-in-2009.html.

2 Michael Norris, a senior analyst at Simba Information, which provides research to publishers, from his presentation, "I'll Never Pay More Than $9.99 for an E-Book! And Similar Lies."

3 The cost of traditional publication of any given book will vary greatly depending upon the number of copies in the initial print run, the amount allocated for publicity, etc.

4 According to the Robert E. Shepard Agency, they, "like most agencies," accept less than one percent of the book proposals they receive. http://www.shepardagency.com/writing_proposals.html. The Levine Greenburg Agency accepts about one percent. http://www.mediabistro.com/articles/cache/a1438.asp.

5 http://news.bookweb.org/news/talking-pod-lightning-sources-david-taylor. http://www.wiley.com/WileyCDA/PressRelease/pressReleaseId-49224.html.

6 http://www.publishersweekly.com/pw/by-topic/industry-news/publishing-and-marketing/article/42826-self-published-titles-topped-764-000-in-2009-as-traditional-output-dipped.html.

7 From a conversation on the Book Marketing Forum.

8 "Four times" if I were using CreateSpace, more if I were using a steeper discount with Lightning Source.

9 http://www.fonerbooks.com/booksale.htm. He gathered these stats from SEC filings, company press releases, and annual reports.

10 http://www.amazon.com/gp/help/customer/display.html/ref=hp_rel_topic?ie=UTF8&nodeId=14101911; http://www.answers.com/topic/barnes-noble-inc - the average Barnes & Noble carries between 60,000 and 200,000 book titles (from Hoovers).

11 http://www.publishersweekly.com/pw/by-topic/industry-news/publishing-and-marketing/article/42826-self-published-titles-topped-764-000-in-2009-as-traditional-output-dipped.html - 288,355. 288,355 titles were traditionally published in 2009. 764,448 titles were published by self-publishers and micro-niche publishers.

12 I credit this observation to Peter Bowerman.

13 From a personal phone conversation with a receiving manager.

14 http://parapublishing.com/sites/para/resources/statistics.cfm - The figures vary from year to year and vary from hardback (more returns) to paperback, between 20% and 36%.

15 Personal conversation with novelist Ray Adkins.

16 While niches have always existed, the Web has given us new ways to find them and make a profit selling to "the long tail." Statisticians have studied the concept of the vast market for niche products since at least 1946, but Chris Anderson popularized this term for retailing on the Web in a *Wired* article and later in his 2006 book, *The Long Tail: Why the Future of Business is Selling Less of More*. Anderson observed that while most businesses concentrate on producing only the most popular products in a field, other businesses (like Amazon.com or Netflix) profit by marketing to the people who'd prefer the less popular, but more specialized products. Thus, since bookstores have limited space and must limit themselves to only the most popular books, Amazon can offer specialty, less popular books. If the larger part of the population prefers specialty books, then brick & mortar bookstores will miss out on the "long tail" beyond the most popular books. Customer demand for niche books has been growing rapidly, so that by 2008, 36.7% of Amazon's book sales were niche books.

17 http://www.publishers.org/main/PressCenter/Archicves/2011_Jan/November2010StatsPressRelease.htm.

18 http://online.wsj.com/article/SB10001424052748704912004575253132121412028.html?KEYWORDS=vanity+press+goes+digital

19 http://latimesblogs.latimes.com/jacketcopy/2010/06/simon-and-schuster-smart-ebook-truman-fires-macarthur.html.

20 http://www.webinknow.com/2010/06/book-publisher-goes-real-time-with-truman-fires-macarthur.html

21 David Meerman Scott, *The New Rules of Marketing & PR* (Hoboken, New Jersey: John Wiley & Sons, Inc.), p. xxvii.

Chapter 3: Write a Marketable Book

1 Jonathan Mahler, *James Patterson, Inc.*, *New York Times Magazine*, Jan. 20, 2010.

2 Ibid.

3 Dale Carnegie, *Effective Speaking* (New York: Association Press, 1962), p. 72.

4 Jack Canfield, Mark Victor Hansen, Bud Gardner, *Chicken Soup for the Writer's Soul* (Deerfield Beach, FL: Health Communications, Inc., 2000), pp. 230 ff.

5 Michael Del, with Catherine Fredman, *Direct from Dell* (New York: HarperBusiness, 1999), pp. vii, 117, 118, 122, 132-134, 139-155.

6 Jack Welch, with Suzy Welch, *Winning* (New York: HarperBusiness, 2005), pp. 25-35. See also Jack Welch, with John A. Byrne, *Jack* (New York: Warner Books, Inc., 2001), pp. 169-184.

7 Sam Walton, with John Huey, *Sam Walton: Made in America* (New York: Doubleday, 1992), p. 210.

8 Stephen King, *On Writing* (New York: Pocket Books, 2000), pp. 76, 77.

9 Motoko Rich, *Christian Novel Is Surprise Best Seller,* November 24, 2008, *New York Times.* http://www.nytimes.com/2008/06/24/books/24shack.html?_r=1&em&ex=1214452800&en=40f16df7490a912f&ei=5070. See also: http://www.forbes.com/forbes/2009/0622/celebrity-09-shack-religious-thriller-paul-young-publishing-miracle.html.

10 Dr. McGinnis – "Fiction is raw creativity, with scientific and factual coercion forcing a new product."

11 Dale Carnegie, *How to Win Friends and Influence People*, Revised Edition (New York: Pocket Books, 1981), pp. xv, xvi.

12 Benjamin Franklin, *The Autobiography of Benjamin Franklin* (New York: Dover Publications, 1996), pp. 45,46.

13 Humphrey Carpenter, J.R.R. Tolkien (Boston: Houghton Mifflin, 2000) pp. 152-155.

14 Dale Pollock, Skywalking: *The Life and Films of George Lucas* (New York: De Capo Press, 1999).

15 Jonathan Mahler, *James Patterson, Inc*. (*New York Times Magazine*: Jan. 20, 2010).

16 Jack Canfield interview with Steve Harrison, aired Oct. 16, 2008.

17 Peter Rubie and Gary Provost, *How to Tell a Story* (Writers Digest Books, 1998), p. 61.

18 Cherie K. Miller, *Writing Conversations* (Acworth, Georgia: Wisdom Creek Press, LLC, 2010), p. 35.

Chapter 4: Write a Title and Subtitle that Attracts Audiences

1 http://www.amazon.com/gp/help/customer/display.html/ref=hp_rel_topic?ie=UTF8&nodeId=14101911.

Chapter 5: Intrigue People with your Cover

1 Dan Poynter, *Dan Poynter's Self-Publishing Manual* (Santa Barbara, CA: Para Publishing, 2007), p. 51. Another source said that, according to the *Wall Street Journal* people spend eight seconds looking at the front cover.

2 Arielle Eckstut & David Henry Sterry, *Putting Your Passion into Print* (New York: Workman Publishing Company, Inc., 2005), p. 225.v

3 J. Conrad Levinson, Rick Frishman & Michael Larsen, *Guerilla Marketing for Writers* (Cincinnati, OH: Writer's Digest Books, 2001), p. 138.

4 Marilyn & Tom Ross, *Jump Start Your Book Sales* (Buena Vista, CO: Communication Creativity, 1999), pp. 7, 8.

Chapter 6: Publish it through the Most Marketable Channel

1 http://michaelhyatt.com/2008/08/advice-to-first.html.

2 http://en.wikipedia.org/wiki/A_Wrinkle_in_Time . See also Madeleine L'Engle and Carole F. Chase, *Madeleine L'Engle Herself: Reflections on a Writing Life* (Shaw Books, 2001).

3 James B. Stewart, *Disney War* (New York: Simon & Schuster, 2005), pp. 486, 487.

4 Ibid. p. 527.

5 http://www.go-publish-yourself.com/community/interview-bollesr.php.

6 Dave Ramsey, *The Total Money Makeover* (Nashville: Thomas Nelson Publishers, 2003) p. ix.

7 http://en.wikipedia.org/wiki/The_Shack.

8 http://www.nytimes.com/2010/01/24/magazine/24patterson-t.html , see also http://www.answers.com/topic/publishing-industry.

9 *Current Biography (1951)*, The H.W. Wilson Company.

10 See http://en.wikipedia.org/wiki/Self-publishing for a list of famous self-published works. See another list in the introduction to John Kremer's *The Self Publisher's Hall of Fame*.

Chapter 8: Optimize Your Amazon and Barnes & Noble Pages

1 http://www.amazon.com/gp/help/customer/display.html/ref=hp_rel_topic?ie=UTF8&nodeId=14101911.

2 Shiv Singh, *Social Media Marketing for Dummies* (Hoboken, NJ: Wiley Publishing, Inc., 2010), pp. 160, 161.

3 Darren Rowse noted this tendency in product reviews. "The best results I've had from affiliate programs are where I give an open and honest appraisal of the product, including both its strengths and weaknesses." Darren Rowse and Chris Garrett, *ProBlogger*, Second Edition (Indianapolis, IN: Wiley Publishing, Inc., 2010), p. 110.

4 For more information on tags, see: http://www.amazon.com/gp/help/customer/display.html/ref=tag_cld_cl_ihlp_wt?ie=UTF8&nodeId=16238571&pop-up=1.

5 Aaron Shepard says that after optimizing your book on Amazon, it may take a year or more for it to rise on lists and reach its full potential. Aaron Shepard, *Aiming at Amazon* (Olympia, Washington: Shepard Publications, 2007), pp. 135, 141.

Chapter 9: Build a Professional Online Presence

1 http://www.facebook.com/press/info.php?statistics.

2 As I write, Google doesn't use "description" or "keywords" meta tags to rank your site, but things can change! http://googlewebmastercentral.blogspot.com/2009/09/google-does-not-use-keywords-meta-tag.html.

Chapter 11: Check Your Attitudes toward Marketing

1 Dan Poynter, *Dan Poynter's Self-Publishing Manual* (Santa Barbara, CA: Para Publishing, 2007), pp. 201, 202.

2 Debbie Allen, *Confessions of Shameless Self Promoters* (Scottsdale, AZ: Success Showcase Publishing, 2002), p.19.

3 Ibid., p. 113.

4 See interview with Canfield here: http://freelancewriterblog.blogspot.com/2008/10/marketing-ideas-from-jack-canfield.html.

5 John Kremer, *1001 Ways to Market Your Books* (Fairfield, IA: Ad-Lib Publications, 1990), p. 19.

6 Ibid., p. 699.

7 http://en.wikipedia.org/wiki/Eragon, http://www.teenreads.com/authors/au-paolini-christopher.asp , http://inheritance.wikia.com/wiki/Christopher_Paolini.

8 http://freelancewriterblog.blogspot.com/2008/10/marketing-ideas-from-jack-canfield.html.

9 Benjamin Franklin: *The Autobiography of Benjamin Franklin* (Mineola, N.Y.: Dover Thrift Edition, 1996, from the 1868 edition by Lippincott & Co.) p.67.

10 Walter Isaacson, *Benjamin Franklin: An American Life* (New York: Simon & Schuster, 2003), p. 257.

Chapter 12: Let Basic Principles Guide Your Choice of Initiatives

1 Stephen Manes and Paul Andrews, *Gates: How Microsoft's Mogul Reinvented An Industry - And Made Himself The Richest Man in America*, Simon & Schuster, New York, 1994, pp. 199,200.

2 See especially Malcolm Gladwell on "the law of the few" and the power of connectors, mavens, and salesmen in producing tipping points. Malcomb Gladwell, *The Tipping Point* (New York: Little, Brown and Company, 2002), pp. 21, 30-88. See also Shiv Singh, *Social Media Marketing for Dummies* (Hoboken, NJ: Wiley Publishing, Inc., 2010), pp. 12-14 on types of influencers, pp. 160 and 161 on studies, and pp. 139ff on courting influencers.

3 Charles W. Lamb, Joseph F. Hair, Jr., Carl McDaniel, *MKTG2*, Instructor's Edition (Mason, OH: South-Western Cengage Learning, 2008), p. 219.

4 Shiv Singh, opt. cit., p. 160. In October 22nd and 23rd (2010) conversations with social media experts Olivia Blanchard (BrandBuilder) and Marla Erwin (Interactive Art Director for Whole Foods), we discussed the wisdom of low profile authors interacting with already popular blogs rather than devoting significant time to trying to build their own followings. They tended to concur with this approach. Also reference Dan Zarella, *The Social Media Marketing Book* (Sebastopol, CA: O'Reilly Media, Inc., 2010), pp. 165-169. Zarella suggests that starting and maintaining a forum can be too time consuming for many companies. Rather, they should consider participating in already-popular forums that are maintained by others. In other words, go where people already gather.

5 Our ability to reach niches in "the long tail of the web" has made it possible to better target those who are already interested in our products, rather than having to broadcast to everyone, annoying the disinterested in order to reach the interested.

6 http://www.nytimes.com/2010/01/24/magazine/24patterson-t.html?_r=1&pagewanted=2. TV ads can serve many purposes in marketing beyond producing immediate sales. They can inform, persuade and remind. While some decry the death of such forms of marketing, the amount of money spent on TV ads grew 28% from 2000 to 2005. (*MKTG*, opt. cit., pp. 212ff.) Many smart business people obviously believe that these still pay off for certain products.

Chapter 13: Seek Reviews from the Most Respected Early Book Review Source

1 http://www.ala.org/ala/aboutala/offices/publishing/booklist_publications/booklist/insidebooklist/booklistproc/proceduressubmitting.cfm.

2 Phone interview, 7/27/10.

3 Personal e-mail from a Discoveries Editor, 7/27/10.

4 Phone interview with Mike Harvkey, 7/30/2010.

5 Their website says that 8,500 are received in one place and 7,500 in another, so I averaged it to 8,000. An editor told me in a 7/30/2010 conversation that they receive from 500 to 700 titles per week, so I used the average of 600 per week.

6 I asked editor Kent Turner, "How do you know if it's self-published?" He replied that he doesn't trace down ISBN's or search for the publisher in Literary Marketplace. Rather, if he sees something obvious, like the author is John Smith and the publisher is "John Smith Publishers," he assumes it's self published and not appropriate for their review.

7 http://articles.sfgate.com/2007-03-03/news/17237363_1_book-review-times-publisher-david-hiller-times-staffers.

8 http://en.wikipedia.org/wiki/New_York_Times_Book_Review.

9 http://www.bookmarket.com/newspapers.htm.

10 http://en.wikipedia.org/wiki/New_York_Times_Book_Review.

11 http://www.qcknightnews.com/2.10350/the-man-behind-the-criticism-sam-tanenhaus-1.1377318.

12 http://www.nytimes.com/2009/01/29/books/29post.html - "The *Los Angeles Times* lost its stand-alone Sunday section in 2007, when it was combined with the paper's opinion section and the Sunday pages devoted to book reviews dropped to 10 from 12. At the end of 2008 the newspaper was redesigned again, moving the book reviews to the second of a two-part weekly calendar section devoted to the arts."

13 http://www.publishersweekly.com/pw/by-topic/industry-news/publishing-and-marketing/article/43875-los-angeles-review-of-books-to-launch-this-fall.html ; http://chronicle.com/blogPost/The-Los-Angeles-Review-of/25674.

14 http://www.nytimes.com/2009/01/29/books/29post.html.

Chapter 14: Get Exposure on Busy Blogs

1 Example: www.techcrunch.com boasts over 10 million unique visitors. Over 100 countries have less than 10 million inhabitants (http://www.worldatlas.com/aatlas/populations/ctypopls.htm).

2 Malcomb Gladwell, *The Tipping Point* (New York: Little, Brown and Company, 2002), pp. 30-88.

3 http://federatedmedia.net/authors/boingboing.

4 http://www.exalead.com/search; http://www.lib.berkeley.edu/TeachingLib/Guides/Internet/SearchEngines.html.

5 Darren Rowse and Chris Garrett, *ProBlogger* (Indianapolis, IN: Wiley Publishing, Inc., 2010) p. 146. "There is a high probability your email will not be read past the first few lines, so make them count."

6 On buyers responding to reviews that include negatives as well as positives, see Darren Rowse and Chris Garrett, *ProBlogger*, Second Edition (Indianapolis, IN: Wiley Publishing, Inc., 2010), p. 110.

7 I mentioned this campaign to John Kremer, who replied, "Don't forget to follow up again with the ¾ that didn't respond the first time. People are busy. They miss things they really want to respond to. A second offer helps to remind them that they intended to follow up. The best intentions to follow up often go astray because we are all busy. Something set aside to act on later, unfortunately, rarely gets acted upon. It's too easy to forget something when you set it aside."

8 "Success in blogging means having great content backed by solid promotion...." Rouse and Garrett, opt. cit., p. 141.

9 Stats from http://www.blogpulse.com.

Chapter 15: Seek Reviews and Exposure from Other Publications

1 John Kremer, *1001 Ways to Market Your Books* (Fairfield, IA: Ad-Lib Publications, 1990), p. 138.

2 Lisa Rogak, *The Man Behind The Da Vinci Code* (Kansas City: Andrews McMeel Publishing, 2005) pp. 93, 94.

3 http://www.condenastmediakit.com/wir/circulation.cfm. This is their "rate base" – the average net paid circulation guaranteed to their advertisers. Actual "paid and verified subscription" was 754,574 as posted in August 2010.

4 http://www.magazine.org/CONSUMER_MARKETING/CIRC_TRENDS/1318.aspx - the July 2009 US Census reported the US population as 307,006,555. 1975

magazine subscriptions were 166,048,037. Subscription averages are reported each year by the Magazine Publishers of America, calculated by Audit Bureau of Circulations statements. Annuals, international editions, and comics have been excluded.

5 David Meerman Scott, *The New Rules of Marketing & PR* (Hoboken, New Jersey: John Wiley & Sons, Inc.), p. 30.

6 From Lynda O'Connor in a Book Marketing Network discussion on Ning.com.

7 Marilyn & Tom Ross, *Jump Start Your Book Sales (Buena Vista, CO: Communication Creativity, 1999)*, pp. 58, 59.

Chapter 16: Attract Attention through Social Media

1 On finding and using the most effective social media outposts for your product, see Shiv Singh, *Social Media Marketing for Dummies* (Hoboken, NJ: Wiley Publishing, Inc., 2010), pp. 105-137.

2 http://www.facebook.com/adsmarketing/#!/adsmarketing/index.php?sk=targeting; http://www.facebook.com/adsmarketing/#!/press/info.php?statistics.

3 From e-mail correspondence with Karen O'Toole, 10/20/2010.

4 Personal interview with social media specialist Olivier Blanchard, 10/23/2010.

5 http://www.myspace.com/pressroom/2010/10/meet-the-new-myspace.

6 http://www.youtube.com/t/advertising_audience_targeting.

7 From e-mail correspondence with Marguerita McManus, October 2010.

8 http://musingsonminutiae.com/articles/promoting-marketing-shelfari.

9 http://musingsonminutiae.com/articles/promoting-marketing-goodreads.

10 http://twitter.com/about.

11 http://business.twitter.com/twitter101/case_bestbuy.

12 http://business.twitter.com/twitter101.

13 http://www.youtube.com/t/about.

14 http://www.facebook.com/#!/facebook.

Chapter 17: Offer Your Writing in Appropriate Digital Formats

1 According to the 14 publishers surveyed. http://www.publishersweekly.com/pw/by-topic/industry-news/financial-reporting/article/44546-e-book-sales-jump-150-in-july.html.

2 http://www.dailyfinance.com/story/company-news/why- apples-ipad-numbers-are-confusing-and-a-little-misleading/19426612.

3 http://www.publishersweekly.com/pw/by-topic/digital/content-and-e-books/article/43899-amazon-s-e-book-sales-tripled-in-first-half-of-2010-.html.

4 http://blog.logicalexpressions.com/archive/2010/05/28/adventures-with-smash-words-signing-up-as-a-small-publisher.aspx.

5 https://www.smashwords.com/about/supportfaq.

6 http://blog.smashwords.com/2010/07/smashwords-publishes-15000th-indie.html.

Chapter 18: Sell Your Book in Brick and Mortar Stores

1 From personal interviews with David Cady.

2 From e-mail interview with Dr. McGinnis.

3 John Kremer, *John Kremer's Self-Publishing Hall of Fame*, e-book edition, p. 26.

4 Ibid., pp. 264,265.

5 On the importance of personal selling, see Charles W. Lamb, Joseph F. Hair, Jr., Carl McDaniel, *MKTG2*, Instructor's Edition (Mason, OH: South-Western Cengage Learning, 2008), p. 215.

6 John Kremer, opt. cit., pp. 13,14. See also http://www.kathleenantrim.com/74.html.

Chapter 20: Consider Radio

1 Donald Trump, *Surviving at the Top* (Random House, 1990) p. 26.

2 "Late Night," *Pioneers of Television*, 9 January 2008.

3 http://freelancewriterblog.blogspot.com/2008/10/marketing-ideas-from-jack-can-field.html.

Chapter 21: Consider Speaking

1 See especially the classic book on persuasion – Robert B. Cialdini, *Influence: The Psychology of Persuasion* (New York: HarperCollins Publishers, 1984), pp. 17-56.

Chapter 22: John Kremer

1 John Kremer, *1001 Ways to Market Your Books* (Taos, New Mexico: Open Horizons, 2008), pp. 31ff.

2 Ibid., p. 155.

3 John Kremer, *John Kremer's Self-Publishing Hall of Fame*, e-book edition, p. 253.

4 Ibid., p. 72. See also http://www.hankthecowdog.com/erickson.html.

5 Ibid., p. 109. See also http://www.dawnhallcookbooks.com/about.htm.

6 Ibid., p. 9.

7 Ibid., p. 28.

8 Ibid., p. 111.

9 Ibid., p. 128.

Chapter 23: Brian Jud

1 http://www.newsweek.com/2008/12/12/rick-warren-s-the-purpose-driven-life.html; http://en.wikipedia.org/wiki/The_Purpose_Driven_Life. http://scotthodge.typepad.com/scott/2005/09/miracle_or_mark.html. http://www.forbes.com/ 2003/09/17/cz_ik_0917megachurch_print.html.

2 http://www.go-publish-yourself.com/community/interview-bollesr.php.

3 Brian Jud, *How to Make Real Money Selling Books* (Garden City Park, New York: 2009), p. 151.

4 John Kremer, *John Kremer's Self-Publishing Hall of Fame*, e-book edition, p. 231.

Chapter 24: Send News (Media) Releases

1 David Meerman Scott, *The New Rules of Marketing & PR* (Hoboken, New Jersey: John Wiley & Sons, Inc.), p. 169.

2 http://www.siliconvalleywatcher.com/mt/archives/2006/02/die_press_relea.php.

3 Scott, opt. cit., pp. 27ff.

4 http://www.topseos.com/rankings/search-engine-marketing-agencies/evaluation-criteria/press-release-distribution.

5 Scott, opt. cit., p. 30.

6 Ibid., pp. 62, 63.

7 Ibid., p. 64.

8 Ibid., p. 169.

9 Getting your press release on Google Alerts isn't just about achieving a one-time mention in cyberspace. Interested groups subscribe to these alerts and may blog about you, post information about you on forums, etc. It's all about reaching "the long tail" of the web.

10 http://www.topseos.com/rankings/search-engine-marketing-agencies/evaluation-criteria/press-release-distribution.

Chapter 25: Sell Even *More* Books!

1 Jack Welch, with John A. Byrne: *Jack: Straight from the Gut (New York: Warner Business Books, 2001), p. ix.*

2 Jack Welch,with Suzy Welch: *Winning* (New York: HarperBusiness, 2005), pp. 81ff.

3 *Winning*, opt. cit., p. 87.

4 Lisa Rogak, *The Man Behind The Da Vinci Code* (Kansas City: Andrews McMeel Publishing, 2005), p. 93.

5 http://en.wikipedia.org/wiki/Eragon, http://www.teenreads.com/authors/au-paolini-christopher.asp , http://inheritance.wikia.com/wiki/Christopher_Paolini .

6 http://freelancewriterblog.blogspot.com/2008/10/marketing-ideas-from-jack-canfield.html.

7 http://freelancewriterblog.blogspot.com/2008/10/marketing-ideas-from-jack-canfield.html.

8 From personal e-mail interview with Pamela Jackson.

9 http://thebookmarketingnetwork.com/forum/topics/523145:Topic:10404?commentId=523145%3AComment%3A243244.

10 *Winning*, opt. cit., p. 83.

11 http://freelancewriterblog.blogspot.com/2008/10/marketing-ideas-from-jack-canfield.html.

12 http://en.wikipedia.org/wiki/Eragon, http://www.teenreads.com/authors/au-paolini-christopher.asp, http://inheritance.wikia.com/wiki/Christopher_Paolini .